FILM & EVERYDAY ECO-DISASTERS

FILM&EVERYDAY ECO-DISASTERS

ROBIN L. MURRAY AND JOSEPH K. HEUMANN

University of Nebraska Press | Lincoln and London

Library of Congress Cataloging-in-Publication Data
Murray, Robin L.
Film and everyday eco-disasters /
Robin L. Murray and Joseph K. Heumann.
p.   cm.
Includes filmography.
Includes bibliographical references and index.
ISBN 978-0-8032-4874-8 (cloth: alk. paper)
ISBN 978-0-8032-5515-9 (epub)
ISBN 978-0-8032-5516-6 (mobi)
ISBN 978-0-8032-5514-2 (pdf) 1. Environmental
protection and motion pictures. 2. Ecology
in motion pictures. 3. Documentary films—
History and criticism. 4. Documentary films—
Influence. I. Heumann, Joseph K. II. Title.
PN1995.9.E78M88 2014
070.1'8—dc23   2013047064

Set in Scala by Renni Johnson.
Designed by Ashley Muehlbauer.

CONTENTS

ILLUSTRATIONS

ACKNOWLEDGMENTS

Our thanks go to Julia Lesage, Chuck Kleinhans, and John Hess, the editors of *Jump Cut*, for their continued support for our work. Two of our chapters appeared in *Jump Cut* in an earlier form: a revised version of "Oil Drilling and the Search for the 'Golden Shrimp': The Myth of Interdependence in Oil Drilling Films" and a shorter version of "Give Me Shelter: The Ecology of Homes and Homelessness." We would also like to thank Deane Williams (editor) and Sally Wilson (editorial assistant) for including an earlier version of "Contemporary Eco-food Films: The Documentary Tradition" in their *Studies in Documentary Film Journal.* We also appreciate the help and support that our book editor, Bridget Barry, provided us throughout the publication process. Our manuscript reviewers deserve kudos for their useful commentary as well. The publication information for the previously published chapter portions follows:

"Oil Drilling and the Search for the 'Golden Shrimp': The Myth of Interdependence in Oil Drilling Films." *Jump Cut: A Review of Contemporary Media* 53 (Summer 2011). Web.

"Give Me Shelter: The Ecology of the Home in *Blue Vinyl* and *Libby, Montana*." *Jump Cut* 54 (Fall 2012). Web.

"Contemporary Eco-food Films: The Documentary Tradition." *Studies in Documentary Film* 6.1 (May 2012). 43–59. Print.

INTRODUCTION
Cinematic Eco-disasters and Our Basic Human Needs

Steven Spielberg's *War Horse* (2011), an epic antiwar drama confronting the fight for survival of a Devon horse named Joey in the no-man zones of World War I France, addresses our relationship with the environment in a variety of ways. It effectively illustrates the connections between humans and the natural world with its focus on the relationship between Joey and his owner's son, Albert Narracott (Jeremy Irvine). The scenes before, during, and after battles also demonstrate the horrific consequences of modern warfare for people, animals, and the natural world, a devastating human and ecological disaster leaving clear evidence that, as the film tells us, "The war has taken everything from everyone."

But the film moves beyond more traditional disaster themes by illuminating everyday eco-disasters associated with our basic needs. For example, Joey, a swift and strong Thoroughbred, must prove he can plow a field for turnips to ensure that the Narracott family maintains its shelter and the surrounding land that provides its food. When the turnip crop fails and war is declared, Albert's father, Ted (Peter Mullan), sells the horse to the British army to pay the farm lease and, again, secure those basic needs. Joey's horrific war journey, then, is caused by a family's drive to simply survive.

Film and Everyday Eco-disasters examines our basic needs in relation to the changing perspective toward everyday eco-disasters reflected by

How to Boil a Frog: The atmospheric cost of energy production

filmmakers from the silent era forward. Maurice Yacowar provides a base reading of such eco-disaster films in his seminal "The Bug in the Rug: Notes on the Disaster Genre," which delineates eight basic types of disaster films, all of which have as their essence "a situation of normalcy [that] erupts into a persuasive image of death" (261). Yacowar's categories of disaster films include a category most aligned with environmental disaster, "Natural Attack," which pits a human community against a destructive form of nature, such as animal attacks, an attack by the elements, or an attack related to atomic mutations.

The natural attack disaster film has evolved in contemporary film, however, and now includes everyday eco-disasters, such as those associated with industrial farming and energy generation. These films serve as examples of ecocinema, a term that critics, especially ecocritics, are just beginning to debate. Although some define ecocinema narrowly to include only those films that "actively seek to inform viewers about, as well as engage their participation in, addressing issues of ecological import" (10), as does Paula Willoquet-Maricondi, others take a broader approach.

Although we too see the best ecocinema, especially eco-documentary, as inspiring viewer action, we agree with the more general view of ecocinema that Stephen Rust, Salma Monani, and Sean Cubitt postulate in *Ecocinema and Practice*: "All films present productive ecocritical exploration and careful analysis can unearth engaging and intriguing perspectives on cinema's various relationships with the world around us" (3). In other words, every film is potentially an example of ecocinema, one of the media included in definitions of eco-media, a term that encompasses nonprint media from still photographs and cinema to music and videogames.

According to this definition these filmic representations of everyday eco-disasters are ecocinema ripe for ecocritical readings. To begin this study, our work will explore a sampling of eco-films in relation to three primary ecocritical approaches: human approaches to ecology like those of Ellen Swallow Richards, the rhetoric of the eco-documentary, and the repercussions of negative externalities, the term corporations producing everyday eco-disasters use to mask practices that potentially have a negative effect on both humans and the natural world.

Human Approaches to Ecology

This text centers exclusively on films associated with our basic needs (air, water, food, clothing, shelter, and energy) and the everyday eco-disasters associated with their exploitation. Such exploitation is typically associated with a "fair use" model of ecology, which grew out of economic approaches to the environment connected with social Darwinism. Human approaches to ecology, however, maintain the worth of our basic needs, either as separate from or part of the natural world. Whether defined by psychologist Abraham Maslow as physiological needs, by Reality therapist William Glasser as survival needs, or self-determination theory as competence in dealing with the environment, our most basic needs all highlight our connection with our external ecology.

The worth of our basic needs has been calculated in the United States and around the world in the last decade to determine the lowest income necessary for a family's survival. This calculation resulted in the Self-

Sufficiency Standard. According to Diana Pearce and Jennifer Brooks, "the Self-Sufficiency Standard measures how much income is needed for a family of a given composition in a given place to adequately meet its basic needs—without public or private assistance" (1). This standard differs from the federal poverty measure in multiple ways: it takes into account regional differences, changing demographics, and new needs. As Pearce and Brooks explain, "there are many families with incomes above the federal poverty line who nonetheless lack sufficient resources to adequately meet their basic needs" (1–2). For a working adult in Illinois, for example, an hourly wage of at least $8.57/hour was necessary in 2002 to earn the $1,508 per month (with 176 hours per month of work), or $18,096 per year, necessary to meet housing, food, transportation, miscellaneous, and tax expenses (Pearce and Brooks 8). For a family of four, with two working adults, a preschool child, and a school-age child, an hourly wage of at least $10.07 per adult was necessary in 2002 to earn the $3,545 per month (for 176 hours per month of work), or $42,516 per year, required to meet these same basic needs, as well as child care expenses (Pearce and Brooks 8).

This Self-Sufficiency Standard makes clear that at least some of our basic needs have become commodities, which consumers must purchase for survival, a dilemma chemist Ellen Swallow Richards examines in her multiple explorations of human ecology at the turn of the twentieth century. The human ecology movement grew out of the work of Richards, who translated Ernst Haeckel's work from its original German and, according to Robert Clarke, introduced the concept of ecology in the United States. Richards defined human ecology as "the study of the surroundings of human beings in the effects they produce on the lives of men" (*Sanitation in Daily Life* v).

Instead of "fair use" approaches to ecology, with an ultimate goal to maximize benefits of nature for humans, chapters 1–3 explore how Richards's human approaches to ecology are manifested in documentary and feature films addressing air pollution, climate change, water rights, and the clothing industry. This approach also points to sustainable development as an alternative to resource exploitations and the everyday eco-disasters associated with them. Our exploration of everyday eco-disasters demonstrates some of the disastrous consequences of applying an economic approach that condones overdevelopment and exploitative overuse and commodification of resources sustaining our basic needs.

The Rhetoric of the Eco-documentary

Although many would argue that all texts, including documentaries, are inherently rhetorical, since they address an audience from a particular standpoint, historically the rhetorical documentary presents an argument and lays out evidence to support it. In *The Rhetoric of the New Political Documentary*, however, Thomas W. Benson and Brian J. Snee assert, "The rhetorical potential of documentary film . . . relies not on an audience who merely provides the rhetor with resources that might be exploited in persuasion but instead on an audience who is actively engaged in judgment and action" (137).

Audiences do not merely mimic the action on the screen, according to Benson and Snee. They interpret the actions documented, and invent and engage in acts of their own that respond to the film's rhetoric but from the viewer's perspective. Chapters 4 and 5 highlight this rhetorical potential in relation to food industry documentaries. The best of these eco-documentaries fulfill Paula Willoquet-Maricondi's definition of the role of such films, "to play an active role in fostering environmental aware-ness, conservation, and political action . . . , that is, to be a member of the planetary ecosystem or 'ecosphere' and, most important, to understand the value of this community in a systemic and nonhierarchical way" (10).

In the films we explore in this section, documentation of actions also seems to adhere to the criteria Karl Heider outlines for ethnographic film-making, when explaining that "the most important attribute of ethnograph-ic film is the degree to which it is informed by ethnographic understand-ing" (5). According to Heider, first of all "ethnography is a way of making a detailed description and analysis of human behavior based on a long-term observational study on the spot," (6). Second, Heider suggests that eth-nography should "relate specific observed behavior to cultural norms" (6). The individual narratives these films provide also support Heider's third criteria for an effective ethnography: "holism" (6). These interconnected stories are "truthfully represented" (7) according to Heider's final criterion for an effective ethnographic film, all in service to the films' rhetoric.

Repercussions of Negative Externalities in Everyday Eco-disaster Films

The term "externality" comes from economics and refers to "an economic choice or action by one actor that affects the welfare of others who are not involved in that choice or action" (Goodwin et al). Although externalities can be positive, as when "a landowner, by choosing not to develop her land might preserve a water recharge source for an aquifer shared by the entire local community" (Goodwin et al), environmental externalities are most often negative. As Neva Goodwin explains, "a negative externality . . . exists when an economic actor produces an economic cost but does not fully pay that cost. A well-known example is the manufacturing firm that dumps pollutants in a river, decreasing water quality downstream."

Environmental externalities resulting from everyday eco-disasters continue to have negative effects on water, air, and landscapes. For example, oil remains from the 1979 Ixtoc oil spill disaster in the Gulf of Mexico, and cleanup continues after the 1989 *Exxon Valdez* accident, ominous foreshadowing of the possible aftermath of the 2010 BP environmental catastrophe caused by the Deepwater Horizon rig explosion. Negative externalities have a detrimental effect on workers in various industries, including fishing, drinking water, air quality, mountains and forests. See, for example, the December 23, 2008, coal slurry dam breach caused by mountaintop removal mining in Tennessee or the April 10, 2010, West Virginia Massey mine explosion that left twenty-nine dead.

Natural gas drilling also causes negative externalities, as documented in *Gasland* (2010), threatening upper water supplies in the Delaware basin, for example. Genetically engineered seed has produced resistant superweeds, and carp introduced into the Chicago River are threatening other fish in Lake Michigan and the other Great Lakes. Environmental externalities have a global effect negatively impacting water, air, and the quality of human and nonhuman life around the world.

Chapters 6, 7, and 8 examine representations of negative externalities associated with housing and energy production in documentary and feature films. Instead of advocating for the fair use politics associated with the term "externality," however, these films embrace sustainable development. A fair use model rests on conquest more than conservation. In "The Law of Increasing Returns," for example, Ronald Bailey promotes a fair use model when he asserts, "It is in rich democratic capitalist countries that the air and water are becoming cleaner, forests are expanding, food is abundant, education is universal, and women's rights respected. Whatever slows down economic growth also slows down environmental improvement" (Salon.com). Unfettered economic growth, then, promotes environmental conservation, according to Bailey, so resources should be used as needed to advance economic development and thus environmental consciousness. Wise use and sustainable policies, on the other hand, disagree with Bailey's premise. According to an article in *Environment*, "the Brundtland Commission's brief definition of sustainable development as the 'ability to make development sustainable—to ensure that it meets the needs of the present without compromising the ability of future generations to meet their own needs' is surely the standard definition when judged by its widespread use and frequency of citation" (Kates et al. 10).

Illustrating Everyday Eco-disasters in Film

Recent documentaries and feature films explore and argue against these everyday eco-disasters. With explorations of films as diverse as *Dead Ahead*, a 1992 HBO dramatization of the *Exxon Valdez* disaster; *Total Recall* (1990), a science fiction feature film highlighting oxygen as a commodity; *The Devil Wears Prada* (2006), a comment on the fashion industry; and *Food, Inc.* (2009), a documentary interrogation of the food industry, this project explores documentaries and feature films as film art to determine how successfully they fulfill their goals. We assert that the success of the films we explore as arguments against everyday eco-disasters and the negative environmental externalities they produce depends not only on the message the filmmakers convey but also, and most importantly, on the rhetorical strategies they employ.

This work examines both documentary and fictional feature films but provides a unique focus: everyday eco-disasters. With multiple coal-mining accidents, oil spills, and food-borne diseases in recent news, explorations of films examining consequences associated with everyday environmental problems seem not only relevant but also imperative. Scientists agree that our human "carbon footprint" has accelerated global

Happy Feet Two: Mumble's son Eric with the Mighty Sven

climate change, but ecologists from the early twentieth century forward demonstrate that humanity contributes to the toxicity of our planet's food, water, and air primarily by serving what are seen as our daily needs. This work explores filmic representations of everyday eco-disasters, the environmental externalities associated with delivering these daily needs.

Happy Feet Two is a case in point. Even though most reviews of *Happy Feet Two* claim that the film has subsumed the original film's environmental critique of overfishing with an entertaining story of species interdependence, we see it as a powerful critique of humans' toxic contributions to climate change and water pollution in order to fulfill basic needs without the restraint necessary for sustainable development. Lisa Schwarzbaum's *Entertainment Weekly* review of the film argues, for example, that "earnest messages about bad climate change and good parenting skills have been replaced by a we-all-share-a-planet sense of fun that's more *Finding Nemo* than National Geographic." Manohla Dargis of the *New York Times* goes further, asserting that the film is merely "an amiable sequel with not much on its mind other than funny and creaky jokes, and waves of understated beauty."

For us, however, despite the film's weaknesses, *Happy Feet Two* embraces a broader environmental message than the original film. *Happy Feet* illustrates a clear eco-problem: overfishing. But the film offers a single unrealistic solution: human intervention to ensure sustainable fishing practices and protect penguins because they dance and sing like humans. *Happy Feet Two*, however, illustrates at least two devastating everyday eco-disasters caused by humans: oil spills and fires, and, more devastating for penguins and humans alike, global warming, both of which connect with humans' exploitation of resources that meet their basic needs.

With a more subtle approach to its message, *Happy Feet Two* looks more like a subtle enviro-toon than a didactic sermon. As Jaime Weinman argues, a model enviro-toon "never preaches." Unlike cartoons with anthropomorphized animals or plant life alone, what Weinman calls "enviro-toons" not only humanize nature; they comment on abuse of nature and the natural, especially by humans. For us, enviro-toons are animated shorts or feature films that address environmental concerns and embrace an environmental message that responds to their historical and cultural contexts.

Happy Feet Two meets these criteria well. It shows us scenes of Ramon (Robin Williams) struggling to escape an oil spill and watch the spill flame up in a spectacular oil fire. It also explains The Mighty Sven's (Hank Azaria) dilemma to introduce the film's central conflict, the negative repercussions of global warming. Sven has lost his icy home to global warming. With warming temperatures, the ice melted, revealing open waters and green grasses that are uninhabitable for puffins.

The emperor penguins face a similar plight when rising temperatures cause glaciers to break off, or "calve," isolating them in a large crevasse encircled by icy walls. Although the film suggests that the solution to this disaster is cooperation (working together to collapse a wall, so the penguins can relocate), the green patches showing through snow and ice tell a different story: climate change is stealing these penguins' home. Unlike in the original *Happy Feet*, humans' attempts to help the penguins fail. Instead, penguins and their puffin friend are left alone to adapt to a changing landscape caused by humans. Despite the weak link that additional characters like Bill and Will Krill (Matt Damon and Brad Pitt) provide, *Happy Feet Two* succeeds as an enviro-toon and an illustration of the everyday eco-disasters (externalities) associated with obtaining and overusing our resources to meet our basic needs.

By examining fictional and documentary films with these everyday eco-disasters at their center, our work, then, seeks to fill a gap in both film studies and ecocriticism. Works like Jhan Hochman's *Green Cultural Studies: Nature in Film, Novel, and Theory* (1998) and Richard Slotkin's *Gunfighter Nation* (1992) look at the representations of landscape in American mainstream film outside the field of ecocriticism, for example. Most texts that examine environmental movies explore nature documentaries or independent films in which environmental messages are blatant, not popular films where the message is subtle, unintentional, or embedded in relation to cultural context (see Gregg Mitman's *Reel Nature: America's Romance with Nature on Film* and Scott MacDonald's *The Garden in the Machine*).

Our book builds on work begun in David Ingram's *Green Screen: Environmentalism and Hollywood Cinema*; MacDonald's *The Garden in the Machine: A Field Guide to Independent Films about Place*; *Wildlife Films* (2000), Alison Anderson's *Media Culture and the Environment* (1997); Sean Cubitt's *Eco-Media* (2005); Willoquet-Maricondi's *Framing the World: Explorations in Ecocriticism and Film* (2010); and parts of Deborah Carmichael's *The Landscape of Hollywood Westerns: Ecocriticism in an American Film Genre* (2006) and Michael Dana Bennet and David W. Teague's *The Nature of Cities: Ecocriticism and Urban Environments* (1999). *Everyday Eco-disasters* seeks to extend this conversation and examine documentary and fictional features addressing everyday eco-disasters associated with our daily needs from three ecocritical perspectives.

Human Approaches to the Ecology of Air, Water, and Clothing

Chapter 1, "At the Boiling Point: The Aesthetics of Atmospheric Pollution and Climate Change in Documentary and Feature Films," examines the commodification of oxygen in science fiction films such as *Total Recall* (1990) and the consequences of polluting the air in features and documentaries including *Red Desert* (1964), *No Blade of Grass* (1970), *Safe* (1994), and *How to Boil a Frog* (2009) in relation to Ellen Swallow Richards's human approaches to ecology. Since Richards viewed humans as part of nature, she considered urban problems like air and water pollution as products of human activity imposed on the environment and, subsequently, best resolved by humans. This chapter explores the consequences of taking this stance.

Chapter 2, "James Bond and Water Wars in Contemporary Film: A New Eco-warrior?," explores the multiple environmental consequences of an industry devoted to providing drinking water for a price. By examining documentaries such as *Blue Gold: World Water Wars* (2008), *Flow: For the Love of Water* (2008), and *Tapped* (2009), as well as recent and twentieth-century feature films from *Chinatown* (1974) to *The Road to Wellville* (1994), *A Civil Action* (1998), and *Rango* (2011), we evaluate the films' arguments against environmental externalities associated with the water industry with a primary focus on their popularization in *Quantum of Solace* (2008).

Chapter 3, "Ready to Wear? From Fashion to Environmental Injustice," focuses on environmental consequences of the textile and fashion industry in films such as *Norma Rae* (1979), *Ready to Wear* (1994), *Life and Debt* (2001), *T-Shirt Travels* (2001), *China Blue* (2005), *Mardi Gras: Made in China* (2005), *The Devil Wears Prada* (2006), *Maquilapolis* (2006), *The Last Train Home* (2009), *Baytar Environmental Clothing Industry Documentary* (2010), *Thread: A Documentary* (2013), and *Cotton Road* (2013). Although fashion films primarily emphasize their industry's product—high-end fashion—documentaries exploring both textile and clothing production reveal the human and the environmental exploitation behind the clothes.

Eco-documentaries and the Rhetoric of Food Production

Chapter 4, "Contemporary Eco-food Films: The Documentary Tradition," asserts that food documentaries have become popular in the last few years, with films from *Supersize Me* (2004) to *We Feed the World* (2005) and the recent critically acclaimed *King Corn* (2007) and *Food, Inc.* (2008). We assert, however, that *Our Daily Bread* (2005) provides the most effective argument against the move to industrial farming because it eliminates verbal explanation altogether. With only background sounds and voices to support its visual rhetoric, this avant-garde rhetorical documentary conveys its message more effectively than either *Food, Inc.* or *We Feed The World*. Because it relies exclusively on visual rhetoric, we assert that *Our Daily Bread* works as a powerful rhetorical tool, undiluted by either ambivalent multiple viewpoints or a voice-over that sometimes disguises the consequences of industrial farming on display.

Chapter 5, "Flipper? We're Eating Flipper?: Documenting Animal Rights and Environmental Ethics at Sea," explores differences between animal rights and environmentalism in relation to the fishing industry. Recent documentary films interrogating the fishing industry bring this debate to life, either from a particular case, as in *The Cove* (2009) and *Darwin's Nightmare* (2007), or in the more broadly based *The End of the Line* (2010). *The Cove* draws on animal rights arguments in its strong advocacy for the dolphins of Taiji. *Darwin's Nightmare* and *The End of the Line*, however, immerse themselves in wise-use environmental arguments similar to Aldo Leopold's land ethic. While *Darwin's Nightmare* foregrounds human rights issues in Tanzania and *The End of the Line* more logically connects with long-term global environmental solutions, because *The Cove* meets its goal to end dolphin slaughter, at least temporarily, at the film's site and slow its progress elsewhere, the film employs the most effective rhetorical strategies, strategies grounded in the animal liberation movement's claims that all animals are equal because, like humans, they feel pain.

Negative Externalities of Housing and Energy Industries

Chapter 6: "Give Me Shelter: The Ecology of Homes and Homelessness," highlights the environmental externalities associated with the housing industry in films such as *Dark Days* (2000), *Blue Vinyl* (2002), and *Libby, Montana* (2004). These films examine multiple externalities associated with the housing industry, from toxic building materials to overdevelopment, but they also explore the concept of housing in relation to environmental justice.

Chapter 7, "Activism in Mountaintop Removal Films: Turn Off the Lights for Sustainability," explores the repercussions of coal-generated electricity on the environment in relation to feature films such as *Gomorra* (2008) and recent anti–mountaintop removal (MTR) mining documentaries including *Razing Appalachia* (2003), *Black Diamonds* (2007), *Burning the Future: Coal in America* (2008), *Mountain Top Removal* (2007), *Coal Country* (2009), and *The Last Mountain* (2011). Although all twelve of the anti–mountaintop removal documentaries we viewed successfully demonstrate the disastrous effects of mountaintop removal mining, only B. J.

Gudmundsson's *Mountain Mourning* (2006) and *Rise Up! West Virginia* (2007), and to a certain extent, *The Last Mountain* (2011) successfully support arguments against mountaintop removal mining while offering viable non–fossil fuel energy alternatives, alternatives that, according to the films, will eventually end America's addiction to coal and Appalachia's over-reliance on a coal mining economy.

Chapter 8, "The Search for the 'Golden Shrimp': The Myth of Interdependence in Oil Drilling Films," examines consequences of our dependence on oil. Although the consequences of the April 2010 BP oil well blowout are still unfolding, the primary example to which this ecocatastrophe is compared is the March 24, 1989, *Exxon Valdez* spill in Prince William Sound, Alaska. We analyze documentary and feature films that examine this event and others like it to make externalities associated with such spills transparent. See, for example, *Dead Ahead: The Exxon Valdez Disaster* (1992), *Crude: The Real Price of Oil* (2009), and *Black Wave: The Legacy of Exxon Valdez* (2009), in the context of films valorizing the oil industry, including *Louisiana Story* (1948) and *Thunder Bay* (1953), in an attempt to restore lost historical memory or environmental destruction.

Our conclusion, "Can the Film Industry and the Environmental Movement Mix?," synthesizes our arguments regarding the aestheticization of environmental externalities in rhetorical and multigenre feature films in relation to the environmental consequences of the film industry. We explore environmental progress made in films foregrounding everyday eco-disasters associated with our daily needs and evidence supporting the greening of Hollywood both in the film content and the production process of recent blockbusters and eco-films.

1

HUMAN APPROACHES TO THE ECOLOGY OF AIR, WATER, AND CLOTHING

CHAPTER ONE

AT THE BOILING POINT

The Aesthetics of Atmospheric Pollution and Climate
Change in Documentary and Feature Films

In *Red Desert* (1964) director Michaelangelo Antonioni's constructed world dominates the film's narrative. Combined with an outstanding and eerie electronic soundscape, the film's female protagonist Giuliana (Monica Vitti) and the contemporary viewer become trapped in a world that is overwhelmed by industrial waste, noise, and fear. The natural world is pushed to the edges of the frame. This world is filled with ghostlike freighters that dock with quarantine flags run up their masts. Her two competing lovers, husband Ugo (Carlo Chionetti) and Corrado (Richard Harris), walk past polluted lakes, laughing about how people now complain that their food tastes of oil. In another scene Corrado and Giuliana walk past a lone fruit and vegetable vendor. His outdoor display is full of ghostlike produce that has turned ashen and gray. Giuliana's son asks why birds avoid the smoke pouring out of factory smokestacks. "It's poison," Giuliana exclaims, and we see a bright yellow smoke streaming into the sky, a clear reference to the human costs of toxic air and a lament for the loss of our most important basic need.

From ancient Rome to the contemporary world, clean air has been a requirement for human and nonhuman life. It is an essential basic need we, perhaps without our knowledge, purchase, and when it is unobtain-

Red Desert: Giuliana (Monica Vitti) alienated by threatening industrial landscape

able, we suffer the consequences of a toxic atmosphere. Although recent political struggles in the United States over cap-and-trade legislation and changes to the Clean Air Act highlight this dilemma, filmic representations of these struggles that draw on human approaches to ecology may be the most dramatic and effective arguments for clean air.

Fictional and documentary films with atmospheric pollution at the center underscore the costs of both clean air and its absence. The Lumière brothers' views of factory emissions and oil well fires in the nineteenth and early twentieth centuries and films from the 1960s and 1970s such as *Red Desert* (1964) critique industrial waste with their narratives and/or aesthetics. Recent documentaries and animated films argue against air pollution and its negative climate change consequences in similar ways, as do the critically acclaimed documentary *An Inconvenient Truth* (2006); an eco-drama, *Safe* (1995); and the animated features, *WALL-E* (2008) and *Happy Feet Two* (2011). Although the messages of atmospheric pollution and climate change merge most powerfully in two of these films (a little-known science fiction film from 1970, *No Blade of Grass*, and a 2009 documentary, *How to Boil a Frog*), *Total Recall*, *Red Desert*, and *Safe* all demonstrate the continuing concern with air pollution and its consequences for humans and the natural world. These films of con-

Total Recall: Reactivated oxygen atmosphere on Mars

trasting genres and periods provide a compelling look at the dire costs of human's exploitation of the natural world that places blame for the Earth's health squarely on humanity and maps out explicitly the consequences of humans' disastrous choices.

These films shed light on not only the economic costs to limit emissions and climate change but also the human costs when these limits fall short. Unlike films showing pollution without commenting on human consequences, such as *How Green Was My Valley* (1941) and *The Molly Maguires* (1970), or documentaries concentrating primarily on environmental rather than human disasters resulting from global warming, as in *An Inconvenient Truth*, some filmic explorations of toxic air demonstrate the importance of clean air as a basic need that must be met to reduce harmful effects on humans and nonhumans alike. They also reveal the continuing truth of Ellen Richards's 1908 assertion: "The essentials of public health are recognized as clean air, clean water, clean soil, clean and wholesome food. When people crowd into a limited space these must be secured by cooperation" (*Cost of Cleanness* 49–50).

Total Recall (1990), for example, explores what might happen if oxygen, now a free and open Earth resource, became a commodity controlled by corporate interests. In the film Douglas Quaid, formerly a secret agent named Hauser (Arnold Schwarzenegger), battles a corporate mining company head on Mars, Vilos Cohaagen (Ron Cox), over air. Cohaagen and his henchman Richter (Michael Ironside) fight to continue mining turbinium rather than activating Martian machinery built half a million years before because it may create a breathable atmosphere around the planet.

Ultimately Doug escapes his enemies, led by Richter, and travels to Mars, where he meets with rebels led by Kuato (Marshall Bell), who are fighting for free air. With Kuato's help Doug thwarts Richter and his superior Cohaagan's attempts to conceal the Martians' machinery, so they can continue to oppress Mars's colonists who mine their needed turbinium. After a series of action sequences that involve a drill truck, explosions, and gunfire, Doug finds the oxygen machine and activates it, shooting himself and his lover, Melina (Rachel Ticotin), out onto Mars's surface, and the ancient machine begins to work, exploding with oxygenated air, until an atmosphere quickly begins to form, and the sky turns blue on a new Mars, where air is free and clean.

Within the futuristic science fiction setting of *Total Recall*, the commodification of oxygen can be explored in explicit ways. Other genre films examine the repercussions of climate change in similar fantastic ways. *Our Man Flint* (1966), for example, an action-adventure spoof of James Bond films of the 1960s, showcases an ecoterrorist plot by a group of scientists to force climate changes that will melt the Arctic and Antarctic glaciers and flood major coastal cities if global governments refuse to comply with their ultimatum to destroy all military forces and agree to become docile "programmed" but peaceful automatons. In this comic action adventure, world leaders rely on a computer program to choose their savior, Derek Flint (James Coburn), an ex-intelligence officer with 007 gadgets and testosterone levels.

As a present-day dramatic action-adventure film, *The Day after Tomorrow* (2004), on the other hand, argues vehemently that we need to combat global warming as quickly as possible to avoid the apocalyptic consequences on display in the film. But the film conveys this message in ways that many find so hyperbolized that it becomes humorous, because in the story, consequences some scientists argue might result from global warming arise almost instantaneously rather than over the course of decades or even centuries. All these films, however, demonstrate the ongoing importance of keeping our atmosphere free of destructive pollutants.

Atmospheric Pollution and Climate Change: A Short History

Although we may date our own country's attention to clean air with the passing of the Clean Air Act in 1970, writers have addressed harmful consequences of dirty air since at least the third century BC, when, according to R. J. Meyers, Theophrastus complained that the "smell of burning coal was disagreeable and troublesome." Some two centuries later Seneca concurred, lamenting the "heavy air" in the city of Rome. In ancient Rome lead, copper, and zinc smelting contributed to conditions that required chimneys of seven to eight meters in height and beach houses that the rich used for an escape from the oppressive urban conditions.

During the Middle Ages Londoners first polluted the air with limestone kilns heated with oak, producing quicklime. Wood shortages, however, led to use of high-sulfur-content sea coal for kilns, industry, and heating, and the soot became so heavy in the air that in 1285 a commission was established to address severe air pollution. In 1306 Edward I banned coal use in lime kilns, but the ban was largely ignored. In 1661 John Evelyn wrote *Fumifugium, or the Inconvenience of the Aer and the Smoake of London Dissipated* in response to London smoke, stating that a traveler "sooner smells then sees the city" (6) and proposing the following solutions: limit use of coal, relocate industries, develop new fuels, and plant green belts around the city. The production of the steam engine in the eighteenth century only exacerbated these conditions so that, according to Christa Clapp, there was a hundredfold increase in coal combustion in Great Britain between 1800 and 1900. According to Clapp air pollution killed seven times more people in Great Britain than anywhere else in the world until coal combustion industries developed globally (quoted in Jacobson 84).

The Industrial Revolution, which increased atmospheric emissions astronomically, also prompted attempts to regulate them. In Great Britain, for example, Public Health Acts passed in 1875 and 1891 and led to a Smoke Abatement Act in 1926 (Jacobson 84). In the United States individual cities passed smoke reduction laws that remained unenforced

(Jacobson 85–87). In 1920 air pollution ordinances existed in 175 cities and by 1940 had grown to 200. Changes occurred in response to
environmental disasters. In London, for example, smoke-fog (smog)
incidents from 1873 to 1962 accounted for thousands of deaths, but the
worst case was in December 1952, when four thousand people died as a
result of exposure to smog (Jacobson 2010).

Los Angeles became famous for smog as populations and car usage
increased, but incidents began as early as 1542, when Juan Rodríguez
Cabrillo called the city Bahia de los Humos (bay of smoke) because of the
smoke produced by natives' fires. In 1903 factory smoke was so thick in
LA that residents thought there was a solar eclipse. Because smog such as
that in LA is photochemical in composition and does not require smoke
or fog, however, it continues to be a problem in cities such as Atlanta, Los
Angeles, Houston, Mexico City, Tokyo, Beijing, and Athens (Jacobson
202) after emission controls have been implemented. Even with passage
of the Clean Air Act in the United States and similar legislation around
the world, CO_2 emissions continue to increase atmospheric temperatures,
contributing to climate change and its negative ramifications for humans
and nonhumans. In fact, as of 2012 the world produces two million
pounds of CO_2 emissions per second.

The Environmental Protection Agency (EPA) makes clear the connection
between atmospheric pollution and climate change in a 2012 report on
climate change and air quality, *Our Nation's Air: Status and Trends through
2010* ("Climate Change and Air Quality"). According to the EPA "just as
air pollution can have adverse effects on human health and ecosystems,
it can also impact the Earth's climate" (22). Greenhouse gases (GHG) such
as carbon dioxide and methane, for example, now "constitute air pollution
that threatens public health and welfare," according to this report (22), and
these gases are also linked to climate change. As the report asserts, "warming of the climate system is unequivocal, and . . . most of the observed
increase in global average temperatures since the mid-20th century is
very likely due to the anthropogenic increase in GHG concentrations" (22).

As Benjamin Ross and Steven Amter argue, however, despite the
evidence, "the emission of greenhouse gases goes on, protected with the
time-honored techniques of toothless laws and twisted science" (171). Both
documentary and feature films highlight the negative repercussions of

atmospheric pollution, including climate change, and invite a collaborative approach to change, demonstrating that the costs to humanity and the environment are worth the communal expense necessary to preserve clean air, a necessity for life.

Ellen Swallow Richards, Human Ecology, and the Fight for Clean Air

Ellen Swallow Richards defined human ecology in the multiple books she published in the early twentieth century. Her *Sanitation in Daily Life* provides the most explicit definition, "the study of the surroundings of human beings and the effects they produce on the lives of men," and outlines the features of the environment that humanity should combat: "noise, dust, poisonous vapors, vitiated air, dirty water, and unclean food" (v). Richards not only delineated the harmful environmental features to which humans contributed; she also promoted their eradication to ensure that all humans obtain their basic needs, or what Richards called "essentials," which include clean air, water, soil, and food (*Cost of Cleanness* 49–50).

More importantly, however, Richards asserts that these essentials should be met through community cooperation that includes accepting taxes to support municipal services deemed necessary for public health. For Richards, then, the monetary outlay necessary for clean air is minimal in the face of the human costs of a toxic atmosphere. Writing in 1908 Richards seemed optimistic that the public would accept clean air as a necessity worth higher taxes, explaining, "Clean food awaits clean air for the most part and depends upon the education of the people" (*Cost of Cleanness* 50). Richards offers this solution to the problem of toxic interior and exterior air: "Clean air implies perfect garbage and wastes disposal, clean streets and alleys, and an atmosphere tolerably free from dust, smoke and noxious odors. In this direction the civic expense has gone about as far as the people will support it. More money must be spent (and more wisely spent) on street cleaning, on schoolhouse and public building cleaning, on smoke suppression" (*Cost of Cleanness* 50). To obtain the trust of taxpayers and industry heads, Richards recommends hiring friendly female inspectors to enforce sanitation laws, once they were in place, and argues, "There is hope for clean air within the next twenty-five years" (*Cost of Cleanness* 53).

Richards argues vehemently for clean air because it could combat illness and death in urban areas and ultimately save millions of dollars. Based on her research, she presents alarming statistics: "Deaths from preventable diseases due to dirty air, soil and water have averaged in cities about 700 to 1,000 per 100,000 inhabitants. Each death means also the *sickness* and recovery of others, expenses for medicine, nurses, etc., and is frequently reckoned as a cost to the state of $10,000." Richards also places a price tag on the loss of productivity associated with these deaths, asserting, "This is an economic waste—unproductive—effort—of $7,000,000 to $10,000,000 for every 100,000 persons" (*Cost of Cleanness* 69).

In *The Art of Right Living*, Richards also highlights the importance of clean air for life, including the food we eat (15). Toxic air affects humans in multiple ways, Richards asserts. In *Air, Water, and Food*, for example, Richards and Woodman explain, "In the neighborhood of factories, smelting works, ore-heaps, and of cities burning soft coal there is a noticeable amount of sulphurous and sulphuric acids, sometimes considerable as to destroy vegetation" (16).

Richards work for the human ecology movement, however, moves beyond defining the harmful consequences of a toxic atmosphere. She also offers solutions: public agreement to pay taxes to implement and enforce a variety of sanitation laws to control industrial emissions and urban waste. As a member of the Committee on Standard Methods for the Examination of Air, for example, "she urged ventilation and air purification systems in factories, better air and humidification for homes, schools, and other public buildings" (Clarke 224–25). And Richards also argued that building materials for factories should be based in science, "subjected to scientific tests in the factory and for the factory" (Clarke 124). Films from *Red Desert, No Blade of Grass,* and *Safe* to *How to Boil a Frog* draw on these elements of human ecology. The costs of a toxic atmosphere are too great, these films illustrate, for the health and life of humans and the natural world that sustains them.

Red Desert: Connecting Humanity with a Toxic Environment

The director of *Red Desert*, Michelangelo Antonioni, once said, "There are people who adapt, and others who can't manage, perhaps because they are tied to ways of life that are now out of date" (Godard 20). Clearly the heroine of *Red Desert* (1964) has failed to adapt. Antonioni's film focuses on the psychological disintegration of Giuliana (Monica Vitti), who finds herself in an industrial hellhole that dominates the Italian landscape where she lives. Her husband, Ugo (Carlo Chionetti), is busy running a large factory and is seemingly oblivious to her recent suicide attempt while he was away on business in London. He is content to accept the story that Giuliana was in an auto accident. Their young son has a large erector-set robot with glowing eyes that prowls his bedroom at night, and the boy ultimately mirrors some of Giuliana's anxiety by feigning paralysis for a few hours, which pushes his mother deeper into despair.

Only Corrado (Richard Harris), another prosperous industrialist, notices Giuliana's condition and becomes sympathetic to her despair. Since he appears to be the only human being in a world dominated by smokestacks and enormous factories belching pollution who is interested in her feelings, she is willing to develop a relationship with him as long as it provides her with some measure of support. The fact that they have a brief affair is meaningless. Giuliana's existential crisis, her suicidal despair, her unwillingness to accept her polluted, blighted environment is usually read by critics as Antonioni's aestheticization of an Italian industrial city, but it is also presented as an eco-nightmare, one that might provide a surface mirror to Giuliana's troubled soul.

Critics both in 1964 and today have marveled at how Antonioni shaped the visual world with overdetermined colors that made the world his own. Gary Morris notes in *Bright Lights Film Journal*, for example, "Antonioni uses color throughout to tantalize the viewer with higher possibilities." Leonard Quart of *Dissent* observes, "Antonioni makes masterful use of color in the film, his first not in black-and-white. The grays and whites of a hotel corridor evoke a sterile solitude, in sharp contrast to the erotic red walls of a shack along the water." And Richard Brody asserts in a *New Yorker* DVD review, "Though the chilly design of the couple's apartment reflects the clean yet barren lifestyle that advanced industrial technology sustains, Antonioni celebrates the alluring abstractions of high-tech industry itself, with its pure geometry of spheres, arcs, and planes."

These critics and others demonstrate that Antonioni was determined to paint his world with the exact palette he envisioned, and in this, his first color film, he was enormously successful. But it is naive to assume that he was not also determined to define the post–World War II success story of industrial Italy as a nightmare of success, a "painted wasteland," according to Michael Atkinson of the *Village Voice*, and what Jaime N. Christley of *Slant Magazine* calls a "morass of modernity" and Christopher Sharrett suggests is "a landscape of doom." Giuliana walks through this landscape, her son in tow, as if she were witnessing the aftermath of an enormous warscape. She may not have succeeded in adapting, but she is also falling apart in a world that gives her no room to breathe or see. She is out of date, and Antonioni succeeds in creating a credible character who makes us feel what she is seeing, touching, tasting, and smelling. And it is the taste and feel of waste, a waste, Ellen Richards would argue, "produced by human activity" (*Sanitation in Daily Life* v).

No Blade of Grass: A Bleak Eco-warning

Based on the 1955 John Christopher novel, *The Death of Grass*, *No Blade of Grass* provides a blatant and bleak picture of the costs of a toxic atmosphere to human and nonhuman life that brings to mind postapocalyptic films such as *Silent Running* (1972), *Soylent Green* (1973), and *The Road Warrior* (1981). In *No Blade of Grass*, however, those effects include both atmospheric pollution and deadly climate change.

Reinforcing Richards's definitions of human ecology, the film powerfully illustrates the human causes of the disaster people now face: because humans have polluted the Earth's air, water, and soil, a strange new virus has appeared, which only attacks strains of grasses such as wheat and rice, and the world is descending into famine and chaos. When the virus reaches London, architect and former military officer John Custance (Nigel Davenport) escapes the city with his wife, Ann (Jean Wallace); daughter, Mary (Lynne Frederick); and Mary's boyfriend, Roger (John Hamill). Together with those who join them along the way, they fight their way to John's brother's farm, where survival seems possible. Despite this hopeful road film narrative, however, the film maintains its fierce critique of humanity's destruction of the natural world.

As in films such as *Soylent Green*, *No Blade of Grass* opens with a montage of polluted scenes: factories spewing smoke, dead birds, arid land,

No Blade of Grass: One of the factory sources of eco-disaster

traffic jams, and armed masses of people while in the music soundtrack, Roger Whitaker sings, "Gone with the dawn." An image of Earth from space pans into a crowded football stadium, and a voice-over explains that the environment has been destroyed. More scenes of dilapidated cars, factory smoke, car exhaust, and crowded city streets lining a smog-filled city of high-rise apartments and human masses prove the narrator's claim. These shots are reinforced by another montage of industrial wastewater, toxic smoke emissions, pesticides, strip-mining, oil spills and red tides killing water birds, starving children, thousands of cars in an airport parking lot, and a nuclear explosion. "It's the end of life," the soundtrack tells us, and after a focus on the explosion, the camera pans back into space while the narrator exclaims, "And then one day, the polluted Earth could take no more."

Because the eco-disaster has reached London, the military plans to close the city, so John and his family pack to leave, and a flashback reveals the reason for their departure. In a restaurant a year earlier, John and Roger share a lunch while a television in the background broadcasts images of famine in Southeast Asia and a message about a grass disease killing all the world's grain. This famine contrasts blatantly with the plentiful plates of food in the restaurant. In the scene we learn that the world's ecology has been poisoned by pollutants and pesticides in the soil and atmosphere, causing a grass disease that can be contained only by fire. In some areas, martial law has been invoked to control the chaos. These dire warnings are juxtaposed with images of Londoners eating large forkfuls of food. One woman, who is oblivious to the real eco-disaster around her, even suggests that the disease is caused by the Chinese because they "fertilize everything with human shit."

In the film's present the Custance family comprehends and fears the environmental destruction that has now reached London. As they leave the city, they hear a radio report that starvation deaths have reached six hundred million, an astronomical human cost of a toxic atmosphere. After a series of mob and police incidents, they do escape the city, taking another couple, Pirrie (Anthony May) and Clara (Wendy Richard), with them from a gun shop to the school of the Custances' son, David (Nigel Rathbone). As they drive through the country, the landscape is brown and dying and festooned with dirty water full of industrial waste and smoking factories. Now in two cars, the Custance family and their friends kill for survival along the road.

They kill soldiers to get through military barriers and a group of rapists at a railroad crossing, but the polluted environment outside the car window is even more horrifying than this human violence. More polluted rivers and industrial smokestacks provide the terrible backdrop for a truth exposed by the boy, David, who explains, "Earth gets warmer because of pollution," and he maps out the aftermath of melting glaciers and polar ice causing flooded coastlines and cities, "so we all drown," he exclaims. Humans have created the toxic atmosphere that has bred a grass disease that may destroy humankind. According to radio broadcasts it has caused cannibalism in Africa, Asia, and Europe and uncontrollable panic in England because people fear they will be slaughtered with nerve gas. They must fight to live in this poisoned world. The human costs of this man-made environmental disaster are great, but the environmental losses are massive. Every animal that feeds off the diseased grass dies: calves, cattle, sheep, birds, and deer.

Even when the group combines with a community that has lost its village and the accompanying score crescendos with hope, the tragic tone continues, with multiple scenes foreshadowing violent events amplifying the film's sense of dread. As the group walks through a dying field, they pass an ancient Roman aqueduct that contrasts with lines of electric wires along a road. Ultimately the group must win two more battles for the chance to survive, one against a motorcycle gang called the Huns and one against John's brother and his community within a gated pastoral fortress. After both John's brother and Pirrie are killed, the last battle ends and the communities combine, but the film ends here without a sense of hope for humanity's future. Instead, the film's voice-over explains, "This is not a documentary, but it could be," and Whitaker's song of eco-disaster ends the film, highlighting the film's connection with a human ecology that studies humans' surrounding environment and its effect on their lives, especially externalities such as climate change and the greenhouse effect associated with atmospheric pollution.

Safe: Escaping Toxic Air

Safe (1995) updates alienation from the modern industrial world explored in *Red Desert* with a focus on the multiple chemical toxins in the air as of 1995 and their horrific effect on an upscale suburban homemaker, Carol White (Julianne Moore), but the film makes its point by transforming an everyday event into a thrilling eco-disaster. Rita Kempley of the *Washington Post* argues that the film's director, Todd Haynes, "takes what might have been a deadly disease-of-the-week and turns it into a chic postmodern chiller." Desson Howe, another *Washington Post* staff writer, states that Haynes takes a "world of postmodern angst and makes it tremendously affecting and eerily compassionate." And Edward Guthmann of the *San Francisco Chronicle* suggests that Haynes "wants to engage us on a deeper level—to challenge our notions of illness and identity, make us wonder if we aren't all, in some way, allergic to the 20th century."

As in *Red Desert* pollution surrounds Carol throughout the film. She drives down crowded streets and accepts furniture and other goods from delivery trucks. Conversations between Carol and her husband, Greg (Xander Berkeley), or best friend, Barbara (Ronnie Farer), are blurred by the noise of machinery: a vacuum cleaner, a phone, a television or radio. Roger Ebert asserts that this "low-level hum on the soundtrack . . . suggests that malevolent machinery of some sort is always at work somewhere nearby. . . . The effect is to make the movie's environment quietly menacing" ("*Safe* Review").

In a literal homage to *Red Desert* this menacing environment sickens Carol so much that she becomes alienated from it, a response illustrated by long shots of her, even in her own home. She is set apart from her maid and other servants and the painters whose work is accompanied by a television voice explaining that critically ill patients die of chemical exposure. According to Edward Guthmann these "master shots and slow, stately camera moves . . . recall the eerie austerity of Stanley Kubrick's films and suggest a seething menace under the hushed metallic veneer."

Settings associated with chemical toxicity are also shown in long shots. A shopping center where Carol takes her dry cleaning is shown from a distance, for example. Then the connection between toxic air and Carol's sickness is made more palpable when Carol's car is stuck behind a truck spewing smoke. Carol coughs so violently from the smoke that she races into a parking garage to escape. The squeal of her wheels and the car radio heighten the painful coughing until she is gasping for air.

These initial scenes introduce the elements of human ecology explored in the film. Humans are causing toxic air, and humans are suffering because of it. This environmental message is amplified by an image of earth from space and a television message about deep ecology, "a new, more holistic approach."

Within this toxic environment Carol grows sicker, yet the male figures in her life blame her emotional state rather than the state of the environment for her ill health. Her stepson, Rory (Chauncy Leopardi), illustrates the masculine violence these characters embody with a report about Los Angeles gang violence. The family doctor finds nothing wrong with Carol. Her husband reacts angrily to her headache claims and suggests she is withholding sex, even though she is now suffering nosebleeds because of a recent permanent wave at a beauty shop.

A second visit to the dry cleaner, now filled with pesticides being spread by a masked exterminator, sends Carol into a life-threatening event. After Carol is rushed to the hospital and intubated, however, her doctor claims that she has no discernible problems. Her disease is hysterical, the doctor implies, and mollifies Carol by supporting her demand that a nurse cease spraying the room with air disinfectant.

A flyer advertising the Wrenwood Center and its programs seems to offer Carol a solution. "Do you smell fumes? Are you allergic to the twentieth century?" the flyer asks. Instead, Carol's doctor suggests she see a psychiatrist, handing the doctor's card to her husband. Even though the Wrenwood Center's leader, Peter Dunning (Peter Friedman), tells Carol and other audience members attending a seminar that "certain people's tolerance to everyday chemicals" is weakened and an allergy testing session proves her reactions are environmentally based, Carol's stay at the Wrenwood Center seems to worsen her condition. Peter Dunning even tells her and other group members that they have "allowed themselves to get sick."

Carol, not her toxic environment, is at fault for her condition, they all tell her, a message that becomes even more horrific when the film begins to focus more closely on the red sore on Carol's forehead as she tells herself, "I love you" in her safe-house mirror. Overall, however, earlier segments of the film demonstrate well the human causes for a toxic environment and suggest the need to find a safe haven free from poisonous air.

How to Boil a Frog: Documenting Air Pollution and Climate Change

Davis Guggenheim's *An Inconvenient Truth* also documents dangers associated with air pollution, especially as a stimulus for climate change. The Canadian Jon Cooksey's *How to Boil a Frog* (2009), however, takes the nostalgia-based arguments in *An Inconvenient Truth* further. By infusing comedy into arguments that climate change is occurring; about its causes, including atmospheric; and for actions we can take to address it, Cooksey offers a viable argument for change that includes fun activities like making friends and making trouble. He's not trying to save the planet; he's trying to save himself. Ultimately *How to Boil a Frog* provides a complex view of atmospheric pollution because it explicitly connects global warming and climate change with atmospheric pollution.

How to Boil a Frog explores how human activity such as toxic atmospheric emissions has contributed to climate change, combining arguments against air pollution and an industrial complex like those found in *Red Desert* with evidence connecting this human-caused poisoning of the atmosphere to climate changes that threaten both humans and the natural world. In a move toward human ecology, *How to Boil a Frog*

How to Boil a Frog: Power plant cooling tower "corked" for comic effect

not only blames humans for global warming; it also proposes solutions based on the premise that basic needs like clean air "must be secured by cooperation" (Richards *Cost of Cleanness* 50).

As Cooksey makes clear, warnings about global warming caused by air pollution have been around at least since 1827, when Jean-Baptiste Fournier suggested that an atmospheric effect kept the earth warmer than it would otherwise be—he used the analogy of a greenhouse. But Cooksey emphasizes global warming not as a problem but as a symptom of our "overshooting" nature's curve. When we go past things that nature can give us, we "overshoot," Cooksey explains. There are too many of us, but we keep on multiplying, and we consume too many resources.

How to Boil a Frog compares our own experiences with air pollution, climate change, and their repercussions to a frog in a pot of water that starts out cool and then heats up slowly till it boils. The frog doesn't jump out of the pot because it has become acclimated, just as we have become used to our warming environment. The problem with this acclimation is that we're on a death course, the film suggests. But the film doesn't stop there. It demonstrates definitively the horrific mess we've made of Earth's environment through a structured comedic argument. But it also provides multiple solutions that move the film beyond rhetorical documentaries like *An Inconvenient Truth*, which rely on individual and collective nostalgia—a look to the past—for their arguments. This metaphor also demonstrates the film and its filmmaker/narrator's human approaches to ecology. Cooksey asserts, "I'm no tree hugger. I'm a people hugger" and then illustrates what ordinary people can do to save themselves by establishing the problem (human-caused climate change) and proposing viable and simple solutions everyone can implement.

Cooksey first shows shots of a body of water so covered with jellyfish it has turned pink. There is so much CO_2 from atmospheric pollution in the water, he explains, that only jellyfish can survive. He outlines an overview of theorists' discoveries that provide evidence of our negative effect on Earth's atmosphere and comically responds by climbing into a coffin because it seems to be too late. But, as he explains, he "can't give up" because he "has a daughter." Instead, we must determine what we can do to stop its dire effects.

To address the massive problem of climate change, Cooksey connects it with elements that humans can change. For example, global warming is represented as a symptom of a bigger problem associated with exponential growth of populations and their overconsumption, all resulting in toxic atmospheric emissions (air pollution) that "overshoot" what nature can give and purify. The world's population has grown so astronomically, the film explains, that CO_2 emissions in the air have also grown exponentially. Cooksey compares our plight with that of reindeer on St. Matthews Island. In 1913 there were six thousand reindeer on the island, but when the lichen disappeared, all but forty-two died. The last reindeer died in 1982, he explains. For Cooksey this tragedy parallels the "tragedy of the commons": "If no one is in charge of a common resource, people will keep taking it until it is gone." Not only are there too many people, Cooksey explains; there are too many people in the wrong places, just like the reindeer on St. Matthews.

Another cause of our predicament is our war on nature, according to Cooksey, who describes the amount of plastics discarded into the oceans, arguing that it has already killed half of finned fish. In fifty years all ocean fish will be dead or near extinction. These plastic-filled ocean dead zones will never break down, he explains, yet a half pound of plastic is discarded by each person every day in the Western world.

Trees too are being destroyed, so much so that only ten acres remain for every million originally growing on Earth, even though one-fourth of global warming is caused by this loss of trees. Half of Earth's species will be extinct by the end of the century if this waste continues. Pesticides are also cited as a problem, as well as erosion caused by soil overuse and tree removal and industrial pollution contaminating water, air, and land. Like Richards, Cooksey sees "clean air, clean water, clean soil, and wholesome food" as essentials, basic needs that cannot be met if this overconsumption continues.

Production and consumption of goods around the world requires exploitation of natural resources and labor and the release of exponential amounts of CO_2 into the atmosphere in the form of air pollution, and according to Cooksey, developing countries learn about these consumer items from television and other media. The gap between rich and poor may begin to narrow, but widening access to consumer goods may only be bad for the environment. The worst resource exploitation, however, may be oil consumption, which also contributes to air pollution, according to the film. Cooksey explains that oil supplies peaked in the United States in 1970, so we are now accessing oil reserves that may require as much energy to extract as they provide, as with the Canadian tar sands in the province of Alberta. Cooksey asserts that the Earth can only absorb eleven billion tons of CO_2 per year, but we are emitting thirty-one billion tons. This "peak oil," as Cooksey calls it, is exacerbated by massive overconsumption, like "a baby boomer with a Visa card."

These five human-caused problems can be addressed, however, by human action. Overpopulation can be addressed by having only one child or none. Harmful oil consumption can be addressed by boycotting Exxon/Mobil, which accounts for 3 percent of global warming and its air pollution source since 1982. We can also cut our emissions by eliminating beef from our diets, since more than 10 percent of global warming comes from raising cows for food because they too contribute to air pollution. This simple step will also begin to address problems associated with water use and overgrazing. Cooksey also suggests buying used, recycling more, and trading to move toward sustainability. He agrees with Ross Gelbspan's arguments in *Boiling Point* that we should reduce use of coal and oil by 80 percent, since there is no such thing as clean coal. The mercury produced by burning coal will always be in Earth's atmosphere and contributes to numerous problems, including acid rain. As Utah Phillips explains in a song Cooksey mentions in the film, "The Earth is not dying. It is being killed."

To address these bigger problems such as coal and oil consumption and the air pollution and global warming associated with them, Cooksey tells viewers to "make trouble" with YouTube videos against burning coal, for example, a method he demonstrates has worked. In British Columbia, for example, Cooksey claims no new coal plants are allowed. He also proposes a more communal approach to living, with cohousing and smaller communities relying on wind and solar and, when viable, geothermal energy, turning "neighborhoods into small towns that are self-sufficient." And Cooksey notes what he can do personally to contribute to CO_2 reduction. Because he works for Canadian television, he can inform the public about problems and solutions connected with climate change. He rents his home and could walk and bike more. He could also learn to grow his own food. Primarily, however, Cooksey seeks to "make trouble."

This last proposal lines up well with the conclusion of the film, scenes of devastation meant to parallel the crash films from driver's education classes. Cooksey says we should "view it so we don't have to do it" before showing scenes of eco-disasters: garbage, air pollution, nuclear explosions, oil spills, human deaths, and spectacular fires and smoke. Instead, the film tells us, we should "make trouble" and save ourselves by minimizing the root causes of atmospheric pollution that contribute to climate change.

Human Ecology, Atmospheric Pollution, and Climate Change

How to Boil a Frog provides a variety of ways to address climate change and fight for humanity's survival, but its emphasis on saving ourselves aligns especially well with human ecology, an approach that originated at the turn of the twentieth century, rather than more recent approaches to ecology, organismic and chaotic ecology. Organismic ecologists like Aldo Leopold encourage an ecologically centered view of the land as a biotic pyramid in which humans are a part and propose a land ethic that "enlarges the boundaries of the community to include soils, waters, plants, and animals, or collectively: the land" (Leopold 204), an approach that takes the focus away from humanity to highlight a biotic community of all living things sharing an equal place in the natural world.

The chaotic approach to ecology, which emerged in the 1970s, suggests that nature is a potential disrupter of its own ecosystems through natural disasters such as hurricanes and tornadoes but primarily embraces Leopold's biotic community ideal. Another approach, economic ecology, parallels "fair use" approaches missing from all the films explored here because it argues that humans should exploit environmental resources for their own benefit without restraint. Instead, these films, to a lesser or greater extent, reinforce Ellen Richards's assertion that clean air is essential to public health and "must be secured by cooperation" (Cost of Cleanness 49–50). In a clear connection with circumstances of the twentieth and twenty-first centuries highlighted in the films, Richards underlines the costs of a modern, technologically advanced and interconnected world: "Today a passenger landing in New York may be in St. Paul or Helena before [a] disease develops, and perhaps he has scattered seeds all the way. In a crowded quarter, close contact in halls, alleyways, restaurants, and streetcars all demand greater care in cleanliness of both person and quarters. Dust in streets, refuse in shops, smoke in the air, all demand removal by expensive means" (Cost of Cleanness 57). This cost of cleanness is calculated in human terms in films addressing atmospheric pollution.

Red Desert and Safe illustrate the cost to human health and life caused by a toxic environment. They each concentrate on the ecology's effects on one woman primarily and illustrate attempts made by each to alleviate her symptoms. In Red Desert Giuliana seeks solace in a lover, and in Safe Carol escapes a poison Los Angeles for the chemical-free zone afforded by Wrenwood Estates. Although Safe may suggest that eliminating toxins provides few benefits for human health, it does demonstrate that a "clean" environment affords emotional gains.

No Blade of Grass and How to Boil a Frog both complicate issues of atmospheric pollution, not only because of their genres (science fiction and documentary, respectively), but also because they explicitly connect global warming (climate change) with poisoning the air. Again, however, these films take a human ecology approach to atmospheric pollution. Both films clearly blame humans for the eco-disaster they now face. They also focus on humans when illustrating the effects of environmental degradation. *No Blade of Grass* showcases a family's attempts to survive in a postapocalyptic world. It illustrates the toxic environment created by humanity, but it purveys only a message of humanity's preservation, not a biotic community.

How to Boil a Frog also demonstrates well the blame humanity shares for global warming by documenting human-based causes for atmospheric pollution and climate change. It also illustrates the continuing problems humans will face if consumption and population growth continue at the current pace. As a documentary, however, the film also proposes a number of changes we can make, not to save the Earth, but to save ourselves. All these films, then, draw on human approaches to ecology, perhaps demonstrating more effectively the costs of a toxic world.

CHAPTER TWO

JAMES BOND AND WATER WARS IN CONTEMPORARY FILM

A New Eco-warrior?

Chinatown (1974) serves as the quintessential water rights film: murder, infidelity, and incest all become integrally connected with water as a commodity in 1930s Los Angeles, a context established by a picture of FDR in the opening shot of the office of private investigator J. J. (Jake) Gittes (Jack Nicholson). Jake is introduced to an infidelity case but discovers that the lover is Hollis Mulwray (Darrell Zwerling), the chief engineer of Los Angeles's Water and Power. According to Water and Power, Los Angeles is on the edge of the desert. Without water the valley will turn to dust, and the Alto Valley Dam will save it, but Mulwray opposes the dam because it is shoddy and ineffective and because he discovers that his former partner Noah Cross (John Huston) is dumping gallons of water from the Los Angeles reservoir into the ocean to prove the need for the dam. Ultimately Mulwray is murdered by the very water he serves. "Los Angeles is dying of thirst," says a sticker near Jake's car, but as one police officer explains, "Can you believe it? We're in the middle of a drought, and the water commissioner drowns. Only in LA."

While investigating Mulwray's murder, Jake discovers that the water department is not irrigating as it has claimed. A clandestine group is

Chinatown: Jake investigates water disappearance

poisoning the farmers' wells and shooting out their water tanks so they will sell their property to "ghost" buyers who are either dead or elderly relatives of wealthy LA socialites. In fact, Noah Cross has killed Mulwray when he hindered Cross's plan to incorporate the valley into the city of Los Angeles by buying up farmland to grow even richer on its resources. Cross declares, "Either you bring the water to LA or you bring LA to the water," underpinning the continuing connection between water rights and environmental history in *Chinatown* and other films centering on water, especially the 2008 James Bond installment, *Quantum of Solace*.

Quantum of Solace takes water rights issues and human approaches to ecology to the world stage in a genre that draws on the neo-noir of Polanski's *Chinatown*. In *Quantum* a private detective is replaced with a British Secret Service agent. But the mystery in both films incorporates a utility company's attempts to control water and results in multiple action sequences and deaths. Although the corporation wins in *Chinatown*, in *Quantum* its representatives are defeated, and the hero becomes an eco-warrior encapsulating the activist spirit of Bolivian peasants in Cochabamba.

Water Rights: A Short History

Water rights are steeped in environmental history in films with water at their center. *Chinatown* explicitly highlights the continuing influence of the 1877 Desert Land Act and the doctrine of prior appropriation. Water rights in America respond to at least three political, historical, and economic perspectives, all of which have throughout U.S. history addressed water distribution during times of both drought and abundance of water. The first of these, the riparian doctrine, connects water with the land adjacent to it, so that "Riparian land owners can access water for a 'reasonable use,' so long as downstream users are not adversely affected" (Donohew 90).

A second approach, the appropriative doctrine, provides grounding for legislation that opened the West to pioneers. See, for example, the Desert Land Act (1877), the General Mining Act (1872), and the Homestead Act (1862), which rested on the doctrine of prior appropriation: "Water rights with older priority dates are more likely to receive their full allocation and hence are more valuable" (Donohew 89). A third perspective focuses on groundwater rights, which are more difficult to define and measure, so specifications differ from state to state. For example, "in some states, including parts of Texas, unlimited ground water pumping is allowed by a landowner so long as it is put to a beneficial use" (Donohew 91), but in others, state or local agencies regulate groundwater usage more closely.

Water rights also connect explicitly with human approaches to ecology that not only draw on riparian rights and the appropriative doctrine but also helped to foster the EPA's Clean Water Act of 1972. For example, Ellen Swallow Richards explains how human approaches to ecology encourage the right to water, explaining, "In common law, water is held to be a gift of nature to man for use by all, and therefore not to be diverted from its natural channels for the pleasure or profit of any one to the exclusion of the rest" (Richards and Woodman 57). But for Richards it was not enough to ensure that water was available. That water must also be clean; she asserts, "A city or town is under strict obligation to furnish a safe supply of water as it is to provide safe roads" (59). For Richards everyone should have access to water free of contaminants or "objectionable substances, mineral and organic" (61) because it is "a necessary condition of life" (67).

Perhaps because water is both abundant and necessary, it serves as a protagonist in films from the silent era to the present. Water rights take different roles in contemporary feature films. Floods take the center in silent films such as Victor Fleming's *When the Clouds Roll By* (1919), New Deal features such as *Our Daily Bread* (1934), and contemporary features such as Michael Polish's *Northfork* (2003). Drought, on the other hand, serves as the protagonist in features such as the John Ford epic *The Grapes of Wrath* (1940) and contemporary documentaries, including Jim Burroughs's *Water Wars* (2009).

All these films, however, draw on environmental history and environmental law, paving the way for films that are at least partially based on America's sometimes conflicting views of water rights, views almost always grounded in the nineteenth-century American drive for progress. Although this connection to environmental law is most explicitly illustrated by the documentary *Tapped* (2009) and an animated feature, *Rango* (2010), it reaches the mainstream in more subtle and powerful ways in *Quantum of Solace*, an unlikely rhetorical film that not only demonstrates the dangers of commodifying water but also offers solutions that look back to earlier historical visions of water as a right.

Current U.S. Feature Films and the Riparian Doctrine

Water has been considered a natural right around in the world and treated as a usufructary right for thousands of years. Such a right gives temporary possession and enjoyment to those who use water, as long as that use does not cause damage or change it. According to this perspective water can be used but not owned. The riparian doctrine clarifies this natural right. As economist Zachary Donohew explains, because water is typically seen as a usufructary right, rivers and streams cannot be owned, but their water can be accessed by those who live and work beside their banks (90). Although current riparian principles draw on private ownership to define reasonable water use, the doctrine primarily applies to public riparian lands, as activist Vandana Shiva notes in her discussion of communal water use in Colorado's Rio Grande Valley (27). The riparian doctrine still prevails in much of the eastern United States because water is much more abundant there than in the western states, but it also serves as a guiding principle for community rights and water democracies in India (Shiva 29), which hold that "water is a commons. . . . It cannot be owned as private property and sold as a commodity" (36).

Both fictional features and documentaries with water at their center draw on the tenets of the riparian doctrine. Westerns such as *The Ballad of Cable Hogue* (1970) emphasize riparian principles, especially in relation to the Desert Land Act, but contemporary feature films also draw on riparian ideals, which, in these cases, conflict with the Clean Water Act and its roots in human approaches to ecology. In *A Civil Action* (1998), for example, "reasonable use" is under question. The film explores whether those who use the same water source as a leather tanning company have been adversely affected by the company's water use. Although the film primarily centers on Jan Schlichtmann's (John Travolta) failed attempts to sue both Beatrice and W. R. Grace, he ultimately proves that the tannery these companies manage has dumped silicone and trichloroethylene (TCE), toxic waste that has contaminated a town's water supply and caused multiple cancers in its townspeople.

In *A Civil Action* attorney Schlichtmann investigates a case that revolves around a woman whose son had died of leukemia two years before, along with more than a dozen other townspeople, and the city's drinking water is blamed. The townspeople seem unaware of the source of this water pollution, but Schlichtmann discovers that a tannery connected with W. R. Grace is dumping toxins into the river beside the factory. He meets representatives of Beatrice Foods and W. R. Grace, and since they have big pockets, the lawsuit begins. Schlichtmann's investigation is meant to determine that silicone and TCE have been dumped into the water supply by the tannery and are causing the cancers in townspeople. Ultimately Schlichtmann and his law firm settle with both Grace and Beatrice, but Schlichtmann also sends his case files to the EPA, including a report from a worker who has witnessed the cleanup that proves toxic waste had been dumped in the city's water supply. The EPA forces both Grace and Beatrice to pay $69.4 million in cleanup costs because both companies have violated the Clean Water Act.

According to a summary of the Clean Water Act from the EPA, "the Clean Water Act (CWA) establishes the basic structure for regulating discharges of pollutants into the waters of the United States and regulating quality standards for surface waters" but not groundwater sources. Based on the Clean Water Act, the EPA "has implemented pollution control programs such as setting wastewater standards for industry" and "set water quality standards for all contaminants in surface waters," making it illegal to "discharge any pollutant from a point source into navigable waters, unless a permit was obtained." The Clean Water Act helps control one important element of the riparian doctrine, ensuring that downstream water uses are not adversely affected by those upstream. The Clean Water Act and the EPA monitoring it become integral agents in *A Civil Action* and the actual court case it inspired.

The Appropriative Doctrine and Contemporary American Film

In contrast to the Clean Water Act, however, the appropriative doctrine "is a queuing system that rewards first movers." Although those with water rights again hold only usufruct rights, "in this system, the first claimant to a water source has the highest priority to divert water, so long as the withdrawal is for a 'reasonable and beneficial use'" (Donohew 89). The appropriative water rights doctrine, however, serves as "a basis for water markets. The doctrine allows for water to be claimed, diverted and separated from land through which water flows. It can be transported out of a basin for use elsewhere. As such, those who buy water rights or lease water can change the location of diversion, timing of use, and nature and site of ultimate use, subject to regulatory approval to protect downstream claimants" (Donohew 90). Shiva agrees, arguing that "the doctrine of prior appropriation established absolute rights to property, including the right to sell and trade water" (22). Because the appropriative doctrine "gave no preference to riparian landowners," even those far from water sources could compete for water, a principle that "provided the essential ingredients for an efficient market in water wherein property rights were well-defined, enforced and transferable" (Anderson and Snyder 75).

As the title suggests, *Blue Gold: World Water Wars* (2008) also examines the worldwide consequences of commodifying water and offers a foundation for the narrative explored in *Quantum of Solace*. *Blue Gold* is grounded by its opening claim: "This is not a film about saving the environment. This is a film about saving ourselves," narrator Malcolm McDowell declares. "Whoever goes without water for a week cries blood," and a historical overview of ancient cultures' attempts to manage water reinforces the film's premise. The Egyptians and the Romans succeeded where the Mayans did not because the latter had too little water, the film argues. Today water is a source of profit for a few but is necessary for us all. Negotiating a viable resolution between these two worldviews serves as an objective for the film.

To move toward a solution to this conflict between profit and need, *Blue Gold* establishes the problem and supports it with illustrations from around the world. Our water is in crisis, a title card explains, and a World Social Forum in Nairobi is examining the evidence to determine the best ways to ensure that water is available and affordable for everyone. According to Maude Barlow fresh water comprises only 3 percent of the total water on Earth; yet most of that is undrinkable because it is polluted by farms, cars, and industrial wastes that cause miscarriages, low sperm rates, and disease (Barlow and Clarke). The Rio Grande River in the United States, for example, is so polluted that anyone entering it would need eighteen vaccines to survive. Around the world cholera, a water-borne disease, kills more than wars because of this overt pollution, and over 60 percent of the world's wetlands have been destroyed.

The water crisis is a product not only of water pollution; it is also a repercussion of the mining for water by industry, farming, and the bottled water corporations. The world's fresh water supply is becoming polluted so fast that corporations are mining it faster than it can be replenished. Individuals, factory owners, and farmers overuse groundwater, sometimes because of the doctrine of prior appropriation, which states that if farmers or factory owners do not use the water, they may lose their water rights. Urbanization and overdevelopment accelerate groundwater depletion because a paved land devastates the water cycle. Dam projects exacerbate the problem, Shiva states in the film, "choking the artery of the planet" and breaking a sustainable water cycle.

To overcome this water crisis, *Blue Gold* declares that we need to work on a renewable supply, determine how much water we really have at our disposal, and live within those limits. The film asserts that water should be a public commons rather than a privatized source of profit, as it is now around the world—with help from big companies such as Veolia, Suez, Vivendi, and Nestlé. The last scenes of the film highlight ways to solve this water crisis. The title "The Way Forward" introduces multiple examples of local residents usurping the power of these corporate giants.

Uruguay rid itself of the Suez Water Treatment Company by changing its constitution. And Fryeburg, Maine, poured Nestlé's bottled water back into its aquifers. The film ends here, but the suggestion is that with people working together, and primarily on a local level, the water crisis can be solved.

As fictionalized in *Quantum of Solace*, Bolivia expelled its private water companies and began a sustainable water plan, an event Andrew Hageman also examines through a dialectical lens in relation to *The Corporation* (2003), *Even the Rain* (2010), and *Abuela Grillo* (2009) (66). This issue is explored in more detail in *Flow: For Love of Water*, a documentary about the 1999 water privatization in Bolivia forced by the World Bank, which excluded 208,000 people from potable water in Cochabamba. Water was returned to the people of Cochabamba in 2000 and to the citizens of La Paz in 2007, according to the film. Although the Nairobi summit's solutions are not discussed, and the local solutions seem limited, the multiple problems associated with water rights are revealed and illustrated well in *Blue Gold* and reinforced by *Flow*. Contemporary films in a variety of genres reflect the ongoing influence of the doctrine of prior appropriation. *Chinatown* most clearly draws on the doctrine, and *Rango* and *Quantum of Solace* demonstrate the doctrine's continuing influence.

Rango (2011) deliberately addresses water rights issues as it both elucidates the environmental history surrounding water rights in the American desert and critiques current water rights practices in the Las Vegas area. In an obvious homage to *Chinatown* noted by critics from *Time Magazine* to *Salon.Com*, *Rango* explores a hero's attempts to "save a parched Old West–style town from the depredations of water barons and developers" (O'Hehir, "*Rango* and the Rise of Kidult-Oriented Animation"). In fact, the mayor of Dirt (Ned Beatty), the western town that Rango must civilize, modeled his performance on that of John Huston in *Chinatown*. With help from a variety of anthropomorphized western characters, Rango (Johnny Depp) successfully returns water to the desert, defeating the water baron mayor and rehabilitating his henchman, Rattlesnake Jake (Bill Nighy), an obvious homage to Lee Van Cleef's characters in his western films.

Although A. O. Scott declares, "I confess I wanted a tighter gathering of loose ends, and a more thorough explanation of the politics of water and real estate in the fast-changing American West" ("There's a New Sheriff in Town"), *Rango* effectively illustrates the continuing influence of nineteenth-century water rights issues, especially those connected with the Desert Land Act, which offered 640 acres (2.6 km²) of land to an adult married couple who would pay $1.25 an acre and promise to irrigate the land within three years. A single man would receive only half of the land for the same price. Individuals taking advantage of the act were required to submit proof of their efforts to irrigate the land within three years, but as water was relatively scarce, a great number of fraudulent "proofs" of irrigation were provided, a form of corruption evident in both *Chinatown* and *Rango*.

This connection with the Desert Land Act also highlights the film's homage to the western and its typically desertlike setting. As Roger Ebert asserts, "Beneath its comic level is a sound foundation based on innumerable classic Westerns, in which (a) the new man arrives in town, (2) he confronts the local villain, and (3) he faces a test of his heroism. Dirt has not only snakes but also vultures to contend with, so Rango's hands are full. And then there's the matter of the water crisis. For some reason, reaching back to the ancient tradition of cartoons about people crawling through the desert, thirst is always a successful subject for animation" ("*Rango* Review"). Homages to a variety of westerns reinforce this connection, but the references to spaghetti westerns in particular amplify Rango's unlikely heroic persona. The Spirit of the West (Timothy Olyphant) character, for example, is modeled after Clint Eastwood's western roles.

Rango's historical narrative, however, is also connected with the contemporary world and highlights more-current issues surrounding water rights. When Rango is thrown out of his human family's car, he seems to enter the Old West. Yet because the mayor seeks to re-create a desert paradise similar to Las Vegas and its surrounding golf courses in that desert landscape, the Old West becomes connected with the new irrigated deserts of the twenty-first century. Although the film fails to address the fact that "Las Vegas is far more advanced in both water consciousness and water management than almost anywhere else in the country" (Fishman 56), by both integrating innovative computer generated images (CGI) and animation techniques from Industrial Light and Magic and translating the film's narrative to a videogame format, *Rango* also

Quantum of Solace: James Bond (Daniel Craig) fights for water rights

effectively demonstrates the ongoing effects of the Desert Land Act and the exploitation of water rights it sometimes encouraged.

Quantum of Solace: When Water Rights Meet the Mainstream

Contemporary water rights issues come to the fore in *Quantum of Solace*, with control of land and water like that found in *Chinatown* nearly replicating the 1998–2000 Cochabamba, Bolivia, water wars instigated by the World Bank, a connection noted only by Joshua Clover in the *Film Quarterly* review "Cinema for a New Grand Game." These wars began when the World Bank "refused to guarantee a $25 million loan to refinance water services in the city of Cochabamba unless the local government sold its public water utility to the private sector and passed on the costs to consumers" (Barlow and Clarke 154). Bolivia complied, giving control of water to Aguas del Tunari, "a newly formed subsidiary of the U.S. construction and water giant Bechtel," but when water rates increased by almost 250 percent, tens of thousands of Cochabamba citizens protested for a week, with 90 percent of residents opposing Bechtel. This reaction prompted the Bolivian government to break its contract with Bechtel. The World Bank president James Wolfensohn argued against the change, but protest coordinator Oscar Olivera disagreed, declaring, "I'd like to meet with Mr. Wolfensohn to educate him on how privatization has been a direct attack on Bolivia's poor. . . . Families with monthly incomes of around $100 have seen their water bills jump to $20 per month—more than they spend on food" (155).

Quantum of Solace also takes the appropriative doctrine further, since it puts water at the center of an international film genre, the James Bond film. Juxtaposing a secret organization fronted by what looks like an environmental group against Bond and the British Secret Service, *Quantum* constructs water as a commodity worth more than oil, the resource that the organization, Quantum, claims to be seeking on its now environmentally protected lands in Central and South America. Most notably, however, the film addresses water rights issues in Bolivia, drawing overtly on the 2000 Bolivian water wars for its narrative. The film merely replaces the World Bank and Bechtel Corporation of the actual water war with a military coup and a secret organization fronted by Greene Planet, whose mission is to acquire and commodify environmental resources, an act that amplifies the tenets of the appropriative doctrine. Although the film's plot obviously parallels the Cochabamba water wars, only one review mentions this connection. Joshua Clover calls it "wholly plagiarized from the archives of reality" (8), but other reviewers focus on changes to the Bond genre and the Bond character, either praising or lamenting differences from the previous installments. Tobias Hochsherf's *Film and History* review, especially, lauds how well the film transforms the Bond character from "gentleman spy" to "more a tough, rugged and uncompromising agent in the tradition of violent hard-boiled detective" (78). As Clover declares, "None of [the reviewers] manage the word 'Cochabamba'" (8).

Even though James Bond films are rarely topical, they do sometimes tackle environmental issues. In *A View to a Kill* (1985), for example, James Bond (Roger Moore) must stop a greedy industrialist from triggering a massive earthquake to destroy California's Silicon Valley and corner the microchip market. In *The Living Daylights* (1987), Bond (Timothy Dalton) combats an organization trading clearly non-conflict-free diamonds for weapons. And in *The World Is Not Enough* (1999), Bond (Pierce Brosnan) must protect a beautiful oil heiress from a notorious terrorist.

Quantum of Solace, however, goes further. It not only examines a contemporary environmental issue, whether water is a resource to share or to sell, but also individualizes that issue, connecting it explicitly to an actual event, the Bolivian water wars, which began less than a decade before the release of the film.

Many reviewers highlight the film's topical nature, but they fail to connect water rights with the particular water war that sparks the film's narrative. Roger Ebert scoffs at the film's villain, a "fiend [who] desires to corner the water supply of . . . Bolivia" ("*Quantum of Solace*"). Stephanie Zacharek describes Greene as "a baddie who poses as an environmentalist so he can pull off crazy schemes, like causing drought that will allow him to barter a deal with a creepy exiled South American general." And Anthony Lane describes Bond's role as "fussing about with water supplies at the back end of Bolivia." These reviewers, like most others, either laud or lampoon Bond's changing character as well.

Clover, however, documents in detail *Quantum*'s connection with the Bolivian water wars, declaring that in the film, "Bechtel returns as Greene Planet, ecopolitics merging with corporate cynicism" (8). Clover explains the water war and its source well: "In 1999, Cochabamba . . . privatized its water supply—as a condition of receiving a loan continuation from the World Bank. The Aguas del Tunari consortium, as it was called, was an international combine including a couple of local corporations but led by International Water Ltd., a subsidiary of Bechtel Corporation. Their pricing meant that the Bolivians were paying in some cases a quarter of their income for water" (8). With these devastating repercussions of privatization, the citizens of Cochabamba revolted, so that "midway through 2000, the 'Bolivian Water Wars' ended with the eviction of the consortium and, shortly, the fall of the government itself" (8), paving the way for the election of Evo Morales and his Movement for Socialism. Shiva sees the outcome of this water war as a great victory for "the people's democratic will" and proof that "privatization is not inevitable and that corporate takeover of vital resources can be prevented" (103). For Clover the film "comes closer to telling the Bolivian story than the critics were able to address, or notice" (8).

Like most James Bond installments, *Quantum* opens with a series of action sequences involving car chases and footraces that continue the narrative of the last Bond feature, *Casino Royale* (2006), and introduce the film's conflict: a battle against an organization that "is everywhere" but remains nameless and without a clear motivation until Bond (Daniel

Craig) connects it to Dominic Greene (Mathieu Almaric) through one of the film's two female protagonists, Camille (Olga Kurylenko). A. O. Scott argues that this first sequence is "speedy and thrilling" but declares that "the other action set-pieces are a decidedly mixed bag, with a few crisp footraces, some semi-coherent punch-outs, and a dreadful boat pileup that brings back painful memories of the invisible car Pierce Brosnan tooled around in a few movies ago" ("007 Is Back").

Ultimately, however, the sequences move the plot forward, introducing the film's eventual Bolivian context and its connection both to Greene and to Bolivia's ex-dictator, General Medrano (Joaquin Cosia). When Medrano seems surprised that Greene can easily recover his Bolivian dictatorship for him, Greene reveals his connection with corporate control: "Well, look at what we did to this country. The Haitians elect a priest, who decides to raise the minimum wage from thirty-eight cents to a dollar a day. It's not a lot, but it's enough to upset the corporations, who were here making T-shirts and running shoes. So they called us, and we facilitated a change." Greene's "organization" can give back Medrano's government as long as Medrano ensures that it will gain access to what looks like a worthless desert in Bolivia. Medrano declares, "You won't find oil there. Everyone has tried," but Greene explains, "But we own everything we find."

Greene's purpose for this newly acquired Bolivian desert becomes clearer once M (Judi Dench) outlines Greene's file for Bond, explaining that he serves as CEO of Greene Planet, a utility company, and also does "a lot of philanthropic work, buying up large tracts of land for ecological preserves." But "there's a firewall around his other corporate holdings," and the Americans claim they have no interest in his work. Because M's phone call was transferred to the section chief of South America immediately, however, she realizes that Greene is "a person of extreme interest." Suspicions regarding Greene's motives and his connection with the FBI and the CIA have now been established without a clear sense of his actual purpose for the land he acquires in Bolivia. The Americans believe they will gain access to leases for any oil found in Bolivia if they do nothing to stop its coup, but Greene hints at his aim when he tells the CIA, "You don't need another Marxist giving national resources to the people, do you?"

In a conversation Bond overhears at a performance of the opera *Tosca*, clues to Greene's objective become more explicit: "This is the world's most precious resource," Greene declares. "We need to control as much of it as we can. Bolivia must be top priority." Even though Greene blames the Bolivian government for water problems at a fund-raising party, asserting, "They cut down the trees; they act surprised when the water and the soil wash out to sea," Camille's intervention in the discussion places Greene's claims in question: "Somehow the logging rights went to a multinational corporation that cut down the forests, but only after our last government sold the land to Greene Planet," she declares. Now both Bond and Camille are Greene's enemies, so they leave the party quickly. The ensuing motorcycle chase leads to the loss of Bond's friend Mathis (Giancarlo Gianini). Bond's recklessness also leads to the death of fellow British agent Strawberry Fields (Gemma Arterton).

Bond and Camille escape by plane after another action sequence and parachute into Greene's Bolivian eco-park, where they discover the real reason for Greene's establishing nature preserves: "They used dynamite," Bond exclaims. "This used to be a riverbed. Greene isn't after the oil. He wants the water. . . . It's one dam. He's creating drought. He'll have built others." With control of water, Greene and Quantum, the clandestine company he fronts, can charge exorbitant prices for the resource. When Bond and Camille walk through a nearby village, they see firsthand the results of this manufactured drought: an empty water tank and a line of peasants coaxing drops from a dry faucet.

Although Bond is now seen as a rogue agent, he and Camille elude the Americans with M's approval and finds Greene's hideout, where Greene and Medrano are finalizing their deal. Greene tells Medrano he must sign over the land. Greene's phantom organization, Quantum, owns more than 60 percent of Bolivia's water supply, and Medrano's "new government will use [Quantum] as [its] utilities provider." When Medrano objects because the cost is double what the people are now paying, Greene illustrates the consequences Medrano might endure if he refuses to sign: "You will wake up with your balls in your mouth and your willing replacement standing over you."

The film's action-filled plot resolves in conventional ways. Camille kills Medrano to avenge her family, and Bond saves her from a series of fantastic explosions and fires. Greene tries to escape, but Bond leaves him in the desert with nothing but a quart of motor oil to drink. His organization ends up killing him. The eco-plot, however, is resolved in ways that again highlight the film's connection with the Bolivian water wars: "Well, the dam we saw will have to come down," Bond declares. "And there'll be others too." Ultimately, however, *Quantum of Solace* most effectively illustrates the repercussions of the appropriative doctrine and its solution: a water democracy like that established in Bolivia after the recent water wars there.

Interpreting Groundwater Rights in American Documentary and Feature Films

Films highlighting mining of water from aquifers demonstrate the broadening effects of viewing water as a commodity but draw on the same appropriative doctrine underpinning the eco-conflict of *Quantum of Solace*. Because groundwater rights are less easily defined than those associated with either the riparian or the appropriative doctrine and vary greatly across states and countries, they are even more easily exploited: "Differences in recharge rates, interaction with surface water and the size of groundwater basins makes groundwater rules difficult to apply across the board." Perhaps because groundwater rules are less explicitly defined, "groundwater is more like an open-access resource, subject to wasteful extraction" (Donohew 91), as well as increased toxic pollution by corporations that exploit it.

Groundwater takes center stage in both contemporary fictional and documentary films. In most fictional films, groundwater is exploited by large companies dumping toxic waste. Based on a contemporary case against the Pacific Gas and Electric Company, *Erin Brockovich* (2000), for example, dramatizes the fight to expose the energy company's negligent leakage of toxic chromium 6 into groundwater and failure to compensate area residents negatively affected by the poisoning of their drinking water. In 1996, as a result of the largest direct action lawsuit of its kind, spearheaded by Erin Brockovich and Ed Masry, the law firm for which Brockovich worked, the utility giant was forced to pay the largest toxic tort injury settlement in U.S. history: $333 million in damages to more than six hundred Hinkley residents. *Erin Brockovich* provides a sometimes exaggerated picture of Brockovich and her determination to unearth evidence to ensure that the firm wins the case,

Gasland: Banjo serenade to fracked gas wells

but it also highlights some possible dangers associated with confusing groundwater principles.

Gasland (2010), a well-regarded documentary, highlights the dangers to groundwater aquifers caused by natural gas drilling. As Robert Koehler of *Variety* asserts, "*Gasland* may become to the dangers of natural gas drilling what *Silent Spring* was to DDT" because it so effectively demonstrates and illustrates the horrific repercussions of injecting chemicals into and extracting natural gas from underground shale: toxic water and poisoned aquifers. Visions of flaming water faucets and dying cattle, dogs, and aquatic animal and plant life make it clear in the film that hydraulic fracturing, or "fracking," at least without effective regulations, may have catastrophic results for a region's drinking and agricultural water. The film concentrates on the problem, however, without offering a solution other than perhaps eliminating hydraulic fracturing altogether.

Gasland begins from the premise that natural gas supplies in the United States are a virtual ocean in the shale basins of the East and the West. The assertion from gas companies is that natural gas is good for the nation, our economy, and our environment and poses no credible threat to drinking water because hydraulic fracturing, "fracking," occurs deep underground and is regulated by the EPA. Filmmaker Josh Fox, however, calls these claims into question by telling his and his region's own "fracking" story. Fox first tells the story of his house in Milenville, Pennsylvania, built in the 1970s near a stream connected to the Delaware River during the time when Richard Nixon signed the Clean Water Act into law. But the house is now atop the Saudi Arabia of natural gas, Fox explains, the Marcellus Shale Formation of the Appalachian Basin, and he is being offered nearly one hundred thousand dollars for leasing his nineteen acres. The goal, he is told, is for Americans to adopt natural gas as the fuel of the future.

Because natural gas is considered such a necessary energy source, however, an energy bill passed in 2005 for Halliburton Technology, the source of some hydraulic fracturing technology, exempted "fracturing" from the Clean Water Act and local, regional, and national drinking water laws. The film explains "fracking" in detail, demonstrating that the process requires the use of chemicals such as diesel fuel, which contains benzene, ethylbenzene, toluene, xylene, and naphthalene, as well as polycyclic aromatic hydrocarbons, methanol, formaldehyde, ethylene glycol, glycol ethers, hydrochloric acid, and sodium hydroxide. The process also requires approximately seven million gallons of water each time fracking is used to drill a deep shale gas well. Fox attempts to talk to Halliburton—or any other company—about this process, including T. Boone Pickens. But none of the companies will speak with him, so Fox draws on the nostalgia that opens the film, providing memories of the stream near his house before the rush for natural gas as "alternative" fuel.

The images contrast dramatically with the 2010 context in which more than forty gas wells have been drilled in Pennsylvania in a few months. The hydraulic fracturing process now is poisoning landowners' water supplies. According to Fox complaints are growing about wells going bad around the natural gas sites in Pennsylvania. A well explodes on New Year's Day. Animals lose their hair and begin vomiting. A cat now refuses to go outside. Horses now have no good water to drink. One family complains that they can ignite their drinking water as it comes out of the faucet. If they turn on the water, it could explode because it is contaminated with natural gas. Water produced from the fracking process has been dumped into fields and onto streams, poisoning water for humans and their animals and crops. Fox finds similar repercussions in Nebraska,

Wyoming, and Texas. *Gasland* reveals many of the disastrous repercussions of "fracking," but as *Sight and Sound* reviewer Sam Davies asserts, "The effect is to leave the viewer with the disturbing sense of the sheer quantity of evidence amassed by Fox, and what *Gasland* has had to omit," an assertion that may point to the lack of solutions offered by the film.

Tapped: Democracy and Community Action versus Groundwater as Commodity

A documentary focused primarily on the dangers of mining water to sell, *Tapped* (2009) more effectively addresses the groundwater issue than does *Gasland*. Like *Quantum of Solace*, *Tapped* establishes the problems related to our water use but also proposes a viable solution based on the premise that meaningful change comes from local grassroots movements. According to the film's narrator, by 2030 two-thirds of the world will lack access to clean drinking water because water is being treated as a commodity. When we treat water as a commodity, the film asserts, we end up with corporate control and thirty-nine billion plastic bottles of water per year in the United States alone. Member of Congress Dennis Kucinich takes this premise further when he argues, "When we start commodifying necessities, serious political instability may result." *Tapped* effectively illustrates some of the negative consequences associated with turning water into a product or commodity.

The first problem the film documents is the water mining itself. A case in Fryeburg, Maine, serves as an ample example of how difficult it is for a small town to battle a large corporation over water rights. Scenes of a pristine lake and a small waterfall highlight the idyllic Maine setting where Nestlé is bottling water nearly for free. The narrator explains that Nestlé is mining water and compares Nestlé's exploitation of resources to the oil rush of the 1930s. In Fryeburg the town is waging a losing battle against Nestlé because, whereas surface mining of water is controlled, groundwater is covered by different rules. In Maine the rule of absolute dominion is followed, so the biggest pump takes the most water. No one was notified in town when Nestlé arrived. The company just bought land in places where water was assumed to be and started pumping. Instead of working with the townspeople, Nestlé refused to pay taxes at the wellhead of one cent per gallon. Because of the rule of absolute dominion—a rule based in the appropriative doctrine—Nestlé has precedence over the town, even if aquifers that supply the town's drinking water are in jeopardy.

According to *Tapped* Arkansas, Colorado, Florida, and other states are affected by this greed for water as well because Nestlé defines control of water in relation to these state laws and has overwhelming legal resources. The people in Fryeburg had been out of water for days when their reservoir ran low, but Nestlé kept on pumping. Other documents reinforce the film's arguments. A March 12, 2010, article in the *Portland Press Herald* documents Nestlé's success at the Maine supreme court level: "The decision by the Maine Supreme Judicial Court clears the way for Poland Spring to build the facility that it had hoped to begin four years ago. The pumping station would be capable of filling up to 50 trucks each day with water piped underground from aquifers in Denmark [a small town near Fryeburg, Maine]," a decision that Fryeburg's Western Maine Residents for Rural Living had been fighting for more than four years.

To reinforce the repercussions of this ruling and others, the film asks, is water a basic human right? According to the film it should be. According to corporations such as Nestlé, the narrator explains, water is a moneymaking commodity that should be mined and sold for, according to the film, nineteen hundred times the cost of tap water. The World Bank estimates that water resources are worth $800 billion. Water is a commodity to those in power, even though climate change is causing more drought and deluge. We must protect our fresh water supplies, the film asserts. Other corporations mine water in similar ways, seeing it as blue gold. Pepsi's Aquafina and Coca Cola's Dasani brands are highlighted in the film. Because of their powerful advertising arm, these company's bottled waters became increasingly popular with little criticism until recently, even though bottled water is rarely tested, and at least 40 percent of bottled water is tap water.

A second problem highlighted in *Tapped* is related to the plastics used in the bottles themselves. The plastic used in these bottles is stamped with a PET (petrochemical) recycling code. Companies manufacturing these bottles use seventy-four million gallons of oil to make them and release benzene into the water and air around them. Because 80 percent of PET manufactured in the United States comes from Flint Hills in Corpus Christi, Texas, the effects of toxic waste in air and drinking water there have been devastating. Cancer rates have increased dramatically. Birth defects have increased by 84 percent. Yet by law the EPA could not inform citizens that they could complain, the film explains. Only one person oversees all the bottled water at the Food and Drug Administration, so the production is virtually unregulated.

The film also reveals the negative environmental hazards associated with polycarbonate plastics used in large bottles and sports and baby bottles. These bottles contain bisphenol A (BPA), which acts like an estrogen and damages reproduction systems, even at low doses, affecting other cancers and obesity rates. According to the film's narrator there are thirty billion bottles in landfills. We recycle only 20 percent of bottles in the United States unless states have return deposit policies. We use eighty million plastic bottles in one day in the United States, so sand on beaches is now plastic, and as of 2007, oceans have forty-six times as much plastic as plankton, so fish are being poisoned and our food web is under attack.

These problems seem overwhelming; yet according to the film, we can take steps to change them. Activists around the United States are shown successfully battling big companies. Action in Corpus Christi prompted EPA action against the Flint Hills plant. Fryeburg, Maine, residents are still fighting as well within the film's context. And residents in rural western Maine have won some battles against Nestlé and Poland Springs. Residents of Shapleigh, Maine, passed an ordinance that gives its citizens the right to local self-governance and gives rights to ecosystems but denies the rights of personhood to corporations. This ordinance allows the citizens to protect their groundwater, putting it in a common trust to be used for the benefit of its residents. Other solutions include new bottle deposit laws, but democratic common trust rights serve as the ultimate goal of the film. According to *Tapped* water is not a commodity. It is a basic human right.

Quantum of Solace, Human Ecology, and the Fight for Ecological Democracy

Contemporary films with water at their center illustrate the ongoing power of human approaches to ecology in an environmental legal context. Some water rights films focus on the ramifications of riparian rights, especially when they are less effectively regulated by the 1972 Clean Water Act and organizations such as the EPA. In *A Civil Action*, for example, water rights are represented as the right to clean, drinkable water, and a clear legal solution is provided: EPA intervention. In *Gasland*, however, filmmaker and activist Josh Fox reveals the negative externalities attached to hydraulic fracturing, or "fracking," for natural gas, a new oil and gas extraction process seemingly condoned by legislatures in both the western and the eastern United States. Other contemporary feature films explore water rights in relation to water not as a resource but as a commodity. In *Rango* water is exploited for personal gain and constructed as a product to be stolen or bought and sold. *Rango* demonstrates the consequences of usurping riparian rights with an appropriative doctrine, effectively revealing the long-term ramifications of commodifying water, turning it into a product that can be owned and sold. It also proposes a viable alternative that returns water to its democratic community roots. *Quantum of Solace* makes similar arguments, but within an action-adventure genre that amplifies the message, not only with near-death car chases and maximum explosions but with a narrative grounded in current affairs described in contemporary water rights documentaries released the same year (2008), *Blue Gold: World Water Wars* and *Flow: For Love of Water*. *Tapped* illustrates the dangers of an appropriative doctrine in conjunction with groundwater rights.

Tapped also connects well with both the eco-narrative of *Quantum of Solace* and the Bolivian water wars on which it is based. Like *Quantum*, *Tapped* ends with possible solutions to the commodification of water, all of which include locally based battles against powerful corporations. Although Bond acts as an eco-warrior rather than a citizen activist in the film, he too must win a battle against a powerful corporation, a shadowy and corrupt company that in many ways resembles Nestlé and other industry giants highlighted in *Tapped* and other water rights films. In the Bolivian water wars that inspired *Quantum*, Bechtel Corporation gained temporary control of water rights because of its connection with both the World Bank and the Bolivian government. Maude Barlow and Tony Clarke explain, "As the story of Cochabamba reveals, the World Bank's demands were designed primarily to benefit global water corporations like Bechtel. It also shows how much the major corporate players in the water industry depend on these international financial institutions to build a worldwide water market." These corporations and financial institutions collude with governments as well: "The close ties between corporations and governments have created a network of institutions for global economic governance, which has established a body of rules for finance, trade, and investment that can now be effectively used by both water service companies and water exporters" (Barlow and Clarke 156).

As in both *Tapped* and *Quantum*, however, these corporations and the powers that support them can be defeated and control of water returned to the local communities it serves. In Cochabamba water services were given back to workers at the local water company, Servicio Municipal del Agua Potable y Alcantarillado, and the community's citizens. After years of hard work, community control has become a reality in Cochabamba. According to an E-Source article titled "Bolivia," "[the] Community Association for Drinking Water and Sanitation was formed on April 22, 2007, as a public service community association with charitable status. Its primary purpose is to administrate, operate and maintain the drinking water system and keep it clean. This association has managed to supply water to the districts between the rivers, Trafalgar, Santa Fe and part of Bello Horizonte (Villa Payer-District 14), about 45 minutes bus ride from the city centre."

Whether through the actions of citizens or their eco-warrior representatives, ecological democracies are a viable solution to a commodification of water that places the price of water out of reach and drains aquifers instead of encouraging sustainable water use. As Shiva explains, "Higher prices under free-market conditions will not lead to conservation. Given the tremendous economic inequalities, there is a great possibility that the economically powerful will waste water while the poor will pay the price." Instead we should strive for water democracies: "Community rights are a democratic imperative—they hold states and commercial interests accountable and defend people's water rights in the form of decentralized democracy" (31). That may be at least one message of *Quantum of Solace*: only by returning control of water to the commons, to a democratic community, can it be both affordable and abundant.

CHAPTER THREE

READY TO WEAR?

From Fashion to Environmental Injustice

Near the middle of *The Devil Wears Prada* (2006), Miranda Priestly
(Meryl Streep) reacts to Andy Sachs's (Anne Hathaway) sniggers over
her assistant's struggle to decide between two similar belts for an outfit,
asking her blithely, "Something funny?" And when Andy remarks on
how similar the belts look, declaring, "You know, I'm still learning about
all this stuff," Miranda illustrates the enormous effect that the clothing
industry has on our daily lives:

> This . . . stuff? Oh. Okay. I see. You think this has nothing to do with
> you. You go to your closet and you select . . . I don't know . . . that lumpy
> blue sweater, for instance, because you're trying to tell the world that
> you take yourself too seriously to care about what you put on your back.
> But what you don't know is that that sweater is not just blue. It's not
> turquoise. It's not lapis. It's actually cerulean. And you're also blithely
> unaware of the fact that in 2002, Oscar de la Renta did a collection
> of cerulean gowns. And then I think it was Yves Saint Laurent . . .
> wasn't it, who showed cerulean military jackets? I think we need a
> jacket here. And then cerulean quickly showed up in the collections
> of eight different designers. And then it filtered down through the
> department stores and then trickled on down into some tragic Casual
> Corner where you, no doubt, fished it out of some clearance bin.

Mardi Gras: Failed human ecology

However, that blue represents millions of dollars and countless jobs and it's sort of comical how you think that you've made a choice that exempts you from the fashion industry when, in fact, you're wearing the sweater that was selected for you by the people in this room from a pile of stuff.

Miranda's brief history of the cerulean sweater and its origin begins to reveal the massive size of the clothing industry, here in relation to fashion. Andy's sweater demonstrates well that fashion fabric color choices in 2002 trickle down first to other designers, and then to department stores, and finally to the discount store.

Miranda's speech also makes the point that the fashion industry benefits everyone, providing clothes for multiple socioeconomic classes and stimulating the U.S. economy with billions of dollars in profits and "countless jobs" as illustrated well by multiple clothing and fashion industry films. Miranda's claim is explicitly reinforced, for example, by Robert Altman's *Ready to Wear* (1994), a film that attempts to reveal some of the problems with the fashion industry by focusing on various characters' reactions while preparing for a Paris fashion show. *Ready to Wear* provides an uncomplimentary portrayal of the fashion industry, a "hate letter" according to Richard Corliss, but a "comedy crossed with a home movie," according to Roger Ebert ("*Ready to Wear* Review"). What stands out amid the personal injustices and competitions, however, is a nod to the environment missing from most films. At the ready-to-wear show, one reporter asks a designer, "How do you feel that 50 percent of the world's pollution comes from textile mills?" shocking the designer and prompting the viewer to wonder if she's right. Do the fashion and clothing industries contribute this significantly to everyday environmental disasters such as air and water pollution? This chapter examines films that either peripherally or explicitly address this question: the labor films *Norma Rae* (1979), *China Blue* (2005), *T-Shirt Travels* (2001), and *The Last Train Home* (2009) examine environmental issues primarily from a tangential perspective, but *Mardi Gras: Made in China* (2005), *Maquilapolis* (2006), the dissertation documentary *Baytar Environmental Clothing Industry* (2010), *Cotton Road* (2013), and *Thread: A Documentary* (2013) overtly explore the negative environmental externalities associated with the textile and clothing industries.

Although Miranda's soliloquy, and the films that illustrate its points, address only parts of the fashion, clothing, and textile industries, it also begins to illustrate the industry's effects on a people and their economy. Like other films addressing the fashion and clothing manufacturing industries, *The Devil Wears Prada* not only reveals the complexity of the design and manufacturing process but also begins to expose and illuminate the environmental justice issues associated with this industry, which helps us meet one of our basic human needs. Similar to other clothing industry films, *The Devil Wears Prada* highlights and typically critiques the exploitation of labor and valorizes textile and garment industry workers' efforts to organize, either formally or informally. The film provides a demonstration and multiple individual illustrations of the clothing cycle through personal narratives. It shows the contrast and conflict between urban and rural values and validates figures who become heroic in spite of their humble backgrounds, foregrounding their successful attempts to overcome adversity.

What is hidden in *The Devil Wears Prada* and other films addressing the fashion and clothing industry, however, is an explicit discussion of how environmental justice underpins the films' narratives and rhetoric. Although sometimes obscured by the human rights issues examined by the films, both documentaries and fictional films with clothing at the center address environmental issues across races, classes, and genders, beginning to broach the question, how do gender, class, and race intersect with the environment in the clothing industry? Do problems with cotton production enter these films, or do the water and toxicity issues associated with cotton remain hidden? Do the films address our throwaway society and its effects on local industry in developing countries? Do they highlight problems with sweatshops, air pollution, fabrics made with oil? Although most clothing films focus primarily on heroic individuals and class and race conflict, this chapter seeks to show how some clothing films go further and effectively reveal how social justice issues interconnect with environmental justice concerns.

Human Ecology and Clothing Industry Labor Films

Although textile and clothing industry films such as *Norma Rae*, *China Blue*, *T-Shirt Travels*, and *The Last Train Home* focus primarily on issues related to the rural/urban divide, labor, and globalization, they also peripherally highlight the importance of human approaches to ecology constructed by Ellen Richards more than a century ago. *Norma Rae* tackles social, economic, and environmental injustices related to the textile industry in the rural American South. *T-Shirt Travels* documents the turn to "recycled clothing" forced on Zambians when International Monetary Fund (IMF) policies destroyed their own burgeoning clothing industry, and *China Blue* and *The Last Train Home* highlight the continuing negative effects of the industry on lower-income rural women in China. Each film, however, also includes glimpses of the environmental consequences of unfettered clothing production.

These glimpses coincide with the human ecology movement spearheaded by Richards. In her 1911 text, *The Art of Right Living*, for example, Richards includes environmental conditions in and outside the home in her definition of right living, "the means at hand for mitigating climate when it is too severe for health, the means of improving soil and water supply, for suppressing noise, dust, and for eliminating hurry" (35). To help implement this definition, Swallow asserts that labor laws "are wholly a matter for regulation by the community, made up of individuals whose consensus of opinion rules" (39). For Richards a place of work should be sanitary and clean enough to maintain a healthy and consequently more efficient workforce. To ensure these conditions, Richards suggests, communities must implement labor laws and regulate them, arguments that are still being made in recent films about the textile industry.

More-recent applications of human ecology approaches provide even more explicit parameters for health and wellness in the workplace. In her study of indoor ecology from fall 1990, for example, Sheila Danko explains how "management is recognizing that their competitive edge lies in attracting, maintaining and fostering a work force that is healthy in body, mind, and spirit" (3). Other recent studies in the *Human Ecology Journal* examine ways to protect workers from toxic chemicals in a workplace. Metta Winter summarizes a study conducted by Charlotte Coffman that demonstrated how "operators who use correct protective clothing and well-designed closed transfer systems experience negligible exposure to pesticides" (21). Joe Wilensky provides an overview of research toward "a model that predicts the comfort and protective qualities of nonwoven fabrics" for workers (5). Human ecology approaches, then, attempt to make the workplace environmentally safe and sanitary for workers, if only to increase production and worker health and well-being. By improving environmental conditions "indoors," however, nonhuman life also reaps benefits.

Norma Rae, China Blue, and *T-Shirt Travels* highlight some of the inhumane working conditions addressed by these human approaches to ecology. One of the earliest examples of a clothing industry film with environmental justice issues at its center is *Norma Rae*, a social justice drama drawing on the J. P Stevens textile mill and its sixteen-year battle against union organizers in Roanoke Rapids, North Carolina. Like *The Pajama Game* (1957), a Doris Day musical about workers in a pajama factory organizing a union for a seven-and-one-half-cent raise, the film highlights working-class struggles and racial and gender issues, and addresses the ongoing conflicts between urban (northern) and rural (southern) values as they relate to both culture and nature, but it also broaches environmental concerns that a human approach to ecology would remedy. As Henry Giroux asserts, "If we view the concept of class as not only the objective and structural relation of a group to the means of production, but also as differing sets of values, practices, and meanings shaped through the prism of everyday life and struggle, we will get a better idea of what *Norma Rae* is about."

The conflict between modernity associated with the urban North and romance and Jeffersonian values associated with the rural South is played out in the film with contrasting scenes in the mill and in the rural home of Norma Rae (Sally Field). Partly filmed in a unionized mill in Opelika, Alabama, the film opens with a view of the exterior of the fictional O. P. Henley Textile Mill, reinforcing the modern mechanized and exploitative end of this dualism, as well as the more expansive conflict between the values of the urban North and the rural South. John A. Alonzo's cinematography reinforces this dualism by juxtaposing the rural homes with the hopelessness of the southern mill town atmosphere. As Henry Giroux explains, "He has photographed this southern mill town in grayish whites and dirt brown tones that convincingly capture an environment filled with a mixture of hope and despair: the grimy town motel, the peeling paint on the houses, the life-draining atmosphere of the factory." The images of the town contrast with the vibrant life that Norma Jean brings to her parents' house and her home with Sonny (Beau Bridges).

The characters of union organizer Reuben (Ron Leibman) and Norma Rae embody the dualism on display. According to a review of the film in *Variety*, the "pairing of Jewish radicalism and Southern miasma is the core of *Norma Rae*, and is made real and touching by the individual performances of Leibman and Field." Shots of the interior serve as an illustration of the means of production and a contrast to the rural area around this tiny mill town.

Inside the mill, however, the environmental consequences of poor working conditions are evident when we learn that Norma Rae's mother, Leona (Barbara Bakley), is deaf because of the loud mill. A *Variety* staff review suggests that in the film, management-labor struggles are "being waged in Southern textile mills, where the din of the machinery is virtually unbearable, and workers either go deaf or suffer the consumptive effects of 'brown lung' disease." In one scene, for example, Norma Rae speaks with her mother about opening her lunch sack, but the factory has deafened her, so she doesn't answer. As Norma Rae tells her supervisor, "She didn't hear one word I said!" When the supervisor tells her, "It happens all the time," and "it's just temporary," Norma Rae explodes: "Well, it doesn't happen to my mama!" The only solution the supervisor provides is for her to find another job in a town with no other opportunities. As Vincent Canby explains, "the highly publicized industrial boom in the post–World War II South was largely the result of cheaper (nonunion) wages that lured manufacturers away from the Northeast and mid-Atlantic states."

A union meeting reveals some of the other environmental consequences of working at the textile mill. Women workers talk haltingly about not being allowed to sit down when they have menstrual cramps, "which come pretty hard. They say you gotta keep to your feet unless you bring a note from the doctor. We wouldn't say we was sick if we wasn't." Other workers complain about their low pay, poor working conditions, and the pressure to speed up production. But the most powerful environmental statement comes from a woman who lost her husband, Averil, to "brown lung," or byssinosis, an occupational lung disease caused by exposure to cotton dust in inadequately ventilated working environments. The horror of the mill's environment becomes personal for Norma Rae, however, when her father has a heart attack and dies at his work post because the floor manager forces him to hang on for his fifteen-minute break before seeking help.

Ultimately Norma makes her case, convincing her husband that she loves him and her fellow workers that a union will protect them all. The film takes the time to show the union vote and ends with its results. Although 373 vote against the union, the other 427 vote for it, and the mill is now unionized. Reuben leaves, but Norma stays behind as a stronger and more confident leader in her family, her community, and her job. This optimistic ending parallels the reality of the Roanoke Rapids mill a year after the film's release. According to Robert Nathan and Jo-Ann Mort, "union members finally forced J. P. Stevens to the bargaining table. The film was a key factor in the nationwide boycott against Stevens" (3). Reverend David Dyson, a key member of the boycott, explains, "The movie came along at the two-year point in the boycott, which hadn't picked up any steam. We found Crystal Lee Jordan [now Crystal Lee Sutton, the worker who inspired the Norma Rae character]. . . . We put on a tour, including a great event in Los Angeles with Sally Field and Crystal Lee. The lights would come up and there would be the real Norma Rae and people would leap to their feet" (quoted in Nathan and Mort 3).

In the wider context, however, conditions may have grown worse. According to Nathan and Mort, "the only remaining Stevens factory in the United States (owned by its successor company, Westpoint Homes) is a unionized blanket mill in Maine" (1). Other textile mills have closed, with companies moving the plants to China or Free Zones in Central and South America. As of 2006, "more than 23,000 Americans were fired or penalized for legal union activity" (Nathan and Mort 1). Perhaps these conditions coincide with Sally Field's commentary in a documentary issued with the DVD of the film: "You live there, and you become one of them, and you try to stand at their machine and thread it and run it, and . . . you learn to appreciate how difficult their lives are, and chances are you're never getting out."

Micha X. Peled's *China Blue* powerfully updates the *Norma Rae* narrative and documents the consequences that 130 million peasants, mostly women, face when they leave their rural homes to make and produce clothing in Chinese urban industrial centers. By contrasting the nearly pristine farmlands these peasants leave to the polluted and densely populated cities where they go to find jobs that will help offset rural poverty faced by their family members, the film illustrates the negative consequences workers face when human approaches to ecology are not in place. It also presents characters with whom we are expected to sympathize after its opening photograph of working women and their managers: Mr. Lam, the factory owner, tells his story of rising to the business class from a low-paying job as a farmer and a police chief, and individual female workers in his factory give a face to the masses of clothing industry laborers. Jasmine is a thread cutter, Orchid a zipper installer in Mr. Lam's Lifeng Factory in Shanxi. Jenny provides public relations for this jeans plant, where Mr. Lam plays music to inspire these women to be the hardworking and courageous Chinese citizens the lyrics describe. Working from 8:00 a.m. to 7:00 p.m., when overtime begins and may run until 2:00 in the morning or later, the women struggle to maintain their quotas so that they earn the highest paycheck possible to send home to their overburdened farm families.

According to Dennis Harvey's *Variety* review, this individualized approach strengthens its case against such exploitation. In the opening of his review, he declares, "While sweatshop scandals have rocked the increasingly international garment industry for years, Micha Peled's documentary *China Blue* makes a stronger case against worker exploitation than any news item could, simply by showing the everyday lives of some Mainland China factory girls." These individual stories also illuminate the girls' struggles. For example, Jasmine tells us about her family farm with ducks, goats, and chickens, where they work from dawn to dusk growing soybeans and winter wheat. When she went out to work for her family, she had to travel by train two days and nights away from her home in the Sichuan region through Canton in southern China to the Pearl River Delta.

Jasmine explains that her employer deducts food costs from pay and gives the workers no place to eat, so she finds a space with a roommate, Jade. Other women tell her to use her free time to do her chores, and the supervisor decides the rate per piece because these women are girls ranging in age from fourteen to seventeen who use fake ID cards to get and keep their jobs. These workers cannot afford to buy the clothes they make. According to the documentary's narrator, 70–80 percent of the goods made in China go to the United States and Western European countries. To cope with this inequity, the young women laugh at the enormous size of the jeans they make for Westerners and relish their free midnight snacks when they work overtime hours until dawn. They tell each other stories or drink "energy medicine" to stay awake but must avoid laughing too hard, or fines will be deducted from their meager salaries. Only specialty sewers such as Orchid, who inserts zippers, earn more money per month, and she sends most of her check to her family to support her brother's college tuition. They all must work even harder to complete orders at even faster rates after Mr. Lam negotiates a deal with a British customer in Shanghai.

The documentary *The Last Train Home* builds on the narratives of *Norma Rae* and *China Blue*, illustrating the continuing injustice of poor working conditions in its focus on a family of factory textile workers who attempt to travel to their rural home annually for the New Year month. The power of the film is heightened by the personal perspectives of a mother, a father, and their daughter before she too leaves the farm to work in an urban factory. After a climactic fight with her father, however, Qin goes to Shanghai, where she works in a bar and dances in discos, while her mother and father continue to work in the clothing factory until her brother, Yang, enters middle school. When the mother returns to her family home, the father stays behind. The trains continue running even after the 2008 financial crisis, and this family continues to struggle, illustrating well the social and environmental injustices it must endure to succeed in China's increasingly industrialized culture.

Shantha Bloemen's *T-Shirt Travels* explores recycled clothing as another aspect of the clothing industry. Although recycling T-shirts seems like a positive environmental step to take and a safe alternative to expanding landfills, *T-Shirt Travels* reveals some of the negative economic, social, and environmental consequences of clothing recycling as it documents an African study of the history of a T-shirt as viewed by a volunteer working in a Zambian village. Where did all these clothes come from? According to the film, in the United States T-shirts and other clothing go to Goodwill, the Salvation Army, and other charities, where 95 percent of them are not unpacked. Instead, they are sold to distributors, who, once free trade opened, ship them to Africa, where sellers buy bales at ten to fifteen cents per pound and take them to factories. The largest export from the United States is used clothing.

This process explains why there are no new clothes in Zambia. In 1991, when the country's markets were opened to free trade, clothes began arriving in Zambia by the container load, so local clothing factories went out of business. Zambia was colonized by companies that forced locals to work on colonial plantations and mines, driving citizens to famine. These colonizers built economies outside the African continent, so Zambia did not gain any of the financial benefits from the exploitation of its valuable commodities. Every American T-shirt has become a metaphor for Africa's dilemma: Who will be left to make good on the debt? According to *T-Shirt Travels* globalization has exacerbated disparities between rich and poor and encouraged economic and environmental injustices that may destroy a country and its people.

A Brief Overview of Environmental Justice Issues in the Clothing Industry

Most would agree that fashion is fun, and "fast fashion," clothing available at such a low price that consumers may see it as "disposable," has become the norm, especially for young women. As Luz Claudio explains, fueled by fashion magazines "disposable couture appears in shopping mall after shopping mall in America and Europe at prices that make purchase tempting and disposal painless." With clothing production and disposal, however, come environmental costs, "with each step of the clothing life cycle generating potential environmental and occupational hazards" (Claudio). Polyester, a widely used petroleum fiber, requires intensive energy and large amounts of crude oil during the manufacturing process, in which "emissions including volatile organic compounds, particulate matter, and acid gases such as hydrogen chloride" and wastewater that includes volatile monomers, solvents, and other by-products are emitted.

Cotton is "one of the most water- and pesticide-dependent crops" (Claudio). During the cotton fabric manufacturing process, the produced "effluent may contain a number of toxics," which flow into stagnant ponds. Not surprisingly, "the EPA, under the Resource Conservation and Recovery Act, considers many textile manufacturing facilities to be hazardous waste generators" (Claudio). The globalization of the clothing industry and the rise in consumption associated with it have also increased the amount of clothing disposed of as waste. According to the EPA Office of Solid Waste, "Americans throw away more than 68 pounds of clothing and textiles per person per year," translating to 4 percent of municipal solid waste in 2007.

Environmental justice seeks to address these dire conditions in the clothing industry. According to the EPA "environmental justice is the fair treatment and meaningful involvement of all people regardless of race, color, national origin, educational level, or income with respect to the development, implementation, and enforcement of environmental laws. Environmental justice seeks to ensure that minority and low-income communities have access to public information relating to human health and environmental planning, regulations and enforcement" ("Environmental Justice Definition"). The EPA explains this definition further, asserting, "Environmental justice ensures that no population, especially the elderly and children, are forced to shoulder a disproportionate burden of the negative human health and environmental impacts of pollution or other environmental hazard" ("Environmental Justice Definition").

This broad definition breaks down into three categories of environmental equity issues. As Robert D. Bullard explains in his article "Waste and Racism," these categories include the following areas: 1. procedural inequity, which involves "the extent that governing rules, regulations, and evaluation criteria are applied uniformly"; 2. geographical inequity, which concerns where factories and waste disposal facilities are placed, suggesting that some areas receive direct benefits, such as jobs and tax revenues, while for others, such as those that become waste disposal sites, the economic benefits may be offset by environmental degradation and other problems; and 3. social inequity, which encompasses how and where noxious facilities are located sometimes mirrors racial and class bias, so that low-income areas become "sacrifice zones."

These categories serve as the basis for the UN Draft Principles on Human Rights and the Environment, which states:

Human rights, an ecologically sound environment, sustainable development and peace are interdependent and indivisible.

All persons have the right to a secure, healthy and ecologically sound environment. The right and other human rights, including civil, cultural, economic, political, and social rights, are universal, interdependent and indivisible.

All persons shall be free from any form of discrimination in regard to actions and decisions that affect the environment. (quoted in Cifuentes and Frumkin 1–2)

Clothing Films and Environmental Justice

A few clothing films take a more explicit approach to illustrate the detrimental environmental consequences of the clothing industry and argue for environmental justice for both humans and nonhumans. *Mardi Gras: Made in China* provides explicit evidence of the serious environmental consequences associated with manufacturing Mardi Gras beads. *Maquilapolis* foregrounds the dire environmental conditions in the communities surrounding a Mexican free zone where pantyhose and other products are manufactured with no governmental controls. *Baytar Environmental Clothing Industry Documentary* explicitly outlines and substantiates the social and environmental impacts along the clothing supply chain.

Thread: A Documentary illustrates and explains the adverse environmental impact of the clothes we wear through expert testimony, and *Cotton Road* provides an overview of the clothing industry "from dirt to shirt," revealing environmental consequences of the industry through visual representations and conversations with workers in the industry.

Mardi Gras: Made in China focuses on the brutal work required to make Mardi Gras throwaway necklaces for the annual New Orleans festival, illustrating how two cultures clash and converge. Excess in the West is built on the backs of young women laborers, who are both exploited by uncontrolled management and poisoned by toxins they inhale every day in the Tai Kuen Bead Factory. The beads are made from polystyrene and polyethylene, which are both petroleum products associated with the Chevron bags shown in the film. The filmmakers explain that styrene is a narcotic and a central nervous system toxin according to the National Institute for Occupational Safety. Studies also suggest that styrene causes cancer when melted and inhaled, a process necessary to produce the beads. The film shows scenes of workers melting the beads to connect them in chains. Close-ups of workers' burned hands emphasize other dangers of this procedure.

A similar sweatshop atmosphere is discussed briefly in *Life and Debt* (2005), a documentary written narrated by Jamaica Kincaid and directed by Stephanie Black that highlights the history and effects of globalization on Jamaican industry and agriculture. Here, these sweatshops appear in "free zones," because of the Caribbean Base Initiative instituted by the IMF, which was meant to bring employment to Jamaica. Because the Jamaican government is paying back money loaned by the IMF for the zones, however, the textile mills and clothing factories are not liable to increased taxes or local control and operate as if they were not in Jamaica. Factory owners follow the same practices as their Chinese counterparts, and employees work like slaves in hazardous environmental conditions.

Free zones are also the focus in *Maquilapolis: City of Factories*, a documentary that not only illustrates the destructive environmental conditions associated with these lawless work areas in Mexico but also demonstrates possible solutions provided by women activists. In the neighborhoods surrounding the factories, water has become toxic, changing colors according to the chemicals strewn in the streams that overflow into the

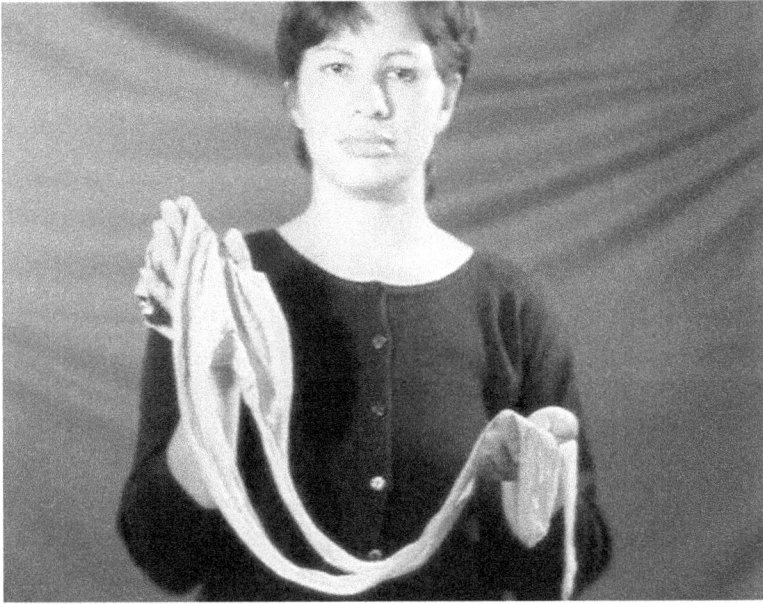

Maquilapolis: Pantyhose as product

streets. The chemicals produce sores on the legs and feet of residents. Women and children struggle to breathe inside and outside the factories. Workers are told they are at risk for leukemia. Drainpipes from factories discharge untreated waste straight into the river. Smoke pours out of stacks with no filters. The factory workers' clothes are so contaminated that they can't wash them with their children's. Ultimately, however, the films shows how a collective for environmental justice comprised of female workers has begun the work to solve these environmental disasters.

Baytar provides an informative overview of the environmental disasters associated with manufacturing clothing and offers viable solutions for fashion-conscious consumers. The film's narration explains a graph showing the social and environmental impacts along the clothing supply chain. Materials used in the fashion industry pollute the environment and exploit natural resources through pesticides used in cotton growing, water use, genetic modification, and oil used to produce synthetic materials. During fabric and garment production, chemicals are used for textile dying and printing. Workers, water, and energy are also exploited, and waste is discharged from factories where there are few, if any, environmental controls. The retail market where clothing is sold also uses large amounts of energy and produces waste from packaging.

Consumers also damage the environment with detergent, exploit energy, and produce waste in landfills from discarded clothing. According to the film, on average Americans discard sixty-eight pounds of clothing and textiles every year, the equivalent of 7 percent of all waste. Sending clothing to developing countries undermines their textile industries and increases environmental degradation there as well.

The film offers solutions to these problems, however, showing ways to build toward sustainability, "attempts to contain all activities toward reducing our negative social and environmental impact." It suggests we reduce, reuse, and recycle. We can reduce waste and the environmental impact of the clothing industry by buying less, using less, and keeping clothing production and sales local. We can reuse by using elements from discarded fabric to update old clothing. *Baytar* also highlights companies like Wendy Skinner's Sew Green, which uses recycled materials to make its clothing. Buying organic is not enough, the narrator tells us, and shows us a list of websites where we can find sustainable clothing. "Look for meaningful ways to consume," the film proposes.

Thread: A Documentary explains how consumers have given little thought to the environmental impact of the clothes they wear. The environmental disasters associated with the clothing industry are manifold, the film explains. For example, Linda Greer of the National Resources Defense Council (NRDC) tells us that most of our clothing is made in China and other developing nations that have very poor environmental standards. One scene in the film shows a truckful of clothing waste piled in a warehouse. Model and entomologist Summer Rayne Oaks declares that the textile industry is one of the two largest polluters in the world. Water specialist Stella Thomas tells us that the industry is one of the largest consumers and the biggest polluter of water of any manufacturing group in the world.

Emphasis on water consumption introduces the environmental impact associated with the cotton production segment of the clothing industry. Shots of leaves and cotton plants accompany the narrator's explanation that "growing cotton requires a tremendous amount of water." Indian environmental activist Vandana Shiva asserts in the film, "What has happened today is the total destruction of more than 1,500 varieties of cotton." We see workers picking cotton in a field. Shiva continues, "There's only toxic seeds with Roundup-Ready genes or toxic seeds with BT [Bacillus thuringiensis] genes. Ninety-five percent of all genetically changed genes around the world is Monsanto owned."

We see workers in India weighing cotton in cloth bags. "Use of Monsanto genetically modified seed does increase herbicide use," concedes Daniel Ravicher, executive director of the Public Patent Foundation, while viewing cotton plants in the film. "America is one of the few places that actually allows unfettered use of genetically modified seed," he tells us while we view cotton fields in Lubbock, Texas, with wind turbines in the distance.

The film's shift to the United States introduces another environmental consequence of the industry, diseases associated with toxins. As organic cotton farmer LaRhea Pepper explains on camera, "My husband grew up on a conventional cotton farm. And at the age of forty-eight, he was diagnosed with agleoplastoma brain tumor stage 4. Our neurosurgeon said that he's diagnosing one of these brain tumors every week. Organic cotton and conventional cotton is to me the difference between life and death"; a shot of a sign appears beside a variety of containers labeled as pesticides: "Danger Pesticides. Keep Out" in both English and Spanish.

The film offers solutions, as well as illustrating problems associated with the industry, however. As couture and up-cycler Gary Harvey asserts, "It only seems right to be as sustainable and eco-friendly as possible," and a model displays a designer sweater produced from recycled materials. Anna L. Chen of Parsons School of Design in New York tells us, "I do believe there's a way to make mass production that isn't at the cost of our health." But model and actress Amber Valletta cautions, "People won't start buying differently unless the design is great." As Linda Greer asserts, "It's not all grim. There are possibilities. It's just awareness, and if there's awareness, then we can find a solution."

Unlike *Thread*, *Cotton Road* shows us the hidden costs behind the clothes we wear from the perspective of those in the various parts of the industry. For example, the film shows us a South Carolina cotton farmer, Carl Brown, and his assistant Grover planting more than one thousand acres with genetically modified cottonseed. Carl picks up a handful of soil to show the cottonseed and declares, "It's very particular. It doesn't like cold soil. It doesn't like to be planted too deep. And it likes moisture." He calls his assistant and tells him about a row that needs work. We see him pouring genetically modified seed into his machine. Another scene shows Carl and Grover spraying Roundup and Staple on his cotton field to kill grass and weeds. The worst culprit, pigweed, is becoming resistant to glyphosate, the main ingredient in Roundup. The cotton they grow is GMO (genetically modified organism) Roundup Ready. Neither man wears gloves as they handle the chemicals, nor do they wear masks when they spray the toxin on their crop. The scenes are presented without commentary from experts or the filmmakers. Instead, they let the facts speak for themselves.

Another scene shows a yarn factory in Chanzhou, China, where workers stack spindles of yarn from machines together for dyeing after drying and dusting them. Female workers clean the yarn, sweep the floor, and check the spindles. They have hairnets but no masks. There is no narration. We just see what they do in close-up with more-distant shots of the machines. Spools of yarn are stacked after they are filled, and an overhead shot shows the dirty factory where workers' hair is covered with cotton dust. The clean white cotton yarn offers a startling contrast.

After they are stacked, thousands of spools of yarn are lifted onto a winch and taken to another area by male workers to be prepared for dying. There the yarn is dropped into large vats. Workers remove the spools from the vats by hand with no protection from toxins. The dyed yarn is next piled into carts by color. Female workers then clean the spools and prepare them for shipping. The workers use an air hose to spray off the spools. The air is full of dust, some particles large enough to be visible to the eye, but the workers wear no masks. Female workers fill cotton bags with the yarn spools in another room where a male worker seals them and weighs them. He stacks them up for shipping, and the bags are then piled on the back of a truck. As in the preceding sequence, the film provides no narration, allowing the images to speak for themselves.

These scenes lay out parts of the clothing industry process, illustrating the environmental and social problems associated with all its elements.

The film's trailer includes a title card that asks, "What if you could see where your clothing was made? And learn about the hidden costs behind the clothes you wear? Is this the real price?" The answer in this film seems to be no, but its series of scenes may not clearly illustrate the environmental costs of the clothing we wear. Unlike *Thread*, the film does not explain the problems behind the images presented throughout the clothing supply line. As a supplement to *Baytar*, *Thread*, and other clothing films, however, *Cotton Road* offers compelling visual representations of an industry in need of a cleanup, perhaps like that proposed by Richards and her human approach to ecology.

The Environmental Costs of Fast Fashion

These clothing industry films illustrate some of the social, economic, and environmental injustices associated with at least part of the fast-fashion industry. Whether the textiles are natural or artificial, they are made from products that require high levels of water, chemical, and energy usage. Exposure to chemical and energy wastes is extremely detrimental to the health of farm workers in cotton fields, who acquire respiratory illnesses and cancers. The fields displayed in some of these clothing industry films show us that the southern United States, China, India, and Africa are all large producers of cotton. China and India are the largest producers of cotton but use most of it in their own textile mills. The United States and Africa, however, are the largest exporters of raw cotton, growing large crops of cotton sent primarily to textile mills in China. Zambia is one of the largest cotton producers in Africa, but its cotton gins are owned by the U.S.-controlled Dunavant Corporation, and the raw commodity only returns as the secondhand clothing shown in *T-Shirt Travels*. Polyester and rayon, too, require enormous water and energy usage as well as exploitation of petroleum products with their own human and environmental problems.

Clothing production also results in a variety of environmental injustices. Globalization has either limited or decimated the textile industries in the southern United States and Africa, for example, while the less lucrative and environmentally dangerous cotton farming continues. This practice, encouraged by free trade rules instituted by the IMF and the World Bank

I feel like a Christmas tree,
all covered in snow.

Maquilapolis: Unbridled pollution from pantyhose factories

and through generous farm subsidies in the United States, demonstrate all three categories of environmental injustice: 1. procedural inequity, 2. geographical inequity, and 3. social inequity. Procedures determining the placement of textile mills facilitate economic and social inequities, and their placement in countries outside the southern United States and Zambia, for example, has a negative effect on both of these regions. The advantages maintained for rich Westerners also produces social inequities based on class, race, and region. *Norma Rae, T-Shirt Travels*, and *Maquilapolis*, especially, foreground these continuing injustices.

In developing countries such as China, which has both cotton farms and factories, similar environmental injustices prevail, this time based on the advantage that urban centers have over rural communities and the age and gender of factory workers. *Thread* and *Cotton Road* show us that China is not only the largest producer of cotton in the world but also "the biggest user of pesticides" and has not banned the importing of chemicals defined as "extremely hazardous" by the EPA (Snyder 74). Cotton production itself is thus dangerous for laborers and their surrounding environments. *China Blue, The Last Train Home,* and *Mardi Gras: Made in China* reveal how rural girls must leave their homes to find work in distant cities, where they make such small wages that they have fallen to the level of bare subsistence, as does Jasmine in *China Blue.*

These injustices may be hidden in fashion industry films such as *The Devil Wears Prada,* but the interconnected pieces of this industry all point to the environmental injustices brought to light in these clothing industry films. *Norma Rae, China Blue, T-Shirt Travels,* and *The Last Train Home* (2009) broach environmental issues primarily on the periphery. *Mardi Gras: Made in China, Maquilapolis, Baytar Environmental Clothing Industry* (2010), *Cotton Road,* and *Thread: A Documentary,* however, demonstrate well the true environmental and social costs of fast fashion.

2

ECO-DOCUMENTARIES AND THE RHETORIC OF FOOD PRODUCTION

CHAPTER FOUR

CONTEMPORARY ECO-FOOD FILMS

The Documentary Tradition

Documentaries focusing on the production of food have become popular in the last few years, with films from Morgan Spurlock's personalized examination of the consequences of a fast food diet, *Supersize Me* (2004), to the critically acclaimed documentary *Food, Inc.* (2008), directed by Robert Kenner. A blatantly rhetorical documentary and adaptation of Michael Pollan's exploration of factory farming, *The Omnivore's Dilemma*, *Food, Inc.* contrasts imagery of a mythic agrarian United States with horrific portraits of an industrial food system. Through the voice-over that explains the problematic consequences of this shift from traditional farming, the film asserts that this system began with the move to fast food in the 1950s. Another response to Pollan's work, the film *King Corn* (2006) documents the process that filmmakers Ian Cheney and Curt Ellis follow when planting, cultivating, and harvesting an acre of corn, as a way to interrogate the consequences of corn's predominance in American diets.

This trend extends beyond American documentary traditions. Erwin Wagenhofer's Austrian documentary *We Feed the World* (2005) also provides a nostalgic view of traditional farming methods as a contrast to industrial

Blood of the Beasts: Preindustrial processing of slaughtered sheep

methods currently employed in Europe, but instead of a voice-over, the film foregrounds a diversity of voices providing multiple perspectives on the food industry. Although most of the film's experts lament the loss of traditional methods, the film provides a more ambivalent and, to a certain extent, evenhanded approach to its exploration of the transition to industrialized food production. Several National Film Board of Canada films continue this approach, as in *Beef, Inc.* (1999), *Bacon: The Film* (2002), and *Animals* (2003). German director Nikolaus Geyrhalter's *Our Daily Bread* (2005), on the other hand, argues effectively against the shift to industrial farming by eliminating verbal explanation altogether.

With only background sounds and voices to support its visual rhetoric, the avant-garde rhetorical documentary *Our Daily Bread* conveys its message differently than do *Food, Inc.*, *King Corn*, or *We Feed the World*. By relying exclusively on visual rhetoric, *Our Daily Bread* works as a powerful rhetorical tool, undiluted by ambivalent multiple viewpoints, a voice-over that sometimes disguises the consequences of industrial farming on display, or nostalgia for a better, cleaner world. Whereas *Food, Inc.*, *King Corn*, and *We Feed the World* draw on environmental nostalgia, a nostalgia found in *The Plow That Broke the Plains* (1936) or *An Inconvenient Truth* (2006), *Our Daily Bread* invokes an avant-garde and direct-cinema-influenced rhetoric, a powerful nonlinear visual rhetoric without the limits imposed by nostalgia. Environmental nostalgia is by definition limited, since a pure, untouched, and unpolluted past projected onto a now lost wilderness cannot recover frontier history. Only *King Corn* gains rhetorical force when an environmental nostalgia with emotional appeal is evoked within a comparison-and-contrast mode that argues powerfully for sustainable environmental policies by invoking both personal and universal ecological memories. But its arguments may lose strength because they too are subject to the limits of nostalgia, despite the film's more synthetic approach.

Modes and Types of Food Documentaries

Documentary films are categorized in a variety of ways but typically align with two types of form: categorical form, which conveys information in an analytical fashion, or rhetorical form, which makes an argument to convince audience members to change an attitude or opinion and, sometimes, to take action to move toward change or eradicate what filmmakers see as a problem. Within these two forms, documentaries may draw on a variety of types. At the lowest level of control, some documentaries are compilations; they are produced by assembling images from archival sources, as in the 1982 film *Atomic Café*. Some food documentaries integrate such archival or "found" footage to serve a variety of purposes. In *Food, Inc.*, for example, archival footage provides a historical view of farming and food purchasing changes from World War II to the present. Some of these segments draw on nostalgia for a more pastoral approach to food. Others illustrate particular points in time when that approach began to deteriorate. The French documentary *The World according to Monsanto* (2008) also includes compilation segments.

Some documentaries rely on interviews or "talking heads" to record testimony about events or social movements. Both *Food, Inc.* and *We Feed the World* include this documentary option. Other documentaries take a direct-cinema approach in which filmmakers record an ongoing event as it happens with minimal interference from the filmmaker. Frederick Wiseman's *Meat* (1976) and *Our Daily Bread* employ this documentary option. Nature documentaries magnify and explore the worlds of nature, as do the Disney Earth Day epics, *Earth* (2007), a full-length version of the television series *Planet Earth*, and *Ocean* (2009), an ecological drama/ documentary that meditates on the vanishing wonders of the subaquatic world. Portrait documentaries center on scenes from the life of a compelling person, as does *The Real Dirt on Farmer John* (2005), but most documentaries pursue several options at once, mixing archival footage, interviews, and material on the fly as synthetic documentaries, as do, for example, *Food, Inc.*, *We Feed the World*, and *Bacon: The Film*.

Food as a basic need has played a central role in documentary films as early as the Lumière brothers' 1895 short film, *Repas de bebe* (*Baby's Dinner*), but Cricks and Martin's 1906 nonfiction film, *A Visit to Peek Frean and Co.'s Biscuit Works*, an industrial process piece that documents tinned biscuit baking, packing, and distribution from start to finish may arguably be the first food documentary. The film provides a glimpse of each step of the process of biscuit making in a British factory, showing workers completing each task with help from bright indoor arc lighting. The film even includes a scene in which workers clean the tins for reuse before a transition to a packing sequence.

Later documentaries take a more ethnographic approach to food acquisition and preparation, as in Robert J. Flaherty's *Nanook of the North* (1922), *Moana* (1926), and *Man of Aran* (1934). As Jack Ellis and Betsy McLane note in their book, *A New History of Documentary Film*, in *Nanook of the North*, we see Nanook "spearing fish, catching and rendering walrus, [and] hunting seals" (16). In *Moana* Moana and his family are seen "snaring a wild boar, collecting giant clams, gathering coconuts, capturing a huge tortoise, making custard, scraping breadfruit, and baking little fish" (16). In *Man of Aran*, too, food takes the fore in multiple fishing scenes, even though the controversial shark hunt is meant to capture shark livers for fuel instead of food.

Each of these Flaherty films also aligns with Karl G. Heider's definition of ethnographic film as "film, which reflects ethnographic understanding" (8). As in *Nanook of the North* (1922), in which archaic Inuit hunting practices are reenacted to highlight a romanticized more natural state, and Merian C. Cooper and Ernest B. Schoedsack's *Grass* (1925) and *Chang* (1927), which show us how civilization has corrupted the native, Flaherty's films reconstruct (both literally and figuratively) the stories his subjects tell, providing viewers with a romantic narrative that foregrounds progress. Heider argues that Flaherty's and Cooper and Schoedsack's works "reflect the romanticism of the period" (26).

Bill Nichols's *Introduction to Documentary* and Jack C. Ellis and Betsy A. McLane's *A New History of Documentary Film* expand documentary categories to embrace different modes and genres, all of which are applied in food documentaries. Nichols illustrates his explanation for reflexive documentaries, for example, with an overview of Luis Buñuel's *Land without Bread* (1933), a portrait of a remote region of Spain where local peasants fight to survive. His expository category lines up well with interview or talking-head documentaries, and his observational documentary aligns with the direct-cinema work. Poetic documentaries, on the other hand, move away from "objective" reality to approach an inner "truth" that can be grasped only by poetical manipulation, as in Flaherty's *Man of Aran* (1934). According to Nichols other documentaries are performative, like Spurlock's *Supersize Me* (2004), and stress subjective experience and emotional responses to the world. Nichols last type, the participatory documentary, was first defined as *kino-pravda* by Dziga Vertov, who emulated the approach of anthropologists in silent films like *Man with a Movie Camera* (1929). Russian for "cinema truth," the *kino-pravda* approach transitioned into "cinema verité" once both lighter camera and sound equipment were available to capture an encounter between filmmaker and subject.

Television food documentaries tend to take a synthetic approach, as do the UK's Channel 4 screened films, *The End of the Line* (2009) and *The Cove* (2009). PBS's *Point of View* (*pov*) documentaries such as *Sweetgrass* (2009), a portrait of the last traditional sheep ranch in the United States, and *Farmingville* (2004), an exposé of the unfair treatment of immigrant farm workers, also take this synthetic approach. Documentaries aired on the U.S. Food Network and the BBC, including *The History of Ready Meals* (2011), provide a historical overview of certain foods and traditions using a variety of documentary approaches.

Contemporary food documentaries adhere to a variety of these documentary types or modes. *Our Daily Bread*, for example, may align more closely with a categorical documentary form than with a rhetorical one. This documentary reveals each step in the production process for each of the food products examined through an indirect but fragmented direct-cinema approach that combines the nonlinear form of an avant-garde cinema calling for social action with the ultrarealism of Georges Franju's *Blood of the Beasts* (1949) and the observational approach of films like Wiseman's *Meat*. Like *Our Daily Bread*, both *Blood of the Beasts* and *Meat* documented the modernization of food production. *Blood of the Beasts* was released a year after *Red River* (1948), a Western examining changes to the post–Civil War cattle drive system after the expansion of the railroad, and juxtaposes portraits of idyllic Paris life with images of slaughter that suggest humans can accept and institutionalize acts of almost surreal cruelty. *Meat* turns the Old West into a factory where cattle are prodded, vaccinated, and then fattened up for slaughter in enormous feedlots that are overseen by modern-day cowboys with electric cattle prods. Because of the film's observational approach, we witness the efficient slaughterhouse and the salesmen taking orders for the product from all over the country.

The Limits of Nostalgia

Most food documentaries, however, draw on an expository talking-heads approach and a rhetorical form that argues through a nostalgic vision of the preindustrial farming period. The environmental nostalgia evoked by films such as *We Feed the World* and *King Corn*, however, may be limited because the past evoked by a nostalgic view is not only unobtainable but also cast in an unrealistic innocence. The reality of the past is lost in its present-day nostalgic translation, even when, as in *King Korn*, emotional appeals draw on both personal and universal ecological historical memories.

Nostalgia has been critiqued, reified, and recovered in the past few decades, with a resurgence of research in memory studies complicating negative views of nostalgia built on postmodern views. Postmodern responses to nostalgia critique its move toward essentialism. In her 1988 article, "Nostalgia: A Polemic," Kathleen Stewart engages postmodern cultural critics' views that consider nostalgia a social disease. According to Stewart "nostalgia, like the economy it runs with, is everywhere. But it is a cultural practice, not a given content; its forms, meanings, and effects shift with the context—it depends on where the speaker stands in the landscape of the present" (227). Drawing on the work of Roland Barthes, Jean Baudrillard, Walter Benjamin, Pierre Bourdieu, Jonathan Culler, Donna Haraway, Fredric Jameson, and Raymond Williams, Stewart elucidates why nostalgia is such a powerful rhetorical tool; she argues that "on one 'level' there is no longer any place for *anyone* to stand and nostalgia takes on the generalized function to provide some kind (any kind) of cultural form" (227, emphasis Stewart's).

According to Stewart nostalgia serves as a powerful rhetorical tool that placates and paralyzes the disenfranchised: "Nostalgia is an essential, narrative, function of language that orders events temporally and dramatizes them in the mode of 'that's what happened,' that 'could happen,' that 'threaten to erupt at any moment'" (227). Stewart sees the seductive nature of nostalgia in a postmodern culture not only as culturally situated but also as reductively negative, resulting in what she calls mirages—either a "grand hotel" of affluence or a "country cottage" of romantic simplicity. For Stewart, then, nostalgia is a negative consequence of attempting to replace postmodern relativism with an essential past based in recovery of an essential "self."

More-recent work, especially in anthropology and cultural studies, complicates visions of nostalgia as inherently and inescapably bad. Ethel Pinheiro and Cristiane Rose Duarte, for example, argue that nostalgia may itself be a way not only to learn from the past but to recuperate real community in the Largo da Carioca. And Sean Scanlan, in his *Iowa Journal of Cultural Studies* introduction to the topic, asserts that "postmodernism's negative critique only partially illuminates its various links to memory, history, affect, media and the marketplace, only partially accounts for nostalgia's continuing power." Yet other cultural critics in the journal condemn the use of nostalgia as a rhetorical strategy because it has "abused individual and collective memory and . . . problematized the relations between producers and consumers." Although *King Corn* most effectively invokes nostalgia by drawing on both the personal memories that Cheney and Ellis recover on the family farm and the collective

Food, Inc.: The costs of factory farming mass production of chickens

memories of the ubiquitous family farm and farmer, *King Corn, Food, Inc.*, and *We Feed the World* essentialize a pastoral past as a solution to factory farming, a solution doomed to failure because it rests on the limits of environmental nostalgia.

Food, Inc.: An Expert's Pastoral Fantasy

Following a pattern similar to Michael Pollan in *The Omnivore's Dilemma*, the talking-heads documentary *Food, Inc.* attempts to illustrate how the American supermarket reflects both the changes in our food and our nostalgia for a pristine agrarian past when, at least in what the narrator claims is "a pastoral fantasy," the fruits, vegetables, meat, and dairy we eat came directly from the family farm. Images of farmers and farms are used to sell a multitude of supermarket products, 47,000 in an average grocery store, according to the narrator. In a store where tomatoes are sold year round, and meat and poultry are sold without bones, however, according to this narrator, a "deliberate veil" has been constructed between food and its source. In reality food is produced in a factory, not on a farm, the film claims, so that "now food is coming from enormous assembly lines where both animals and workers are abused." With help from contrasting images of these factory farms, interviews, and voice-over narration, *Food, Inc.* attempts to show how corporations control food from seed to supermarket. The film's assertions are weakened, however, not only because of an overreliance on the authority of a narrator but also because the film argues its points from single examples, moving from the whole to the particular with a clear point of view that remains unsubstantiated.

Many critics, however, regard the information that the film attempts to convey in general as "important." For example, Owen Gleiberman of *Entertainment Weekly* argues that the film is "one that nourishes your knowledge of how the world works." John Anderson of *Variety* asserts that *Food, Inc.* "does for the supermarket what *Jaws* did for the beach— marches straight into the dark side of cutthroat agri-business, corpora- tized meat and the greedy manipulations of both genetics and the law." According to Andrew O'Hehir, "the food-activism movement in 2009 is roughly where the environmental movement was in 1970. . . . 'Food, Inc.' is meant to be an opening salvo that gets people's attention, not the battle that wins the war" ("Behind the Food Industry's Iron Curtain").

Yet other critics find the film derivative rather than groundbreaking. Kyle Smith of the *New York Post*, for example, asserts, "The film offers very little that food radicals don't already know. Journalists Eric Schlosser . . . and Michael Pollan serve as the packhorses, turning up to say things on camera they've been saying in print for years." Smith also argues that charges made in the film remain unsubstantiated. Instead, we assert that the film does attempt to support its "charges" but relies too heavily on individual examples to make its case. As an illustration, the film begins with a more generalized image of a factory and a businessman in a wheat field meant to reinforce the connection between farming and factories, as a narrator explains, "They don't want this story told." According to images and narration, however, industrial food production's cause is connected to one company, McDonald's, which now controls our food system, from beef, potatoes, and pork, to tomatoes and apples. From here the film high- lights example areas of food production controlled by McDonald's, from chicken and beef production to the corn production that sustains both.

Food, Inc. stands up as an adaptation of Pollan's nonfiction book *The Omnivore's Dilemma*, even following a similar narrative structure that begins with an interrogation of industrial farming and its relation to corn, then moves nostalgically to the pastoral alternative where cattle feed on field grass instead of feedlot corn. Pollan's work, however, offers an extensive bibliography of resources to support his claims. In *Food, Inc.*, on the other hand, broad-based evidence is replaced with single-case support, so individual examples are meant to support assertions about both the control of the market and the negative consequences of such vertical integration.

The film's exposé of the chicken industry is a case in point. In this segment the narrator asserts that Tyson isn't "producing chicken; it is producing food and is mechanized so chickens are grown to be almost the same size." He explains that Tyson produces "lots of food on little land for the least money." Then an example of a Tyson farm in McLean, Kentucky, is used to support this claim. The conditions in the henhouse seem to make the case against four companies controlling 80 percent of the market. According to this chicken farm owner, mass production leads to excessive dust and feces, as well as chickens with bones and internal organs that grow so fast the chickens are unable to stand. To protect herself from these conditions, the farm owner wears a mask while applying antibiotics to the chickens' feed. Yet, according to the owner, "bacteria work up resistance, so it's not working." She also claims that undocumented laborers work at plants and come to work even if they are sick. According to the narrator the Perdue Chicken Company also keeps chicken farmers under its thumb, but we do not see an example of a Perdue farm because the company will not allow the filmmakers to document workers on the farm. Instead, this one example of a Tyson chicken farm gone wrong is used to illustrate a problem with much broader consequences.

Food, Inc. also includes individual examples of cattle production and corn production before offering an alternative: organically grown foods that are meant to help viewers reminisce nostalgically about a pastoral past now beyond our grasp. Again the film provides an individual example to support its assertion that growing and consuming food in traditional ways is a viable solution to factory farming. Joel Salata's Polyface Farms is shown in stark contrast to the factory farms like those of Tyson Foods and Smithfield. On the Polyface Farm cattle eat grass instead of a feedlot diet of corn, dead cows, chickens, and manure, Salata explains. Manure fertilizes the grasses. According to Salata factory farms "hit the bulls-eye at the wrong target—plant, fertilize and harvest corn with satellites when they should be asking if we should feed them corn at all." After highlighting problems with genetically altered corn and soybeans like Roundup Ready, the film ends with a series of solutions to the industrial food problem: respecting the season, buying organic and non–genetically modified foods from local farmers and farmers' markets, growing one's own food, and allowing food stamps at farmers' markets are just a few recommendations. But the film's message is almost undercut by the voice-over narration and overreliance on individual examples to substantiate claims. Although *Food, Inc.* does provide a plethora of information about industrialized farming and argues from a clear position, its message is weakened by both its nostalgic vision and the rhetorical strategies the filmmakers choose to employ.

King Corn: Process-Driven Nostalgia

By concentrating on one element of Pollan's work, corn production, and adding humor to the chilling information it conveys, *King Corn* provides a more engaging process-driven narrative that attempts to reveal why corn now comprises such a large percentage of the American diet. Dennis Harvey's *Variety* review provides a positive perspective of the film, asserting that Cheney and Ellis's "low-key antics, their affectionate regard for the small-town milieu, some delightful stop-motion animation and an excellent rootsy soundtrack by the WoWz all make 'King Corn' go down easy, even if you might regard your burger, fries and Coke with suspicion afterward." Ann Hornaday of the *Washington Post* agrees, asserting that the film is "gorgeously filmed in digital video and Super-8, using clever stop-motion corn kernel animation and a lyrical score by the 'anti-folk' band the WoWz." According to Hornaday, with help from its "engaging guides," Cheney and Ellis, "*King Corn* takes what could be a tiresome agri-civics lesson and delivers a lively, funny, sad and even poetic treatise on the reality behind America's cherished self-image as the breadbasket of the world." Andrew O'Hehir's review of the film also highlights the lessons of *King Corn* but concludes, "This information arrives via a graceful and frequently humorous film that captures the idiosyncrasies of its characters and never hectors" ("Beyond the Multiplex").

Through their naive attempts to grow corn in Greene, Iowa, their ancestral home, Ian Cheney and Curt Ellis reveal the extent to which corn has entered the American diet, so much so that, when tested, both men's bodies chemistries evidence more than 50 percent corn. To expose how corn has become an ingredient in nearly every food source found in the supermarket, Cheney and Ellis plant, grow, and harvest one acre of corn. During the process the two learn not only about corn growing but also about the farm subsidies that support the corn industry, especially since changes in subsidy legislation during the Nixon administration. Like *Food, Inc.*, *King Corn* relies on nostalgia as a rhetorical tool, contrasting the industrialized corn production expected today—with powerful fertilizer, government aid, and genetically modified seed to support it—with traditional farming techniques practiced in the same area when their great-grandparents farmed the land. By primarily maintaining this focus on corn production and its entrance into the American diet through high-fructose corn syrup and other corn-based ingredients found in almost every food item in the supermarket and the fast food restaurant, the film successfully demonstrates the power of corn.

What weakens the film's argument, however, is its reliance on the logical fallacy of causal oversimplification. Like Michael Pollan, Cheney and Ellis blame this corn epidemic on the policies of one man, Earl Butz, the secretary of agriculture under Richard Nixon, because he released farmers from decades of production controls and encouraged them to plant "fence row to fence row" to meet the global demand for their corn, soybean, and wheat crops, especially. In an interview with the then-ninety-six-year-old Butz in his nursing home apartment, Cheney and Ellis attempt to challenge the modern food system that his policies had helped create and the policies that led to food subsidies for corn equaling $51 billion between 1995 and 2005 ("What's the Plan?"). When Cheney broaches the subject, asserting, "We've heard from some people that they think there is too much food," however, Butz counters with his own unchanged perspective on his policy: "Well, it's the basis of our affluence now, the fact that we spend less on food. It's America's best-kept secret. We feed ourselves with approximately 16 or 17 percent of our take-home pay. That's marvelous, that's a very small chunk to feed ourselves. And that includes all the meals we eat at restaurants, all the fancy doodads we get in our food system. I don't see much room for improvement there, which means we'll spend our surplus cash on something else." Butz argues that cheap food has eased hunger and increased disposable income, so everyone, for example, can afford a car. After the interview Curt Ellis concludes that "Earl Butz was a product of his time" ("Meeting King Corn") because he had finished college in the middle of the Great Depression, when scarcity was the norm, but he continues to blame Butz for the consequences of cheap corn, cheap soy, and cheap food, including type 2 diabetes and obesity.

But it was the 1996 farm bill that, according to David Moberg, "ended the old policy of managing both prices and production through a system of loans, target prices and stored surpluses" and "provided subsidy payments to farmers that were 'decoupled' from production." And those subsidies continued after 2002, when prices crashed and subsidies became seen as a political necessity. Blame for the shift to high-fructose corn syrup also does not belong solely on Earl Butz's shoulders, since the move occurred in 1980 after sugar tariff and quota policies failed during the Carter administration. Ethanol, an area of corn production overlooked by the film, became a centerpiece of the Carter administration, as an alternative energy solution to ongoing oil embargo problems. *King Corn* entertains and partially illuminates the issues surrounding corn production, but it falls short because, like *Food, Inc.*, it draws too much on nostalgia, and its argument is oversimplified.

We Feed the World: Veiled Nostalgia

We Feed the World also provides abundant information about industrialized farming, this time from multiple expert perspectives, a point placed in a positive light by many reviewers. Its distributor, Bullfrog Films, asserts that the film "vividly reveals the dysfunctionality of the industrialized world food system and shows what world hunger has to do with us." As Dalia Perelman, a nutrition professor from San Jose State University, explains, "The film effectively reveals the paradoxical disparity between the prevalence of hunger and the overproduction of food, sometimes within the same country." In an article titled "Food for Thought," the *Lumière Reader* calls the film "visually striking," even though "drawn out montages of agricultural production often slow the documentary's pace to a crawl." According to this review, the film "does . . . make its case convincingly—if somewhat bleakly," but it also notes some problems with the film, suggesting that the documentary is a "series of talking head interviews" that "might occasionally feel like a sermon to the converted."

Both the extended montages and the series of talking heads slow the pace of *We Feed the World*, but, for us, the interviews do more than slow down the film; they also counter the film's point of view by attempting to take an evenhanded approach to a controversial issue, industrialized food production. We agree in part with Joe Leydon's assertion in a *Variety* review: "*We Feed the World* is sincere but monotonous as it decries the excesses of globalized food industry," so much so that "even sympathetic viewers may find themselves casting eager glances at their watches during the ponderous progression of talking-head interviews, statistic-crammed titles and globe-hopping reportage." More importantly for us, however, the message the film asserts is diluted by the multiple points of view it foregrounds. The film's attempt to provide an evenhanded overview of the food industry and its consequences veils the case that the film seems to be making, one harking back to the pastoral paradise of a preindustrial food production world.

Divided into sections introduced by titles, *We Feed the World* seems to draw on nostalgia as a rhetorical strategy, similar to the individual and communal nostalgia that Al Gore employs in *An Inconvenient Truth*. The first segment introduces factory farming and its consequences by contrasting it with a farmer's nostalgia for his father's twelve hectares of land. Now it takes six times that to sustain his father's standard of living, the farmer explains. That same strategy is in place when the film explores the consequences of turning the fishing industry into factory farming. According to Dominique, a fisherman in Brittany, the European Union has turned farming of all types into an industry that is mechanized and scientifically controlled. Dominique laments the EU's requirement that he replace his more natural approach with the EU's dictates. Dominique observes nature and notices how creatures follow the sun, from foxes to fish in the sea. Nets must be cast at the same time, "like nature herself."

He counts the number of waves in the sea to determine the right sea height. By observing he decides when and where to fish. It is still dark, but he and his crew prepare the nets at sea and record their catch in the EU logbook. Investors and financiers have made fishing an industry, he says. He believes that the EU brings in scientists to steal the fishermen's knowledge. They keep track of what they catch and what they earn. According to Dominique the sea is divided into zones, and the EU allows certain amounts of fishing and profits from each. Everything is controlled.

That control is amplified when the fish make it to shore. First an inspector makes sure that all the fish are fresh when they return. According to the inspector some of the fish are too fresh and need aging; some are of good quality; others do not meet standards. He shows the difference between a small boat's catches and those of an industrial boat, which trawls so deep the fish's eyes pop when brought to the surface. Industrial fish, Dominique contends, have no flavor—"ratfish only for selling, not for eating." Commercial fishing is moving toward complete industrialization, even though the catches of small ships are much better, the inspector asserts. The EU's rules are making it too difficult for smaller fishermen. This inspector declares that Dominique and the small boats could save the fish and conserve better than industrial fishermen, who are only out for a profit without considering nature's flow and food quality, but the EU disagrees.

The film juxtaposes industrial and traditional farming techniques in similar ways when exploring other foods: tomatoes, sunflowers, eggplants, and onions. According to one expert natural vegetables are better tasting and more efficient because farmers can reuse the seed, but seed companies are owned by a few companies and are subsidized, so genetically modified seed and hybrid vegetables have become the norm in European countries.

But when the film discusses changes to soy production, it emphasizes not nostalgia for GMO-free seed but also another consequence of industrialized farming: a smaller number of companies control distribution. According to one expert few foods are GMO free, including animal feed and chocolate. All this food is not sent to countries that need it, so one hundred thousand people die of starvation every day. One giant food company, Pioneer, has operations in 120 countries, including China; its slogan is

"We feed the world," but according to UN special rapporteur Jean Ziegler, the heartless company prioritizes selling to the highest bidder rather than feeding a starving world. Ziegler asserts that 842 million people are malnourished, so "any child who dies of starvation is in effect murdered."

Soy manufacturing is especially problematic. According to one expert, because they are fed on Brazilian soy, European livestock are, in a sense, eating up the rainforest of Amazonia, causing an ecological imbalance. In Brazil an area the size of France and Portugal combined has been cleared since 1975, while children starve in Somalia, Sudan, and rural Brazil, where women feed their children stone soup. In northeastern Brazil water is contaminated, and women can feed their children only goat's milk once they have been weaned. These illiterate rural Brazilians have virtually no employment opportunities, and now they can grow little food; even though Brazil is one of the largest exporters of soy and one of the richest agrarian states, its people are starving. Europeans import 90 percent of the soy for their livestock from Brazil, the expert explains, since European corn and soy are used to generate electricity.

The film attempts to reveal some of the dangers of industrialized chicken and egg production, but it ends with a portrait of Nestlé's CEO and his claim that the company feeds the world. Avene Nestlé, the company's current CEO, asserts that "Nature is no longer pitiless" and advocates for genetically modified rather than organic food, since it will more quickly and readily feed the hungry. Although Nestlé explains that his responsibility is to ensure a profitable future for the company and its shareholders, his point about feeding a starving world seems to be an answer to the starvation problem highlighted in the film. The film ends with this portrait, leaving the viewer with mixed reactions to the film's images of industrialized food production. Instead of the single message and point of view of Gore's *Inconvenient Truth*, *We Feed the World* relies on a series of experts to make its point about the social and environmental consequences of turning food production into a massive industry. Yet the film loses its edge when it ends not with a clear rearticulation of its thesis but with an opposite, contrasting, and conflicting message of a new kind of hope: the hope that with efficiency and high-production counts that include genetically modified seed and the end of food production as a family business, factory farming can feed the world.

National Film Board of Canada Food Documentaries: A Synthetic Approach

Nostalgic reminiscences also serve a central role in a series of National Film Board of Canada documentaries. *Beef, Inc., Bacon: The Film*, and *Animals* all focus on the meat industry and its negative consequences, sometimes by connecting the negative environmental consequences of animal fecal matter and governmental policy. These three films draw on nostalgia to emphasize the dangers of industrializing meat production, but they also individualize the animals being prepared for slaughter, applying an animal rights argument that constructs beef, hogs, and other food-source animals as sentient. To make their arguments, all three films take a synthetic approach to documentary that pursues interviews, portraits, and nature documentary approaches.

Carmen Garcia's *Beef, Inc.* and Hugo Latulippe's *Bacon: The Film* both rely on tropes of unveiling and talking-head interviews to demonstrate problems with fecal waste and slaughtering practices. Although the filmmakers for *Beef, Inc.* did not have access to the slaughterhouses, the absence of visuals and critical commentary on blood and flesh may move beyond shielding the self from the source of the foods we eat to the shock of absence of the pastoral cattle image from the process.

Directed by Hugo Latulippe, *Bacon: The Film* concentrates on the negative effects that Quebec hog farming has on air and water toxicity levels. To highlight a nostalgia for both a more animal- and earth-friendly approach to hog farming, the film individualizes the hogs on this industrial farm through broad-based portraits, visuals of artificial insemination and separation from the mother. These practices are constructed as cruel by the filmmakers through scenes of distressed piglets, which become portraits of infants taken by force from parents. These changing practices in industrial hog farms around Quebec are contrasted with pastoral scenes around the farm. But these scenes are devoid of farm animals, and shots outside slaughterhouses and images of hogs as food suggest that there is no place for connections in this hyperindustrialized era.

Directed by Jason Young, *Animals*, on the other hand, provides clear portraits of animals raised on a more traditional family farm. The film looks at the everyday slaughter of animals for food on the farm, where the animals are personalized as pets with names before the slaughter.

Our Daily Bread (2005): Pigs on their way to automated slaughter

Animals are also included in the credits alongside their human filmmaker counterparts, further validating the sentience of these farm animals. These animals' faces are even reasserted onto the meat after their slaughter. In the film actual slaughter of a rabbit and a yearling are shown, but we only hear the sounds of beeves raised for food being slaughtered off camera. The message is ambiguous in *Animals* but still points to the need to realize that our meat comes from sentient beings. Despite their rhetorical weaknesses, these films articulate similar arguments against factory farming, as do popular U.S. food films such as *Food, Inc.* and *King Corn* and European films such as *We Feed the World* and *Our Daily Bread*.

Our Daily Bread: The Success of Visual Rhetoric

Our Daily Bread, however, eschews any voice-over narration or commentary from experts, relying on the sounds and images of factory farming to make its point, a minimalist unveiling that effectively reveals the horrors of the factory food chain. The film makes both the reality and the myth of the pastoral transparent without diluting the powerful visible rhetoric on display. Manohla Dargis highlights the force of these visual images in a *New York Times* review of the film: "Part of the film's brilliance is how it lays out the images and their wells of meaning with such cool deliberation, showing rather than telling through the long tracking shots of which [the director] Mr. Geyrhalter is a master and which underscore the ongoing, mechanized flow of work." According to Dargis, "much like [Geyrhalter's] scrupulous use of perspective, which directs your gaze toward the center of each image, the tracking shots reveal the filmmaker's artistry as well as a deliberate ethics." Leslie Felperin of *Variety* also highlights the film's visual rhetoric, asserting, "Precisely composed lensing and painstaking sound create moments of sublime beauty, even when showing the production line slaughter of animals." Felperin compares the "long-held, wide-angle shots . . . often taken from the prow of tractors or cranes" to paintings, "used to create an eerie, machine-eye traveling view of fields and spaces." For Felperin "the portrait shots of workers at rest, their off-center composition and use of light sometimes recall Vermeer paintings." He also notes how the sparing use of sound contributes to the alienating effect of the film.

But these reviewers' explorations of visual rhetoric in *Our Daily Bread* fall short. In spite of the many examples introduced that highlight the film's strategy "to emphasize the impersonal nature of contempo [*sic*] farming, turning workers into cogs in vast, semi-organic machines," for example, Felperin argues that the film offers a tabula rasa upon which audiences draw their own conclusions, seeing the film as "an indictment of the industry's cruelties," "a realistic depiction of mechanized farming," or "a soft-spoken tribute to manual labor." Instead, we assert that the film's stunning and sometimes shocking visual representations of factory farming provide a more powerful critique of its consequences than the narrative-driven depictions of *Food, Inc., King Corn,* or *We Feed the World.*

Our Daily Bread documents factory farming by carefully revealing its apparatus and thus making the horrific environmental consequences of the contemporary food industry transparent. The film's press notes explain that the factory farms Geyrhalter and his crew documented between 2003 and 2005 willingly allowed him to film every aspect of the production process, perhaps because their farms were so clean and mechanically efficient, but it is the mechanically cold sterility revealed by Geyrhalter's long-held, wide-angle shots of each farm's production process that best highlights its cruelty. Whether a factory farm is producing hogs or tomatoes, *Our*

Daily Bread asserts through its visual representations, it is mechanizing the process, separating even these food sources from their natural worlds. With a constant hum of machinery in the background, the film shows the production process for hogs, tomatoes, peppers, chicken and eggs, potatoes, cattle, olives, apples, sunflowers, lettuce, cucumbers, salt, and fish. Scenes are organized according to steps in the food production cycle, moving toward the harvest, so food products overlap in the film, demonstrating how similar all food production becomes under a factory farming system.

The hog production process is shown in fragments that parallel the process while connecting it with seemingly innocuous farming like hothouse tomato production. Hog farming opens the film but then bridges immediately to tomato farming with the sound of spraying water. In opening wide-angle shots, a worker sprays a floor in a slaughterhouse where hogs hang skinless from the ceiling in a long line of corpses. The hum of machinery and spraying water accompanies the title before the scene shifts to a shot of green water, and the camera pans out to show a broader view of moving hoses. The water is now spraying tomatoes in a hothouse. Vines are growing overhead while a line of trailers rolls by. Human voices are heard only in the background. The scene shifts again to show cattle from overhead, rolling on a conveyor with wagging tails. We hear the cow's moos and the hum of machines with the spray of water in the background.

Fragmented images also connect the hothouse of tomato production with a henhouse, this time in relation to the claustrophobia of closed-in farming. The hothouse is shown once emptied, white and clean, like the white window in a hen house that is opened by a human figure who turns on a light, looks in on chicks from a distance, and turns the lights back off. The white of the chicken house connects with the white of a potato field and with white-suited workers in another greenhouse. The hum of machinery accompanies their tasks, as workers spray vines with chemical solutions while a moving pipe irrigates rows of hanging peppers. The hum of machinery bridges to workers picking tomatoes through rows of hanging vines, and the camera pans out to show a giant collection of greenhouses from a distance at night. When the camera pans out further, we see how large this garden is. It runs for miles, with white hothouses nearly touching one another in a massive industrial complex.

The hum of machinery and sterility of white-coated workers bridges these foods to others: cattle from insemination to slaughter and crops from corn and soybeans to apples and olives from planting to harvest overlap. Shots of fields from the point of view of tractors amplify the mechanical nature of industrialized corporate farming. Even when planting potatoes, human workers are separated from the earth. In a wide shot we see acres of fields covered in plastic, hear the plastic blowing in the wind, and see workers under plastic planting potatoes from a box while sprinklers water the newly planted eyes. With an audio bridge of spraying water and humming machinery, potato planting is connected with hog slaughter. The slaughter is quick, cold, and clean, as if it too were under plastic. In this sterile room workers even clean out carcasses with a vacuum cleaner.

The continuous drone of machinery in the slaughterhouse mingles with the whir of a yellow airplane spraying a field of sunflowers, the roar of tractors in a cornfield, the deafening sound of machinery in a plastic-covered lettuce field, and the hum of milking machines and conveyors in a dairy house. Rows of milk cows blend with rows of plastic-covered fields and hothouses. Even olives are collected on large plastic blankets strewn beneath trees shaken by a mechanical harvester and sucked up onto larger sheets. The sucking sound connects olive harvesting scenes with scenes of deep underground salt mining and seafood farming where fish are literally vacuumed into boat hulls.

In this mechanized world even the human workers are portrayed as alienated, unable to escape the sounds of machinery that accompanies even their lunch breaks. The lunch breaks with which each segment ends highlight the purpose behind this process—food production—but also suggest that the workers are not only implicated in the process but immersed in it, becoming a cog in the very machines they seem to control. With the sound of machinery in the background, a single worker eats a sandwich and drinks coffee in a lunchroom in an early scene. In a later scene workers eat together in a cafeteria, but the setting is institutional and sterile, and the film shows us a view from behind a counter looking out into the vast cafeteria and focusing on a solitary female worker eating a sandwich and drinking coffee, this time out of a Styrofoam cup. In another scene immigrant workers cooking rice in a small living space and ladling it out of a large pot seem less alienated, but they watch television rather than communicate while machinery hums in the background.

This humming continues until the film's shocking end. In its final images *Our Daily Bread* reveals the consequences of sterile mechanized slaughter. Cattle are killed in a steel cage and rolled onto a shelf where a worker clamps their feet to hang them upside down. The next cow goes through and workers continue the process, opening up the carcass to bleed it. Workers are on elevated cranes while skinning the cattle. They barely need to touch the meat, since the machinery is so well engineered. Another worker uses an immense saw to cut through carcasses. Other workers spray down the cows and the slaughterhouse, and the film ends. On this mechanized farm slaughter has become, cold, sterile, and inhuman.

Capturing the Truth?

Ending with this impersonal image reinforces the power of *Our Daily Bread*'s visual rhetoric. Death is clean in the factory farm, the film shows us, and workers are cold and distant, consuming food they prepare and seemingly oblivious to the unnatural state of the food production process. Using an avant-garde direct-cinema approach and a seemingly categorical form, *Our Daily Bread* unwittingly makes a strong argument against factory farming that is driven by multiple source-driven images.

Perhaps, as we previously suggested, all texts, including documentaries, are inherently rhetorical, since they address an audience from a particular standpoint historically; the rhetorical documentary presents an argument and lays out evidence to support it. *Our Daily Bread* does this without the exposition found in most food documentaries, drawing on the work of Thomas W. Benson and Brian J. Snee, who assert in *The Rhetoric of the New Political Documentary* that audiences do not only passively respond to filmic texts. They also engage actively "in judgment and action" (137). Benson and Snee argue that audiences do not merely mimic the action on the screen; they also interpret the actions documented, and invent and engage in acts of their own that respond to the film's rhetoric, but from the viewer's perspective.

Our Daily Bread provides evidence of the negative consequences of industrial farming but offers ample room for audiences to interpret the actions documented to invent and engage in acts of their own. The direct cinema approach invoked by *Our Daily Bread* also supports Heider's third criterion for an effective ethnography: "holism" (6). The industrial farming process is "truthfully represented" (Heider 7) in the film, demonstrating Heider's last criterion for an effective ethnographic film, all in service to the film's rhetoric.

Although *Food, Inc.* and *King Corn* assert clear positions through their talking-heads approach to exposition, and *We Feed the World* and many National Film Board of Canada documentaries provide a depth of evaluation supported by multiple examples missing in both *Food, Inc.* and *King Corn, Our Daily Bread* comes closest to capturing the truth, offering fragmented observations that closely replicate the segmented process of industrial food production, effectively revealing its consequences to humans and the natural world because the intermediary veil has been lifted.

CHAPTER FIVE

FLIPPER? WE'RE EATING FLIPPER?

Documenting Animal Rights and Environmental Ethics at Sea

The Academy Award–winning documentary *The Cove* (2009) captures viewers' attention immediately with its opening shots in Taiji, Japan, where its unlikely hero, Ric O'Barry, explains, "I do want to say that we tried to do the story legally," but he then exclaims, "Shit," as he sees city police nearby and introduces the tale of espionage at the center of the film: "Here it is," Ric tells the viewer, "the town of Taiji, the little town with a really big secret," pointing to a seemingly idyllic village beside the sea where dolphins are memorialized in the Taiji Whale Museum and exalted by both locals and tourists in pleasure boats shaped like smiling dolphins. But as O'Barry reveals, "hundreds of thousands of dolphins have died there," and it is his mission to fight for the dolphins' rights and reveal the senseless slaughter to the world.

The Cove and two other documentaries regarding the fishing industry, *Darwin's Nightmare* (2007) and *The End of the Line* (2010), all grapple with issues surrounding fishing for what *New York Times* seafood writer Paul Greenberg calls our "last wild food" in his *Four Fish*. All three documentaries seek to address what their filmmakers consider environmental catastrophes: dolphin slaughter, biosphere destruction, and

The Cove: Recording the slaughtering of dolphins from one of the secret locations

massive overfishing. But only *The Cove* effects the changes it proposes. Whereas *Darwin's Nightmare* and *The End of the Line* reveal little known eco-disasters, *The Cove* goes further. It not only unmasks the slaughter of dolphins that leaders in Taiji work hard to hide; it also provides a call to action that is both heard and followed, successfully slowing the carnage in the cove.

Highlighting its environmental bent from its opening forward, *Darwin's Nightmare* establishes its setting and introduces its perspective differently than does *The Cove*, contrasting the struggles of impoverished natives with their prosperous Eastern European economic colonizers. The opening song, "Tanzania," for example, is contrasted with Eastern European music accompanying a plane's shadow over Lake Victoria, "the source of the Nile" and "the birthplace of civilization," according to the film. A pan of the town reveals poverty and neglect. Dogs sleep on the sand, while fishermen work on their boats. In the streets one boy runs on crutches, and another cries when a bully punches him. Girls sing to the sound of a synthesizer, while a child sleeps on the sidewalk. "They take the fish to the factory," Marcus, a police officer, explains, and European pilots fly the prepared perch back to their homeland. With these opening shots, the film's focus has been established—an interrogation of the dire economic and environmental consequences of introducing perch into the Lake Victoria ecosystem.

With a blatantly environmental message, *The End of the Line*, on the other hand, contrasts a seemingly pristine ocean with its disastrous future. Close-ups of sea life and sky show the passage of time. Coral, neon-colored fish, and crabs are accompanied by violin music. They are revealing a "Marine Protected Area" in the Bahamas, the narrator (Ted Danson) tells us, "protected from the most efficient predator." The music becomes ominous now, as a shark swims by, but the crescendo rises when the hand of a fisherman brings up a line and nets of fish, trawling that the narrator explains is "like plowing a field seven times per year." We are the predators, the image tells us, and the title, *The End of the Line*, rolls on the screen.

The Cove draws on the emotional appeal of animal rights arguments in its strong advocacy for the dolphins of Taiji, and *Darwin's Nightmare* provides a passionate critique of the human consequences of destroying Lake Victoria's ecosystem, but both *Darwin's Nightmare* and *The End of the Line* immerse themselves in wise-use environmental arguments similar to Aldo Leopold's land ethic. Although *Darwin's Nightmare* and *The End of the Line* more logically connect with long-term environmental solutions, because *The Cove* meets its goal to end dolphin slaughter, at least temporarily, and slow its progress, we argue that the film employs the most effective rhetorical strategies, emotionally appealing strategies grounded in the animal liberation movement's claims that all animals are equal because, like humans, they feel pain.

The End of the Line and *Darwin's Nightmare*: A New Environmental Ethic?

Although they elucidate disparate issues surrounding our hunt for seafood, both *The End of the Line* and *Darwin's Nightmare* draw on the biotic arguments of organismic ecology rather than animal rights ethics to substantiate their respective arguments against humanity's exploitation of marine life. *The End of the Line* asserts and supports a straightforward argument against overfishing in our oceans around the world, and *Darwin's Nightmare* effectively demonstrates the negative consequences of introducing nonnative (and carnivorous) species into a freshwater lake

The End of the Line: Harvested bluefin tuna for sale

(Lake Victoria), but they both highlight the need for a biotic community undisrupted by human intervention, either by industrializing the fishing industry or experimenting with a marine biosphere in Africa.

This perspective draws on organismic approaches to ecology, which are based on Frederic Clements's view of a plant community as a living organism that evolves through succession. According to Clements, as a living organism, a plant community changes over time: "The unit of vegetation, the climax formation is an organic entity. As an organism, the formation arises, grows, matures, and dies. . . . The climax formation is the adult organism, the fully developed community" (Clements 124–25, quoted in Merchant 182). This process of succession is apparent in both the life cycle and the developmental history of the United States, with pioneer species invading ecosystems until climax communities of species were established: the deciduous forest climax, the prairie-plains climax, the mountain range climaxes of the Rocky Mountains, and the desert climaxes of the Southwest. A plant community is also vulnerable to disruption or death by technologies such as those that caused the dust bowl, when humans as pioneer species "had not appreciated or understood the grassland biome native to the Plains" (Merchant 184).

The organismic school of ecology "rejected Social Darwinist assumptions of a nature characterized by Thomas Henry Huxley as 'red in tooth and claw,' for a nature of cooperation among individuals in animal and human communities" (Merchant 184). Warder C. Allee and Alfred E. Emerson, organismic ecologists at the University of Chicago after World War I, saw the workings of the natural world as a model for healing societal problems. Organismic ecologist Aldo Leopold, on the other hand, applied human ethics to the natural world, constructing a manifesto, "The Land Ethic," which encouraged an ecologically centered view of the land as a biotic pyramid in which humans were a part. In Leopold's view humans had "the scientific and ethical tools to follow nature and heal it" (Merchant 185).

An organismic approach to ecology views the natural world as a set of communities where living creatures cooperate in interconnected relationships. Ideally, humans, too, interact with the natural world cooperatively rather than seeking to exploit and ultimately destroy it. For Leopold and other organismic ecologists, humanity should see both nature and society as an organism in which each natural element, both human and nonhuman, contributes a part. From this perspective humans thrive only when they seek to sustain rather than exploit the natural world around them because they too are part of this whole organism, a gestalt of sorts in which the whole is greater than the sum of its parts. Our societies too prove most effective when each member is seen as equally important because he or she contributes to the success of the whole.

Both *The End of the Line* and *Darwin's Nightmare* emphasize the need to work toward sustainable development, sustaining the natural world rather than exploiting it as only a source of food. *The End of the Line* warns us against the corporate fishing that is depleting our seafood supply so astronomically that our oceans will be virtually empty of fish in a few decades. Instead, the film asserts, we should implement sustainable fishing practices that maintain aquatic life and nurture the oceans' biotic communities. *Darwin's Nightmare*, on the other hand, demonstrates how our greed for a particular type of fish—perch—has irrevocably disrupted the biosphere of Lake Victoria. Because of the changes in the fishing industry caused by the overabundance of perch and Westerners' taste for this fish as food, human nature has also been irrevocably disrupted according to the film, demonstrating how interconnected humans and the natural world remain.

Universalizing the Biotic Community in *The End of the Line*

Darwin's Nightmare focuses on one example of species manipulation and human oppression. *The End of the Line* argues more generally for an ethical approach to the ocean environment that embraces sustainability. The film exclaims, "Imagine a world without fish," and declares that based on the current rate of fishing, the world will see the extinction of most seafood species by 2048. By juxtaposing images of protected pristine seas with spectacles of predation, *The End of the Line* successfully argues for organismic approaches to ecology that see the survival of humans indelibly intertwined with that of the nonhuman nature of the seas.

Reviews laud the film's exposé of what Andrew Schenker calls "a new threat to the planet's sustainability." Nathan Lee of the *New York Times* declares that *The End of the Line*, an official selection at the Sundance Film Festival, "expos[es] the damages wrought to the sea by the usual suspects: industrialized food production, unchecked capitalism, and soaring consumer demand," for example, and highlights the film's focus on "an over-fishing so severe that the world's piscatorial stock may be completely depleted by 2048." In a review Roger Ebert also notes the film's documentation of "what threatens to become an irreversible decline in aquatic populations within 40 years."

Measures of how effectively the film conveys this horrific message vary, however. Although Ebert asserts that the film "is constructed from interviews with many experts, a good deal of historical footage, and much incredible footage from under the sea, including breathtaking vistas of sea preserves, where the diversity of species can be seen to grow annually," Lee states that the film's propositions "are slathered in laughable scare music." Schenker goes further, nearly condemning the film's effectiveness, declaring that "the picture fails to build a rigorous enough argument to sustain [its] indignant tone." According to Schenker "if over fishing is to take its place among that growing catalogue of woes already assaulting the American conscience, . . . it will certainly take a far more cogent polemicist than [director] Rupert Murray to make it stick."

For us, however, the film effectively illustrates the consequences of industrialized fishing and consumerism. Despite its flaws, then, the film demonstrates the catastrophic consequences of overusing marine resources by contrasting views of oceans with and without the human impact of "fair use" fishing strategies that exploit the sea's resources without regard for the future of sea life. The film documents evidence that validates this key argument. Human exploitation is killing the sea, changing what was a renewable resource into a death pool.

The Newfoundland, Canada, cod shortage is the first example presented as evidence. In 1992 what had once been the most abundant cod-fishing area in the world had been fished out. Forty thousand people lost their jobs, and cod became an endangered species in Canada; its population collapsed and despite a fishing moratorium was unable to recover. Near extinction of the blue fin tuna serves as a second compelling case supporting the film's horrific assertion. According to the narrator blue fin tuna, once caught in the thousands, have declined by 80 percent, probably in the last twenty-two years. Although *The End of the Line* does focus on a specific species of tuna, it explains that these examples merely particularize a more general trend: species after species of fish have collapsed in the world's oceans because developed nations crave seafood. Even fish in developing nations such as Senegal are sold to developed European countries, forcing West Africans into poverty and starvation. The collapse of marine species also disrupts the oceans' biotic community, destroying a balance of predator and prey found in the ocean food chain. Reasons for these major declines are explored, all related to a move toward large-scale industrial fishing in the 1950s, but the film primarily demonstrates that, at the current rate of fishing, the number of fish available in the world's oceans will hit zero by 2048. Marine life is fragile, a finite resource that will disappear if we do not change the way we harvest fish.

The film offers a variety of solutions to this catastrophic future of our seas, all of which are based in organismic approaches of ecology that embrace sustainable development and biotic community. Alaska's conservation methods are held up as one example of a better way, with a strictly enforced two-hundred-mile fishing limit. Alaska also controls the number of fishing boats and enforces quotas on fishing levels, so that exploitation there is only 10 percent, compared to 50 percent in the

North Sea. In Alaska fishermen are willing to take a cut in the harvest so that they can continue to catch fish. The film also suggests that consumers demand to know where their fish come from and how they are caught to support a sustainable fishing industry like that described by the Marine Stewardship Council. According to *The End of the Line*, some corporations are leading this drive toward sustainability. By 2011 Wal-Mart will sell only Marine Stewardship Council sustainable fish, for example. Two-thirds of the fish Birdseye sells come from sustainable sources, as does 99 percent of the fish served in McDonald's restaurants.

The End of the Line argues against fish farming, however, and suggests instead the establishment of more marine preserves where commercial fishing is off limits. According to the film's narrator a global network of 20–30 percent of the world's oceans kept free of commercial fishing would help the seas regenerate themselves, an enormous change from oceans protected by marine preserves today, less than 1 percent. By implementing and enforcing fishing limits, changing our eating habits, abiding by rules, and decreasing commercial fishing capacity, the film asserts, we can manage the recovery of the sea, and, as the narrator explains, we can act now. With this generalized focus on the biotic community of Earth's oceans, *The End of the Line* moves beyond individualized animal rights arguments and embraces a sophisticated theory of organismic ecology.

Whether the film's rhetoric will result in activist responses from viewers, however, is yet to be seen because the film is available primarily by accessing a website rather than through wide release. Despite multiple positive reviews and awards, including one from Sundance, the film has not found a mainstream distributor in the United States. Dogwoof Pictures, a UK company, is distributing the DVD, available on the film's website (endoftheline.com). The website provides multiple resources for reclaiming the oceans and offers educational screenings of the film, but one screening at a Salt Lake City high school that was documented in a YouTube video (www.youtube.com /watch?v=hQJWPvRbqHM) resulted in laughter rather than outrage. Both *Darwin's Nightmare* and *The End of the Line*, then, demonstrate that arguments against overfishing that are based in organismic ecology may or may not change behaviors.

Darwin's Nightmare: One of the results of the eco-disaster at Lake Victoria

Darwin's Nightmare and Animal Welfare: Ecology Meets Human Rights

Although *Darwin's Nightmare* advocates for human rights rather than animal rights, because the film connects these human rights with ecology, it demonstrates that, as J. Baird Callicott asserts, "animal welfare ethicists and environmental ethicists have overlapping concerns" (249); in this case, the disruption of an aquatic community has had devastating effects on both aquatic and human life. *Darwin's Nightmare* limits its argument to one species, as does *The Cove*, and highlights the need for "rights," but because it focuses on a nonnative species that has become an unwanted predator, it does not extend its human rights argument to animal rights. In fact, the film merely exposes a man-made problem rather than proposing a solution: humanity's intervention in the biosphere of Lake Victoria disrupts the evolutionary cycle and destroys what was once a thriving aquatic biotic community. In *Darwin's Nightmare* the ecological message is clear, but because there is no call to action, the film's ability to connect humans and the natural world falls flat.

Callicott explains how an animal welfare ethic aligns well with organismic ecology. Callicott's work draws on Mary Midgley's argument that "since we and the animals who belong to our mixed human-animal community are coevolved social beings participating in a single society, we and they share certain feelings that attend upon and enable sociability—sympathy, compassion, trust, love, and so on" (252). According to Callicott "Mary Midgley's suggested animal welfare ethic and Aldo Leopold's seminal environmental ethic thus share a common, fundamentally Hume-ean understanding of ethics as grounded in altruistic feelings. And they share a common ethical bridge between the human and nonhuman domains in the concept of community—Midgley's 'mixed community' and Leopold's 'biotic community.' [By] combining these two conceptions of a metahuman moral community we have the basis of a unified animal-environmental ethical theory" (152). This unified animal-environmental ethical theory acknowledges preferences for specific examples of human life or nonhuman life but places more value on community, working from a holistic perspective that rests on the notion that the mixed and biotic community matters.

Films that illustrate an animal welfare ethic like Midgley's provide a way to connect animal liberation and environmentalism and thus work toward interdependence between humans and the natural world instead of valorizing the individual regardless of the disruption to the biotic community. *Darwin's Nightmare* offers an individualized portrait of the need for such interdependent connections. Deemed a "fully realized poetic vision" by David Denby of the *New Yorker, Darwin's Nightmare* highlights the need for interdependence not only between humans and the natural world, but also among human and nonhuman species ("Candid Cameras"). The film chronicles the consequences of a little evolutionary experiment: introducing Nile perch into Lake Victoria. Fifty years after their introduction, the perch have destroyed 210 species of African cichlids that once thrived in the lake and controlled the lake's oxygen levels; now, according to the International Union for Conservation of Nature's International Climate Congress in Kenya, falling oxygen levels coupled with the perch's cannibalism may destroy the fishing industry, turning the lake into a "barren sinkhole."

The perch have destroyed the biotic community of the lake, with one species overwhelming all others, but they have also negatively affected the human community. As David Rooney asserts, the film's director Hubert Sauper "focuses on the ripple effect of a globalized economy in a specific microcosm to weigh the casualties of the New World Order." Their destructive behaviors may ultimately destroy the fishing industry, but their introduction into the lake has already changed the industry and the market that sustains it. With huge perch available for export, countries bordering on the lake, especially Tanzania, can no longer rely on the lake for sustenance. Fishermen no longer catch fish for themselves and their families. They catch perch for a factory where they are prepared for shipment to Europe, where, according to the film, two million white people eat Victoria fish each day.

Tanzanians are starving, then, because their lake has become a Darwinian nightmare marketplace for Eastern European businessmen and their pilots, who fly cargo planes into Tanzania for their load of perch. They provide nothing for the people living near the lake, but they do contribute even further to their impoverished state, since they bring arms to warring African countries, including Liberia, Zaire, the Republic of the Congo, and Sudan, leaving more than a million dead. In return pilots from Ukraine bring perch back to Europe, while hungry and orphaned Tanzanian children sleep on the streets. The human biotic community has disintegrated here. Tanzanians who once lived interdependently on the lake can no longer feed themselves. Their lake has been decimated, first by the Nile perch, and then by the European colonizers who further disrupt their community.

To document the effects of such an evolutionary nightmare, *Darwin's Nightmare* opens and closes on views of the European cargo planes landing in and leaving Tanzania, all piloted by white European men who look well fed in contrast to Tanzanians pulling an out-of-control cart full of perch in the impoverished town or fishing on Lake Victoria, the source of the Nile and the birthplace of civilization. Both fishermen and the boys pulling the cart take them to the factory, explains Marcus, a police officer. The film also shows us how both fishermen and boys suffer because their source of food has become a commodity. Fishermen and their families starve. Some fishermen die on the lake, leaving wives and children to mourn them. Many children end up orphaned and living on the street, fighting over scraps of food and falling into a drug-induced sleep on sidewalks and in doorways.

Women in this colonized community are left with few choices. After their husbands die of AIDS, fishing accidents, or war, they care for their children until they starve to death, die from fumes exuded by smoking perch corpses, or prostitute themselves to the European cargo pilots.

They may then live in brothels and bars constructed for their colonizers, where they sometimes die at the hands of their so-called benefactors, as does Eliza, a beautiful young woman highlighted in the film. The lone fish factory employs only four thousand people and pays as little as possible—a dollar a day for a night guard, for example.

The film personalizes each of these struggles: It foregrounds Eliza's attempts to figure out her life, her glowing smile, and her powerful voice singing her country's anthem, "Tanzania." It also focuses on Raphael, a night guard fearing for his life, since the previous guard had been murdered; Jonathan, a painter who documents the life on the streets he left behind; the group of boys fighting to survive on the street; and the cargo pilots themselves, some of whom even regret their part in the arms sales that contribute to so many deaths.

Director Hubert Sauper suggests that *Darwin's Nightmare* stands as evidence that "the old question, which social and political structure is the best for the world? seems to have been answered. Capitalism has won." For Sauper the changes in the communities around Lake Victoria are evolutionary and demonstrate that "the ultimate forms for future societies are 'consumer democracies,' which are seen as 'civilized' and 'good.' In a Darwinian sense, the 'good system' won. It won by either convincing its enemies or eliminating them." Sauper states in the film's production notes, "In *Darwin's Nightmare*, I tried to transform the bizarre success story of a fish and the ephemeral boom around this 'fittest' animal into an ironic, frightening allegory for what is called the New World Order. . . . It is, for example, incredible that wherever prime raw material is discovered, the locals die in misery, their sons become soldiers, and their daughters are turned into servants and whores. . . . The arrogance of rich countries towards the Third World (that's three quarters of humanity) is creating immeasurable future dangers for all peoples."

Despite the EU's claim that Nile perch from Lake Victoria have not been allowed in EU market countries since 1999, the exporting continues, leaving a Syrian factory owner free to play with a mechanical dancing fish while the UN discusses a food shortage in Tanzania on a television news program and starving children fight for food. As Noel Murray suggests in his review of the film, "only a movie could catch the irony and horror of an office manager proudly showing off his Billy Bass while local children beat each other senseless over handfuls of rancid rice." That irony and horror are reinforced in multiple scenes in the film. Tanzanians rally and pray for food while watching a film about Jesus as a fisherman. Factory workers pack fish into boxes and onto cargo planes, leaving only bones and fish heads for the locals. Eliza is killed, leaving her friends to mourn, and a one-legged boy walks down empty railroad tracks, while a man reads a BBC Focus on Africa magazine claiming that there are no supplies for Tanzania. It would be a good idea for his son to be a pilot, the man explains, so he can bring back supplies from Europe. Boys in the street smoke glue from empty soda bottles and sleep, and another plane takes off in a storm with thunder in the background, as a Tanzanian woman watches from the ground.

Sauper used a minimalist unit to shoot *Darwin's Nightmare*, relying only on himself, his camera, and his companion, Sandor, to document the figures he follows throughout the film. Although Sauper and Sandor faced obstacles when shooting the film, including multiple arrests that required bribes to earn their freedom, Sauper found effective footage to make his point. Sauper explains in the production notes, "When you look out for contrasts and contradictions, reality can become 'bigger than life.' So in a way it was easy to find striking images because I was filming a striking reality," a reality that demonstrates the need for an interdependent biotic community.

Even though Sauper argues that Tanzania's dilemma is a product of evolution, we assert that *Darwin's Nightmare* shows us what happens when the biotic communities of and between nonhumans and humans are disturbed. Unlike *The Cove* the film asserts that a single species—either the Nile perch or the European colonizer—can destroy its environment and even itself. Instead of arguing for animal liberation, the film upholds the need for interdependent community. The consequences of its destruction are monumental and ultimately end in both lake and land turning into barren sinkholes. But the film stands only as a warning against disrupting other biospheres. It is too late for Lake Victoria and perhaps for Tanzania, the film suggests. Both *Darwin's Nightmare* and *The End of the Line*, then, demonstrate that arguments against overfishing based in organismic ecology may or may not change behaviors. Documentaries with animal rights–driven arguments, however, may produce real change.

Animal Rights versus Animal Welfare and the Environmental Movement

Animal rights and environmentalism are sometimes seen as resting on similar values and grounded in similar calls to action: if we save the animal world, we save the environment might be the call. According to Peter Singer, for example, "Animal Liberation is Human Liberation too" (vii), and "human equality . . . requires us to extend equal consideration to animals too" (1) and preserve their rights as we might other human rights, as in the civil rights or women's rights movements. Yet the organismic environmental movement of pioneers like Aldo Leopold advocates for the good of all life as part of an ecosystem, not just those animals that Singer considers sentient, a position counter to the animal rights movement's focus on individual "sentient" animals.

The animal rights movement, however, typically bases its arguments on principles of the human rights movement and nineteenth century utilitarianism, which defined *good* as pleasure and *bad as* pain. Creatures capable of feeling pleasure and pain, in Singer's vision, have the same rights as humans because their "sentience" gives them inherent value. Other elements of nonhuman nature without such "sentience" do not share the same rights and are defined as "vegetables," which are living creatures somewhere between the oyster and the shrimp. According to Rebecca Raglon and Marian Scholtmeijer, "advocates for nonhuman animals note the similarities between human and other animal species and argue for rights for animals based on that closeness" (121). From Singer's groundbreaking 1975 work, *Animal Liberation*, to Norm Phelps 2007 overview, *The Longest Struggle: Animal Advocacy from Pythagoras to PETA*, animal advocates base their arguments on the close connection between humans and nonhuman animals.

The principles of organismic environmentalism, on the other hand, valorize biodiversity and interdependence and draw on Aldo Leopold's land ethic, which "enlarges the boundaries of . . . community to include soils, waters, plants, and animals, or collectively: the land" (204). Thus, as Raglon and Scholtmeijer note, animal advocacy is not necessarily associated with the environmental movement. They posit that, "while environmentalism and advocacy share many concerns, they essentially have developed along separate lines. It is [their] contention that some of

the differences informing the political and ethical debates between environmentalism and animal rights also emerge in the literary treatments of
the two topics" (121). Connecting animal rights and environmentalism,
however, through what Midgley calls "animal welfare" (quoted in Callicott
252) can provide a space for interdependence between humans and the
natural world. Animal rights principles, however, focus on individuals, a
focus that may disrupt Aldo Leopold's concept of the "biotic community"
(quoted in Callicott 252), a principle that rests on the belief that humans
are simply members of a community of living things that interact cooperatively and with equal ethical value. One species—humans or other
"sentient" beings—is constructed not as a conqueror but as a group of
"biotic citizens" (Leopold 223).

Robert H. Schmidt differentiates between animal rights and animal
welfare as a step toward aligning animal treatment with the environmental movement. Schmidt explains, "The animal rights movement has as
its underlying foundation the perception that animals have rights equal
or similar to those of humans (the principle of equal consideration of
interests; Singer 1980). . . . In their view, biomedical, agricultural, and
other uses of animals have no place in society unless the same treatment
could ethically be given to humans" (459). The animal welfare movement, on the other hand, "is particularly concerned with reducing pain
and suffering in animals" (459). Schmidt sees focusing the discussion
on animal welfare rather than animal rights as a way to "follow . . . the
direction of the rapidly increasing numbers of people concerned about
environmental issues in general and animal utilization in particular"
(460). Midgley agrees and grounds the animal welfare ethic in a biosocial
perspective that connects well with the ideas that Leopold outlines in *A
Sand County Almanac* (Callicott 254). Documentaries focusing on animal
treatment, however, sometimes foreground animal rights rather than
animal welfare, potentially discouraging alignment with environmentalism. *The Cove* most effectively draws on this rhetoric.

The Cove and Animals Rights

The Cove has received nearly universal acclaim, earning a 2009 Academy Award for Best Documentary Feature film, perhaps because it is,

according to Andrew O'Hehir, "a grim tale of murdered dolphins and poisoned school kids" that spins into "an amazing, real-life spy story video" ("Bond and Cousteau"). O'Hehir asserts, for example, that the film "raises troubling questions about how badly we have befouled the 70 percent of our planet that's covered with water, and about why we have treated the species closest to us in intelligence with such cruelty and contempt." Justin Chang declares, "Eco-activist documentaries don't get much more compelling than *The Cove*, an impassioned piece of advocacy filmmaking that follows 'Flipper' trainer-turned-marine crusader Richard O'Barry in his efforts to end dolphin slaughter in Taiji, Japan." According to Chang, "it's hard not to feel that there's something uniquely barbaric about the destruction of this exceptionally intelligent, human-friendly species." Even Noel Murray, who calls the film "muddled" in his review, suggests that "*The Cove* offers a lot to think about in terms of the future of fishing, and [director] Psihoyos' gift for fiction-feature conventions does make a seemingly unpalatable subject entertaining."

Murray's critique of the film, however, like other reviewers' accolades, rests on its reliance on the point of view of dolphin advocate Ric O'Barry, who, as Murray suggests, sides with "anyone who wants to protect dolphins, whether they want to shutter Sea World or not." *The Cove*, then, is both praised and condemned because it valorizes an animal rights ethic. Animal rights ethicists like Peter Singer first argue that dolphins as a species deserve the same liberation movements as do human groups. As Singer contends, the film suggests that speciesism should be eradicated, just as racism and sexism should be abolished, primarily because animals are so much like humans.

To support his claim Singer asserts that humans are only considered morally superior because they belong to the species Homo sapiens. Singer also suggests that using this membership to define superiority is completely arbitrary. Instead, then, we should consider sentience— the capacity of a being to experience pleasure and pain—as a plausible criterion of moral importance. If we use sentience as a criterion, we extend to other sentient creatures the same basic moral consideration, the basic principle of equality. Therefore, we ought to extend to animals the same equality of consideration that we extend to human beings. Singer, like O'Barry, also connects selected animals more closely with humans, defining them as persons, a category that includes both sentience and self-awareness over time. In *The Cove* O'Barry defines dolphins as both sentient and self-aware, offering these characteristics of persons as reasons for ensuring their safety and freedom.

The Cove demonstrates dolphins' connections with humans first through Ric O'Barry's recollections of interactions with the dolphins he captured and trained for the television series *Flipper* (1964–68). According to O'Barry he captured and trained the five female dolphins that played Flipper in the series, translating the script into dolphin action each day. The dolphins' skills and intellect surprised and impressed even O'Barry. They even recognized themselves in the show when they saw themselves on O'Barry's television. O'Barry lived in the house at the end of a dock featured in the series, so he came in contact with the dolphins almost every waking hour. When the show ended, however, the dolphins were sold to an aquarium where they entertained crowds, seemingly smiling throughout the show, "nature's greatest deception," according to O'Barry. This connection with humans unfortunately leads to their harm or even death. O'Barry maintains that the aquarium life is so stressful for dolphins, they must take Maalox and Tagamet every day. They travel forty miles a day in the wild. Captivity not only confines them but also interferes with their sonar. O'Barry explains, "When they are captured and put in a concrete tank surrounded by screaming people, the noise causes stress." The sound of the filtration system was found to kill dolphins and had to be modified. O'Barry's commentary demonstrates both their sentience, their ability both to feel pleasure and pain, and their self-awareness, their ability to recognize themselves on television, arguing effectively that dolphins should be preserved because destroying them means destroying beings whose value equals that of humans.

The Cove also valorizes dolphins' intelligence as a connection to humans through information provided by John Potter, who measures intelligence in dolphins. Dolphins respond to signals in American Sign Language, but they also connect with humans on an emotional level. Mandy-Rae Cruikshank, one of the divers in the film, states that a dolphin swam with her and invited her to rub its belly. Surfers recount stories of dolphins saving them from shark attacks. According to the film, then, dolphins have worth, so they deserve to live. They also deserve the freedom that all persons of equal worth deserve.

The film establishes the worth of dolphins but also assumes, because they have historically been viewed as sentient creatures, that viewers will immediately call for action, once the slaughter at Taiji Cove is revealed. "We tried to do the story legally," we're told at the opening of this documentary revealing the dolphin slaughter in a cove in Taiji, Japan, "a little town with a really big secret." Ric O'Barry's attempts to film the slaughter are continually hampered by local authorities until he partners with the film's director, Louie Psihoyos. O'Barry never planned to be an activist, he explains, but after one of the dolphins he had trained killed herself in his arms by cutting off her own oxygen supply, he became a dolphin advocate, freeing as many as possible and preventing their slaughter. But dolphins are such great performers they have become a huge commodity worth $150,000.00 apiece for Sea World shows. Because thousands of dolphins come to Taiji each year, dolphin trainers collect dolphins there, bringing $2.3 million a year to the area. The remaining dolphins herded into the cove are slaughtered for food, O'Barry explains, but he needs filmic proof to present to the world, so he can stop the catastrophe.

Filmmaker Louie Psihoyos and Netscape CEO Jim Clark joined forces with O'Barry to accomplish this mission, helping him build a team of experts to plant cameras and microphones, even hiring George Lucas's Industrial Light and Magic to construct artificial rocks in which they could hide cameras in the cove. They brought in world-class divers, a military expert, and a rock concert organizer to facilitate the mission, and the film documents the process these experts follow to plan and execute their goal to film the slaughter in two stages: they first plant audio equipment, and then, in the stage they call "Mission 2: The Full Orchestra," the team hides cameras around the cove.

The film asserts both logical and emotional reasons why the dolphins should be saved. For example, the film provides practical reasons why humans should avoid dolphin meat if they value their health, explaining that it has toxic levels of mercury; yet dolphin meat is donated to area schools for lunch programs and disguised as whale meat in Tokyo markets. The film documents a history of problems with mercury poisoning to support this claim, including the infamous mercury poisoning in Minamata, Japan, in 1956, when the government covered up toxicity levels caused by industrial dumping. Fetuses were most affected, so children were born deformed and lost their sight and hearing. Dolphins' connection with humans is also used as a reason to stop their slaughter. As perhaps the most intelligent sea creature, dolphins have been known to protect humans, are self-aware, and have the ability to learn language, skills only intelligent creatures can achieve.

The slaughter they captured on film becomes the climax of this powerful documentary, serving as the strongest animal rights argument in the film. Before all the cameras had been planted in the hidden cove, from a distance the team filmed a dolphin trying to get away, leaving a trail of blood in the water in its wake. After the team planted the audio equipment, they listened to the dolphins scream in the cove. The sounds demonstrate that each dolphin was aware of its coming death. They anticipated their own slaughter, O'Barry explains.

But it is after cameras had been planted that the most shocking evidence against such slaughter is revealed. Ric and the team watch monitors showing fishermen on shore around a fire telling stories about whaling missions around the globe. Other shots show fishermen standing in boats and placing barriers across the cove. The fishermen herd in dolphins, disorienting them with constant tapping noises. Once they herd in the dolphins, fishermen begin the slaughter, stabbing dolphins repeatedly with harpoons. The water turns red with blood. Dolphin screams fill the soundtrack. The harpooning continues until all the dolphins are dead. The water is ruby red, but dolphins caught in nets are pierced again and again. They try to escape but are caught in this cove fortress. Carcasses are ripped on board the boats, but fishermen smoke nonchalantly, even diving into the bloody water in search of more bodies. The dolphins are dragged like harpooned whales. These images contrast with majestic shots of dolphins swimming freely in the sea.

The footage of the slaughter becomes O'Barry's proof of dolphins' sentience. Their suffering is clear on the video screen he shows a town spokesman and the members of the International Whaling Commission. And these shocking images get results. Small countries paid off by the Japanese leave the International Whaling Commission, and dolphin meat is no longer allowed in school lunches, for example. By building an argument that first demonstrates dolphins' equality because they, like humans, are both sentient and self-aware, *The Cove* draws on animal rights arguments. It also effectively takes that argument one step further. Because dolphins are sentient and self-aware, their slaughter must end.

An Animal Welfare Approach

The focused rhetoric of *The Cove* succeeds where the environmental ethics perspective of *Darwin's Nightmare* and *The End of the Line* fail to convey the same emotional power. Ultimately, even though animal liberation arguments may privilege some elements of the natural world over others, such an individualized approach has been shown to have more effective results. According to Ric O'Barry, the Taiji dolphin slaughter was suspended in September 2009 because of the publicity surrounding the film *The Cove* ("Save Japan Dolphins"), and as of March 2, 2011, Taiji fishermen were returning to traditional fishing practices rather than dolphin slaughter. Even though dolphin killing continues, it has "drastically decreased compared to previous seasons," O'Barry explains ("Save Japan Dolphins").

Today O'Barry is continuing to garner support from Japanese journalists and local students and community members in Wakayama City, Tokyo, and other towns throughout the country. O'Barry sees this response to *The Cove* as a major victory, noting, "Our Save Japan Dolphins Team and I have been meeting with media for years about the dolphin slaughter in Japan, but now the Japanese media is coming to us!" According to O'Barry, *The Cove* opened in Japan despite intense opposition, and a press conference after the film's release "was attended by over 100 media representatives, including every major broadcast outlet" ("Save Japan Dolphins"). Because of the continuing success of *The Cove*, dolphin slaughter is on the wane.

Perhaps, then, films taking an organismic approach to eco-resistance might learn from the strategies invoked in a powerful animal liberation film like *The Cove*. As Holmes Bolston III explains, "Development in the West has been based on the Enlightenment myth of endless growth. . . . [However,] none of the developed nations have yet settled into sustainable culture on their landscapes" (528). By moving from an animal rights perspective to an animal welfare approach, environmentalists may find a way to individualize environmental issues without diluting the need for a biotic community.

An animal welfare approach can provide an emotional center missing from both *Darwin's Nightmare* and *The End of the Line* and perhaps facilitate an eco-activist response that culminates in the powerful eco-resistance that is central to *The Cove*. *The End of the Line* could have, for example, "humanized" selected species of aquatic life, demonstrating that they, like humans, have rights. A film similar to *Darwin's Nightmare* might highlight both aquatic biospheres in which environmental changes can address species disruption and native species worth saving because of their sentience. Such a focus on both individual species and their biotic communities could have the same result as the animal rights focus of *The Cove*: more than two million signatures on a petition that will, it is hoped, end dolphin slaughter for good.

3

NEGATIVE EXTERNALITIES
OF HOUSING AND
ENERGY INDUSTRIES

CHAPTER SIX

GIVE ME SHELTER

The Ecology of Homes and Homelessness

In *Blue Vinyl: The World's First Toxic Comedy* (2002), codirector and writer Judith Helfand and codirector/cinematographer Daniel B. Gold become comic detectives in their attempt to find a viable solution to the home repair dilemma of Helfand's parents: is it possible to replace rotting wood siding with "products that never hurt anyone at any point in their life cycle" but still provide the economy, endurance, and good looks of cheap but toxic blue vinyl? After convincing her parents to forego their new vinyl siding choice for a more environmentally friendly alternative (as long as it's cheap and looks good), Helfand and Gold embark on an investigative journey that reveals both the dangers underlying vinyl use and the challenge to find a viable, affordable, and environmentally friendly alternative. More importantly, their journey also illustrates the complexity of environmental justice issues. Environmental injustice, lack of human rights, and environmental racism all intersect in the literal study of homes in *Blue Vinyl*. For Helfand and Gold, it's not just how you live and how you build your home; it's where you live and what's around you that contribute to the everyday eco-disasters associated with constructing and sustaining shelter.

Blue Vinyl provides a narrative of discovery in which Helfand and Gold reveal what the dangers pvc (polyvinyl chloride) mean not only for her parents and other suburbanites keen on siding their homes with vinyl,

Blue Vinyl: The Lake Charles, Louisiana, PVC factory at night

but also for PVC chemical plant workers and home dwellers nearby. In this eco-comic documentary, as in other documentaries and fictional films, multiple issues of home and homelessness are explored, revealing a plethora of environmental problems that, according to *Blue Vinyl* and films tackling similar issues, should be addressed no matter how difficult the task. The repercussions of doing nothing are too toxic for both humans and the natural world. Overlooking these eco-disasters may turn the everyday into the catastrophic, these films assert, reinforcing the power of an environmental justice movement grounded in an equitable and humane vision of home.

Ecology and Home in Environmental History and Film

Ecology, literally, "the study of homes," connects explicitly with our notions of shelter as a constructed space where humans live either with or without nature. This distinction between what is completely controlled, artificial, and "dead" and what is natural and alive springs from empirical philosophy of the eighteenth century's "Great Awakening," a view that, according to Gary Lease, "led inevitably to an opposition between reason and nature, a position which Kant in his idealism effectively exploited" (8). In the nineteenth and twentieth centuries, this struggle between a culture controlled by "reason" and a nature seen as "irrational" became further complicated by a focus on scientific pursuit that seemed to eliminate Spinoza's identification of nature with God. But, as Lease suggests, "after wrestling with the notion of nature for well over two thousand years, Western tradition had come up dry: neither an identification of the human species with nature nor a strict dichotomy between the two proved ultimately successful" (8, 9).

These dichotomies, or their deconstruction, are reflected in a variety of American fictional films. Numerous films glamorize urban life and the culture it represents. Musicals such as *Anchors Aweigh* (1945), *Easter Parade* (1948), and *On the Town* (1949), and comedies including *Sex and the City* (2008), *Sex and the City 2* (2010), *Friends with Benefits* (2011), and the remake of *Arthur* (2011) celebrate life in the city with little or no reference to the natural world. Numerous crime films and film noir titles reinforce the dark and corrupt underbelly of urban life as well. Other films emphasize the need to connect further with the natural world, even bringing nature indoors as in *Housekeeping* (1987). On the other hand, *Make Way for Tomorrow* (1937), a Depression-era melodrama, explores the predicament of an elderly couple facing home foreclosure after the husband loses his job and is no longer able to pay the mortgage. They must live separately with family members, who mistreat them and misunderstand them. Unwilling to compromise, their children go back on their word and separate them permanently, forcing their mother to live in a nursing home and their father to live without her in California, on the opposite coast. *It Happened on Fifth Avenue* (1947) explores similar housing issues in a post–World War II context.

Many other American films reinforce the need to connect with the natural world, casting off the stifling emptiness of the city (or at least a tiny apartment with little closet space) for the life of the country. In *Mr. Blandings Builds His Dream House* (1948), for example, led by successful advertising executive and patriarch Jim Blandings (Cary Grant), the Blandings leave their urban New York City apartment to refurbish a ramshackle house in the country, hoping for an ideal pastoral life but finding an expensive challenge. The film's comedy facilitates a narrative that supports the ideals of the American dream without discounting the struggles required to achieve it. *Money Pit* (1986) centers on this theme in a 1980s context with Tom Hanks and Shelley Long in the leads. A *Home of Our Own* (1993) also replays the American dream, this time from the perspective of a single mother and her children in the 1960s. With the help of kindly neighbors and her hardworking kids, Frances Lacey (Kathy Bates) escapes the urban blight of Los Angeles and successfully provides a country home for her family, all built from scraps and dreams. These films demonstrate the power of shelter and place, highlighting a need to construct a home, either with or without nature.

Losing or Leaving Home in Feature Films

Watching televised orders to evacuate the upper East Coast to avoid Hurricane Sandy (2012) and the shores from North Carolina to New Hampshire to escape Hurricane Irene (2011) and its aftermath of flooding, power outages, and flying debris, we are confronted with some of the ramifications of displacement or loss of place and, perhaps, the identity attached to it. We witnessed this same displacement after Hurricane Katrina. Just prior to Katrina (2005), for example, the population of New Orleans was nearly half a million. Five years later, according to the 2010 census, the population was still less than 340,000, an increase from the approximately 255,000 calculated in 2006. An estimated 1,464 people died during the hurricane and its aftermath. Most of the more than 200,000 people who were evacuated never returned. Recent films interrogate displacement from various perspectives and levels of violence but move beyond natural disaster to human rights and environmental justice violations, sometimes at monumental levels. Yet they all highlight the power of place and the yearning for a return to a home. For example, *When the Levees Broke: A Requiem in Four Acts* (2006), *Trouble the Water* (2008), and *Treme* (2010) explicitly address this yearning in a New Orleans context.

Claudia Llosa's *Milk of Sorrow* (2009), a fictionalized account of the repercussions of the Peruvian civil war, centers on a woman's struggle to cope with her mother's experiences with rape as a tool of war, a traumatic incident passed on to her through her mother's songs and, perhaps, breast milk. To protect herself from a similar sexual assault, Fausta (Magaly Solier) inserts a potato as a shield, gingerly cutting off growing vines.

Fausta's displacement is twofold. She must leave her village home when her mother dies and transport her mother's body to her uncle's home in a Lima ghetto. To earn money to bury her mother, however, she also leaves her uncle's home and the ghetto community to work as a maid in a beautiful walled compound in central Lima, where an aristocratic female concert pianist tosses a grand piano out a window and steals Fausta's songs in exchange for the promise of pearls. The post–civil war Peruvian setting clearly bifurcates both rural and urban and rich and poor, but it also illustrates the repercussions of the traumas of war, placing the rape of women, landscapes, and cultures on display in relation to both colonial and postcolonial exploitation.

In Sebastian Silva's *The Maid* (2009), a fictional narrative based on the filmmaker's own experiences with his family's live-in maid, Raquel (Catalina Saavedra) suffers from headaches and an eventual temporary paralysis as a result of her more than twenty years working as a live-in-maid for a rich Santiago, Chile, family patterned on Silva's own and filmed in his family home. The film demonstrates Raquel's loss of identity and family connections and her attempts to replace those losses with her employers and their children, so much so that she wards off her employers' attempts to hire another maid to help her with her grueling tasks of cleaning, cooking, and child care.

Yet the entrance of another maid, Lucy (Mariana Loyola), amplifies the clear displacement suffered by Raquel on display in the film. Lucy enters Raquel's home and is subjected to some of the same games that intimidated other maids hired to help Raquel. Lucy, however, reintroduces Raquel to the concept of family and home, first by becoming her friend and then by inviting her to her own rural family home for Christmas. After a long bus ride, Lucy and Raquel enjoy a holiday on a family farm that contrasts with the city mansion they leave behind and the distant relationship shared between Raquel and the family she serves. What stands out, however, is a phone call between Raquel and her mother during the Christmas celebration. For the first time on screen, Raquel asks her mother about her health and her siblings' well-being, and when her mother seems not to answer, Raquel apologizes—for what we're not sure—highlighting the losses felt by those displaced in quiet but powerful ways.

The Help (2011), a mainstream American adaptation of the novel of the same name, and Live-In Maid (2004), an Argentinian exploration of unexpected consequences of the country's economic crisis, however, highlight both issues of displacement and environmental injustices associated with a home's placement. There is much to critique about The Help. Joe Morgenstern of the Wall Street Journal states that the film "takes us on a pop-cultural tour that savors the picturesque, and strengthens stereotypes it purports to shatter." According to Ben Sachs of the Chicago Reader, "as in many reductive period pieces, there are no real characters here, just archetypes, namely reactionary cretins and sensitive souls who anticipate modern attitudes." While acknowledging its shortcomings, other critics note positive aspects of the film that make the it more palatable. For example, David Denby of the New Yorker notes that the film "is, in some ways, crude and obvious, but it opens up a broad new swath of experience on the screen, and parts of it are so moving and well acted that any objections to what's second-rate seem to matter less as the movie goes on." Lisa Kennedy of the Denver Post asserts, "Thanks to a talented cast—starting with leads Emma Stone, Viola Davis and Octavia Spencer—the movie is often entertaining. But The Help should have been challenging too."

Some of the weaknesses of The Help move beyond its focus on picturesque archetypes instead of well-developed characters, however, and may stem from the film and the novel's popularity and its implications, weaknesses that are reminiscent of constructions of race in both the 1934 and the 1959 versions of Imitation of Life and film and television adaptations of A Raisin in the Sun (1961, 1989, 2008). A statement from the Association of Black Women Historians (ABWH) highlights some of the film's problems. The statement responds to the popularity of the film adaptation, noting it "is troubling because it reveals a contemporary nostalgia for the days when a black woman could only hope to clean the White House rather than reside in it" ("Open Statement to the Fans"). The ABWH provides effective evidence for its stance. Giving adequate

ism that continues near mines, waste dumps, factories with toxic smoke and water emissions, mountaintop removal and natural gas fracking sites, and nuclear and coal-generated energy plants around the world.

Blue Vinyl and Environmental Justice

Blue Vinyl highlights environmental justice and racism issues associated with both production of housing materials and the housing industry. Filmmaker and narrator Judith Helfand introduces these issues by documenting the environmental effects of home construction after talking with her parents about new siding for their home. Their redwood siding is rotten and must be replaced. Helfand's mother believes that the rotten wood will mean her daughter will feel a sense of loss for her childhood home, so she thinks her daughter overreacts to the family's choice to replace their old wood siding with vinyl. But because Helfand has had a rare form of cervical cancer, the result of her mother receiving diethylstilbestrol (DES) during pregnancy, worries about toxic chemicals used in vinyl's PVC production are a priority for her now. In her exploration of the ecology of home building, Helfand wonders, is vinyl siding safe? *Blue Vinyl* documents the detective work that Helfand and her codirector, Daniel B. Gold, perform to discover and reveal their answers.

The film has been both heralded and slammed, primarily because of its rhetoric. It has won a number of awards, including Best Environmental Feature Film for the Activist Film Festival in Los Angeles, The Documentary Award for Excellence in Cinematography at the 2002 Sundance Film Festival, and first prize for Best Documentary at the 2002 Bermuda International Film Festival. It was also nominated for two Emmy Awards: Best Documentary and Best Research. The film also received laudable reviews from the *Philadelphia City Paper* ("*Blue Vinyl* Review") and festival reviewer Tim Stopper. Stopper gives the film 4 ½ out of 5 stars and notes, "With its mix of humor and gravity, accessibility and education, conciseness and common sense, this film has what it takes to move an audience." Stopper leaves readers with only positive impressions of the film and its successful execution of its rhetorical purpose, asserting, "With the hundreds of millions of dollars spent every year on brain-numbing, high budget pictures without an ounce of purpose or honest humanity to them, looking back on this film will give me hope that there are people doing important, real, and truthful things with the medium of film."

According to the *City Paper* "the film, which follows Helfand's quest to investigate the toxic origins of the blue siding installed on her parents' Long Island home, has everything most people want in a muckraking documentary—a compelling first-person story, an easily identifiable villain, and an upbeat conclusion." But the *City Paper* review also suggests that "the story seems to have been if not manufactured, at least jury-rigged." Although Christopher Null calls the film "interesting" and explains that "Judith Helfand and Daniel Gold intercut cute animations about the hazards of vinyl products with interviews with her parents (who installed vinyl siding), industry bigwigs, and presumed victims of PVC-based cancers," he notes at least one of its weaknesses: "it's extremely long." Bill Durodie of the conservative website Culture Wars provides the most damaging review, calling *Blue Vinyl* "a case study in dumbing down." According to Durodie the film "shows how a daughter's obsession with her holier-than-thou moral outlook can trump her aging parents' dignity."

Yet even these negative reviewers agree that PVC and vinyl pose environmental and health risks to factory workers and nearby residents. Durodie admits the dangers associated with PVC, noting that "on a visit to a former industrial plant in Italy, the film turns serious. Here [Helfand] meets an elderly scientist" whose "concerns relate to those who produced vinyl." And the *City Paper* review highlights the strong evidence that indicates "higher risks of cancer for factory workers and those in nearby communities, as well as an ongoing international conspiracy among manufacturers to hush up the adverse health risks."

Although Helfand and Gold's documentary journey to reveal the dangers of PVC production and use may be diluted by Helfand's choice to personalize the issue in relation to her parents' siding and her own health issues, it does begin to illustrate and address the environmental injustices of home construction. Even when Helfand is told that vinyl will not emit chemicals unless a house fire has occurred, she remains skeptical and asks her parents how they feel about the cancer-causing chemicals in PVC, the vinyl component in the siding her family begins to put on their home. To uncover the truth about vinyl, the now-detective Helfand goes to the source of vinyl siding—Lake Charles, Louisiana, where PVC, the main ingredient in the vinyl, is produced—and complicates her reading. Although the toxicity of the contents of Helfand's parents' vinyl siding is an everyday eco-disaster, the production process for the PVC vinyl contains highlights a second level of environmental injustice and a second set of victims: those who work in and live in proximity to PVC plants.

Her investigation of PVC leads her to Louisiana during Mardi Gras celebrations in Lake Charles, with an enormous chemical plant in the background. In costume Helfand shows off and measures her vinyl to the crowds at Mardi Gras while countershots demonstrate that the PVC factory sits beside water and fields where cattle graze. Near the factory the owner of a local restaurant, the Pitt Grill, and workers talk about what causes cancer. It's the smoke in the air, they explain, broaching at least one violation of environmental justice and human rights. Their environment is clearly not "secure, healthy, and ecologically sound." But the plant managers argue that hazards near PVC plants may be a relatively good thing because the company takes care of toxic spills fast.

As evidence of the blatant environmental injustices caused by the plant, however, several area residents note the repercussions of living near this toxic plant. In the town of Mossville, African American resident Dianne Prince, for example, has cancer and believes she acquired it from the factory. She asks, is safety a big issue in Lake Charles? At community risk management meetings questions about raw material falling on residents are discussed. Residents near the factory are unable to breathe. Trees are brown on the side facing the plant, green on the other. The factory owners say they will give residents a tour, and Helfand wants to go, noting that her "father's answer to rotten wood looks like a toxic hazard." When the public relations officer refuses her request for a tour, Helfand's suspicions that the company is acting maliciously are reinforced, especially when the company representative refers her to the Vinyl Institute website, where scrolling graphics extoll the uses of vinyl and its "green" recyclable footprint.

Vinyl is everywhere, "making a difference every day," according to the website.

But fires in the 1970s and 1980s tell a different story. PVC products that melted during house fires killed their residents, so vinyl received bad press, and the industry needed a trade organization. The Vinyl Institute was the result. At a conference devoted to alternatives to PVC, the Vinyl Institute was there to exalt the benefits of its product. Other evidence Helfand uncovers tells a different story: "They say they're not hurting the environment, but 56 percent of the product is chlorine. Is there any proof that it's safe?" Helfand asks.

During the investigation, however, Helfand and her team discover that experts disagree about the dangers of PVC. Yet any benefits of PVC are outweighed by the risks, according to most studies. Helfand calls PVC "the Watergate of molecules," since it is more dangerous than any other plastic. Greenpeace calls it the poison plastic. A single PVC fire can cause disease and death. But the danger doesn't stop there. Dioxin is produced at both ends of the PVC life cycle, so PVC and its vinyl output are not easily recycled. PVC ends up in landfills causing more disease and death. According to Helfand the damage caused by PVC is similar to what DES did to her.

When she shows the evidence to her father, he nonetheless wants a second opinion. Ultimately, however, he agrees that dioxin is an unwanted contaminant caused by PVC, a toxic waste that is not degraded by humans or the environment. If dioxin is getting into the atmosphere, it's getting into the food chain and building up in our bodies, Helfand explains, highlighting the breadth of environmental injustices associated with the use of PVC.

The environmental injustice associated with PVC production, use, and disposal extends to human rights issues when attorney William (Billy) B. Baggett Jr. reinforces Helfand's claims. As a lawyer he can legally film areas where exposed workers have been, but he is allowed only one plant visit. When he enters the factory, he uses five cameras on a platform to get a 360-degree view, hoping to show where workers he is representing might have been exposed to vinyl chloride.

To augment Baggett's evidence, Helfand and her crew provide examples of workers afflicted with cancer and other diseases due to vinyl chloride exposure. One afflicted worker's wife holds a handwritten note on a bill that proves the company's culpability: "Exceeds short-term exposure. Do not include on wire to Houston," the note explains, a message whited out on the versions that Baggett receives from the company. This blatant omission provides proof and lays the groundwork for conspiracy allegations against all PVC manufacturers, with Baggett, the lawyer, leading the charge.

Experts see the company's omission as criminal activity that puts people who work in or live near the factory or live in vinyl-sided homes at risk. The industry's knowledge of the negative effects of PVC exposure is confirmed in the documents that Baggett and his clients find, including internal industry documents from Venice, Italy, to all parts of the United States warning about the dangers of PVC toxins. To find out more about this document, Helfand goes to Venice and talks with former workers and their spouses and relatives; she discovers that the European vinyl industry did research in 1972 and discovered that low doses of vinyl chloride caused cancer in laboratory mice, even in amounts that were less than the legal levels to which workers were exposed. None of this was revealed to the public, however, because a secrecy pact was signed in Europe, and American companies agreed to it.

More examples of even minimal exposure causing cancer are revealed with further investigation. One scientist suggests that more research is needed, so Billy Baggett continues his quest for truth about PVC. To prove that PVC causes cancer and that residents are breathing PVC too, collection buckets are created to test exposure and warn residents. When tested the air is found to be full of chloride and other chemicals, and those toxins have also contaminated nearby water sources.

The most extreme environmental consequence of PVC and dioxin revealed by the film, however, transforms environmental injustice into environmental racism, when residents of Mossville, a predominantly African American community in the region, are forced to leave because PVC toxins from area factories have contaminated their water. As further evidence of blatant environmental injustice and racism, these residents are left not only without a community but also without recourse for future health issues. In order to sell their homes at low prices, the PVC companies required all residents to sign an agreement that they would not file suit against the company if they developed health problems caused by the contamination. Clearly, these residents have lost their right to a secure, healthy, and ecologically sound environment.

To avoid this toxic mess and at least minimize one aspect of environmental justice, the negative environmental consequences of home construction, Helfand looks for alternatives for her parents' home. While investigating the hazards of pvc, she discovers a more far-reaching solution not only for homeowners but also for factory workers and residents living near pvc factories. Despite setbacks (Habitat for Humanity's vinyl homes, funded by the Vinyl Institute, and Helfand's ineffective programmed meeting with the Vinyl Institute), Helfand discovers that other pvc lawsuits have succeeded. In Venice, Italy, the city puts a vinyl company on trial for manslaughter and wins. At least in Venice the arm of environmental justice is wide and strong.

Ultimately Helfand discovers reclaimed wood as an alternative for vinyl that also proves aesthetically pleasing to her parents, but since it costs a small fortune, she pays for the new siding. *Blue Vinyl* provides a clear case that vinyl siding is hazardous to humans and the natural world but ends with an ambiguous view of alternatives too expensive for Helfand's family or Habitat for Humanity homes. Yet it also broaches some wider-reaching solutions to the environmental hazards of pvc, condemning vinyl companies for their knowing endangerment of their employees and residents near their plants. *Blue Vinyl* addresses environmental justice issues on both an individual and a universal level. Helfand's film unearths inequities related to geography and racial and class bias, illustrating the extent to which Lake Charles, Louisiana, has become a "sacrifice zone" in which toxins are tolerated because residents and factory workers lack power. Helfand and Baggett help provide them with a voice in both Helfand's documentary film and the court cases Baggett leads.

PVC, Vinyl, and Industrial Ecology

The dangers of pvc have been widely documented, but so has the viability of safer and affordable alternatives. According to David T. Allen, "billions of pounds of vinyl chloride are produced annually." Yet in their Tufts University study, Frank Ackerman and Rachel Massey effectively document both the hazards of pvc and vinyl and the availability of viable and safe alternatives for pvc products. According to Ackerman and Massey "pvc poses hazards to human health over the course of its life cycle. pvc production exposes workers and communities to vinyl chloride and other toxic substances. pvc products such as medical equipment and children's toys can leach toxic additives during their useful life. Vinyl building materials release hydrochloric acid fumes if they catch fire, and burning PVC creates byproducts including dioxin, a potent carcinogen." They note alternative products for a variety of PVC uses, including pipes and gloves, but for our purposes their arguments regarding vinyl siding are most relevant. As Ackerman and Massey assert, "Vinyl is now the most common siding material for low- and moderate-priced housing. However, wood shingles or clapboard also offer viable siding alternatives, as do fiber cement and simulated stucco. Disadvantages to vinyl siding include poor resistance to temperature, vulnerability to water damage, and chemical hazards when it burns or smolders. Despite claims that vinyl is 'maintenance free,' vinyl can fade with time, can require painting, and can warp. Fiber cement, a relatively new product, is more durable than vinyl and almost as low-maintenance; moreover, fiber cement does not warp or burn."

Although Helfand and Gold conclude that environmentally sound alternatives are available but costly, Ackerman and Massey disagree, challenging "economic arguments for continued use of PVC" and asserting that alternatives to PVC are not only viable but also economical. In their report they "offer four principles of analysis" to counter claims that PVC is the most economical choice:

Alternatives that have higher purchase prices, or higher installed costs, than PVC may still be cheaper on a full-cost accounting or life-cycle cost basis.

Alternatives that look expensive when produced in small batches today will become cheaper when they are mass-produced.

The unique health and environmental damages caused by PVC can endanger the users of a product, as in the case of medical supplies.

Academic studies have shown that the costs of environmental protection are routinely overestimated in advance, and decline rapidly after implementation.

Ackerman and Massey's results are reinforced by the research conclusions of both G. K. Al-Sharrah and his colleagues and David Goldsmith, engineers who highlight the need to insert environmental objectives in industry analyses. Al-Sharrah and his colleagues' study of the environmental feasibility of the petrochemical industry concludes, "Results give an optimal structure for the development and prove that simple indicators can represent sustainability giving good results in selecting environmentally friendly processes and at the same time profitable" outcomes (1). Goldsmith, on the other hand, argues against "an anthropocentric model of nature as a supplier of resources" and instead asserts "that it would be beneficial to critically examine the ethical basis for sustainable built environments." Like Arne Naess, Goldsmith argues "for equal rights for the biotic environment, or biocentrism, that values nature for its own sake and not as a resource for consumption." These studies demonstrate the viability of an environmentally sound approach to PVC and other chemical production.

Shelter and the EPA Superfund: Mossville, Louisiana, versus Libby, Montana

Despite these studies, however, PVC production and consumption continue at an astronomical pace. In fact, in 2011, nine years after the release of *Blue Vinyl*, Mossville, Louisiana, a predominately African American community right next door to Lake Charles, lost its case with the EPA to establish the community and its PVC plants as a Superfund site. According to the EPA Superfund Strategy Recommendation of May 3, 2011, "Based on available information and a site score below 28.5, the site fails to meet the minimum criteria at this time required to be considered for . . . the National Priorities List (NPL) by the EPA." The EPA asserted that the water supplies had "not been impacted by chemical contamination," even though it admitted that "surface water sampling within the AOI (ponds) found contaminants above health based limits" because these "concentrations are within the range of the background for the area." Although "soil sampling found a widespread occurrence of dioxins and furans within the study area," the EPA concluded that these "are all naturally occurring." Even though arsenic levels exceeded "its EPA screening level in almost all of the samples," it too was seen as "reflective of local background," and "chlorinated and aromatic compounds that are emitted in

Les Skramstad and Bob Wilkins both died of asbestos-related disease.

Libby, Montana: Two victims of asbestos mining

the permitted releases from the surrounding facilities were not detected in the soil samples."

Because the EPA bases its decisions to recommend Superfund status for a site on risk-assessment principles rather than the precautionary principle in place in most European countries, no action can be taken to protect Mossville or Lake Charles residents until convincing scientific proof that PVC production causes cancer and other respiratory problems has been provided. A risk-assessment approach requires scientific evidence for a cause-and-effect relationship between dioxins in PVC and human health risks. The precautionary principle, however, states that "when an activity raises threats of harm to the environment or human health, precautionary measures should be taken even if some cause and effect relationships are not fully established scientifically."

Although the EPA has failed to protect them, based on the precautionary principle, residents of Lake Charles have found what they hope will be an effective alternative route to protection, a fight for environmental justice and human rights. Mossville residents seek to address the environmental racism they have suffered for generations by presenting their case to an international human rights commission. In 2010 the "Inter-American Commission on Human Rights of the Organization of American States (OAS) . . . agreed to determine if the actions taken by the U.S. government were a violation of human rights" (Center for Health, Environment and Justice). Although the case is still pending, the efforts of Mossville residents illustrate the complexity of issues surrounding shelter. PVC production predominately occurs in impoverished areas of Louisiana where residents are relatively powerless, especially in an economy stressing the need for jobs without consideration of environmental costs.

Libby, Montana, and the Superfund

Libby, Montana, however, did receive a recommendation from the EPA for Superfund site status. The narrative surrounding the Superfund's implementation is documented in Drury Gunn Carr and Doug Hawes-Davis's *Libby, Montana* (2004), a film that illustrates the dire living conditions in Libby, where the Zonolite Company mined vermiculite for decades. The film takes a historical approach in its narrative, drawing on an environmental nostalgia for a once-pristine region and highlighting the town's surrounding forests, lakes, and mountains. Shots demonstrate how this simpler lifestyle translated to an idyllic town life in the 1950s. According to the EPA, however, "while in operation, the Libby mine may have produced 80 percent of the world's supply of vermiculite. Vermiculite has been used in building insulation and as a soil conditioner. Unfortunately, the vermiculite from the Libby mine was contaminated with a toxic form of naturally-occurring asbestos called tremolite-actinolite asbestiform mineral fibers" ("Libby Site Background").

The film also suggests that the area's resources have been depleted for years, explaining that after fur traders left the area, logging companies came in and overcut and harvested the mountain forests, depleting resources in the Montana region. According to the film there were up to two thousand people working in the timber industry and two hundred in the mine during this seemingly untouched period, and Libby was considered a flourishing community. Yet today Libby is still represented as a good place to hunt and fish. Visitors can tour the Mineral Avenue attractions and social clubs on the downtown main streets. The police are efficient and protect tourists, suggesting that the town has remained untouched by the modern world, and loggers' days and taxidermist exhibits commemorate the logging and fur trading industries of more than half a century ago.

Interviews reveal the pain behind the beauty. One worker in the Zonolite mine, for example, suffered health problems because the Zonolite Company and, after 1963, W. R. Grace Inc., developed vermiculite into products that were found near his farm. To introduce the source of the vermiculite, the film provides shots of the mine from above. Mining for vermiculite began in force in 1919, and the mineral was used to fireproof doors. But a montage of news stories in the film demonstrates the health and safety problems associated with this usage, a series of dangers that are connected with the mine company's owner, Earl D. Lovick, when shots of his trial are shown. The film explains that vermiculite was procured through strip-mining and used for insulation and fertilizer, products managed and distributed by the Scotts Company. What the film reveals, however, is that workers in the mine were dying of cancer at astronomical rates, a horrific truth Earl D. Lovick knew but dismissed for profit. On top of this flagrant act of subterfuge, the mine waste was also uncontrolled because the EPA and its affiliates were downsized during the Reagan administration. W. R. Grace, Inc. embezzled four billion dollars and declared bankruptcy, so that the U.S. government would have to pay for the cleanup.

Because of this complex context, the film asserts that Libby needs a Superfund designation from the EPA in order to finance the cleanup, a claim then EPA chief Christy Whitman supports in spite of the ability of Montana's governor (Judy Murtz) to veto the NPL Superfund funds. In 2002 a guarantee for cleanup but not for health care or insulation removal is approved. A public health emergency declaration has been excluded because of federal funding cuts. The rest of the film documents the reasons for the Superfund designation and its results. The filmmakers first emphasize and describe workers whose health was destroyed because of vermiculite: Bob Wilkins, who worked from 1969 to 1990; a worker now in North Dakota with almost no lungs left; and another miner whose respiratory ailments go unreported despite his getting xrays every year, for example. These workers and others have contracted asbestosis and other forms of cancer.

The film also presents proof that the company had been aware of these consequences since 1948. Corporate heads knew by 1956 that there was asbestos in the dust, but the workers did not know that tremolite in the dust was a type of asbestos. The company had even documented the percentage of workers dying on a graph that only corporate heads would see. According to this graph 92 percent of employees died by the time they had worked for the company for twenty years. And the cancers were not confined to miners and workers in the plant. Workers' whole families have contracted cancer. As of May 2002, according to the film, the EPA study has revealed 246 asbestos deaths and 1,200 diagnoses of asbestos poisoning. Because of these deaths and illnesses, the EPA has designated the town a Superfund site and attempted to clean up the tremolite asbestos in the mine, plants, and surrounding homes. In Libby, as in any town where asbestos insulates a home or fertilizes a garden, a home becomes a hazard rather than a shelter.

The good news is that the situation in Libby, Montana, was dire enough to satisfy the EPA's risk assessment study. The EPA began collecting samples in December 1999, amassing nearly seven hundred "from air, soil, dust and insulation at homes and businesses." It released the first indoor-air sample results in January 2000 to both property owners and the media and general public and located "areas in and near Libby that were likely to have high levels of contamination such as two former vermiculite processing facilities." To determine the extent of the contamination, the EPA "also looked at general asbestos exposures in the community and at health effects seen in people who had little or no association with the vermiculite mine in Libby," working "closely with local, state and federal agencies to understand how people might come into contact with asbestos-contaminated vermiculite and what can be done to prevent future exposures" ("Libby Site Background").

After three years of research, Libby was added to the EPA's National Priorities List in October 2002, providing Libby with a Superfund designation and the assurance of extensive cleanup. In September 2011 a Montana judge also approved a $43 million settlement for the "more than one thousand asbestos victims in the town of Libby, Montana" ("Judge

Approved"). The cleanup continues as of October 2011, with the addition of contaminated woodchips to exacerbate Libby's problems ("More Heartbreak"), problems that affect us all, according to Patricia A. Sullivan. Her study of Libby vermiculite workers revealed "significant excess mortality from nonmalignant respiratory disease . . . even among workers with cumulative exposure" (584). Her study's conclusions, however, demonstrate how far-reaching Libby's asbestos problem might be: "Since vermiculite from the Libby mine was used to make loose-fill attic insulation that remains in millions of homes, these findings highlight the need for better understanding and control of exposures that currently occur when homeowners and construction renovation workers (including plumbers, cable installers, electricians, telephone repair personnel, and insulators) disturb loose-fill attic insulation made with asbestos-contaminated vermiculite from Libby, Montana" (584). Since approximately 80 percent of all vermiculite was produced in Libby, Montana, until its mine and factories closed in 1990, the possibility that insulation has been made with asbestos-contaminated vermiculite from Libby is high and reinforces the need to consider the production content of a home as well as its location.

From *Blue Vinyl* to Environmental Justice at Home?

Ultimately films like *Blue Vinyl* and *Libby, Montana* demonstrate the drive for a better home, a shelter and a place where "no population, especially the elderly and children, are forced to shoulder a disproportionate burden of the negative human health and environmental impacts of pollution or other environmental hazard" (Cifuentes and Frumkin 1–2), a place where environmental justice is the norm, and environmental racism is minimized. Some films make that drive for a better life their central message, highlighting both the injustices subjects leave behind and the dangers they suffer to make their way to a new home.

Children in filmmakers Rebecca Cammisa's *Which Way Home* (2009), for example, make their way across South America and Mexico in search of a better life in the United States, hopping rides on a rattletrap railroad line known to locals as "The Beast." Those who survive the trip may face arrest and/or deportation when they arrive, but they may also make a new life in a better home. Similarly, *Sin Nombre* (2008), a fictionalized dramatization of filmmaker Cary Joji Fukunaga's own life experience follows a Honduran teenager who reunites with her long-estranged father and attempts to immigrate to America with him in order to start a new life away from the gang world in Central America. And *Dark Days* (2000) documents a narrative of environmental adaptation in which homeless adults in New York City build homes and a community in the Amtrak tunnels below the city streets.

These films illustrate the need to escape injustice in search of a literal better home that requires a journey of hardship and danger. Their emphasis on human rights issues extends to an environment so insecure that its residents seek something better, no matter how dangerous the journey. *Blue Vinyl*, on the other hand, focuses on a different search for a better home, one we all can take, but one that also makes transparent the hidden injustices that may underlie vinyl production and home construction. The goal for this journey is a better home for us all, one based on the idea that "human rights, an ecologically sound environment, sustainability development and peace are interdependent and indivisible," a home that is "secure, healthy, and ecologically sound," "free from any form of discrimination in regard to actions and decisions that affect the environment" (Cifuentes and Frumkin 1–2).

CHAPTER SEVEN

ACTIVISM IN MOUNTAINTOP REMOVAL FILMS

Turn Off the Lights for Sustainability

B. J. Gudmundsson's *Rise Up! West Virginia* (2007) opens with an assertion from the late anti–mountaintop removal mining (MTR) activist Julia
(Judy) Bonds that restates one argument against MTR, its destruction of
the Appalachian landscape. According to Bonds, "a sense of place pulls
at you here. It's a trait that makes Appalachians who they are," and that
sense of place is reinforced by pristine images of forest-covered hills,
mountain streams, and wildlife seemingly untouched by the outside
world. This is Appalachia, the images assert, and this view of Appalachia
as a region, a place, and a way of life is validated with the accompanying
mountain music in the background.

   This idyllic vision is shattered, however, when the scene shifts to reveal
gruesome aerial shots of the aftermath of mountaintop removal mining
in their end stages, showing mountaintops with browned, crushed trees
scattered like twigs. Other mountains, having lost their peaks, are as flat
as billiard tables, their remains scattered down on the adjacent valleys
as fill. From the distance, a fifteen-million-pound dragline crane looks
like a child's Tonka toy, but the landscape is gray, brown, and completely
barren. This is the perfect spot for *Gomorra*'s (2008) toxic-waste dump-

Rise Up! West Virginia: The destructive scale of mountaintop removal

ing, except the coal companies have beaten them to the punch. As the film's narrator explains, the mountains' "guts [have been] blown out."

By effectively juxtaposing images of the pristine mountains that may become a memory with the hell that mountaintop removal leaves in its wake, *Rise Up! West Virginia* successfully argues against MTR, but the narrator's claim, "coal mining hasn't saved the state yet," takes the argument further. Although all twelve of the anti–mountaintop removal documentaries we viewed effectively demonstrate the disastrous effects of mountaintop removal mining, only B. J. Gudmundsson's *Mountain Mourning* (2006) and *Rise Up! West Virginia*, and, to a lesser extent because of its attempt to provide a balanced approach, Bill Haney's *The Last Mountain* (2011), successfully support arguments against mountaintop removal mining while offering viable non–fossil fuel energy alternatives, alternatives that, according to the films, will eventually end America's addiction to coal and Appalachia's overreliance on a coal mining economy.

We assert then that *Mountain Mourning* and *Rise Up! West Virginia* succeed where other anti-MTR documentaries fail. *Razing Appalachia* (2003),
The Appalachians (2005), *Keeper of the Mountains* (2006), *Look What They've
Done* (2006), *Black Diamonds* (2007), *Mountain Top Removal* (2007), *Burning the Future: Coal in America* (2008), *Coal Country* (2009), and *On Coal
River* (2010) argue to a lesser or greater extent against mountaintop removal
mining, but coal remains an economic and political necessity in each film,
as long as it is procured differently. Because Gudmundsson's films support
alternatives to coal mining, both MTR and underground, without watering
down their rhetoric with an attempt at a balanced approach (as in *The Last
Mountain*), they provide a map toward a solution unbridled by hope in the
face of hopelessness, destructive visions of progress, and perpetuation of
our addiction to coal-generated energy and the negative environmental and
economic consequences associated with the mining and burning of coal.

Rhetorical Documentary: Classic and Contemporary Views

Like the contemporary eco-food films analyzed in chapter 4, the anti–
mountaintop removal mining films we explore here may also benefit from
the audience-engagement work of Thomas W. Benson and Brian J. Snee,
since almost all the films include a call for action in their conclusions.
They also provide clear-cut models of activism with each of the protestors
documented in each film, demonstrating well that, as previously noted,
"the rhetorical potential of documentary film relies not on an audience
who merely provides the rhetor with resources that might be exploited
in persuasion but instead on an audience who is actively engaged in
judgment and action" (137).

Although we do not examine audiences' reactions to the anti-MTR films
we viewed, we do examine protesters' responses to the MTR activities they
see, somewhat as audience members engaged in judgment and action.
In these films, because the same protesters appear in multiple films,
documentation of their actions seems to adhere to the criteria Karl Heider
outlines for ethnographic filmmaking: "long-term observational study
on the spot," an effort to "relate specific observed behavior to cultural
norms," "holism," and attempts to ensure that all these elements serve
the film's rhetoric (6–7).

The documentaries we viewed attempt to present and support arguments against MTR by foregrounding individual stories of protesters in Appalachia, Appalachians viewed in respect to their culture. In spite of their seeming support of sustainable development, however, these activists' arguments break down under scrutiny because they too embrace the commodities of fair use, energy consumption that fuels the production and use of the merchandise of a progressive corporate philosophy: affordable consumer goods from big-screen televisions to SUVs, highways, clean running water, comfortable shelter, electricity, and consumer development projects like big-box stores and restaurants.

In most of these documentary films, then, Appalachia is constructed as a frontier meant to serve the few (progressive individual corporations) or the many (populist politicians, the United Mine Workers of America (UMWA), and clean-air environmentalists). The Massey Energy Company's drive to mine "clean coal" cheaply through MTR, despite the high costs to the environment and the loss of jobs due to mechanization, highlights this "progressive" style. The "populist" style, on the other hand, "developed in reaction to the emergence of the corporate/industrial economy and the political claims of its proprietors and managers" (Slotkin, *Gunfighter Nation* 22). Solutions in most of these films—an end to MTR and a return to underground mining—better serve the community but perpetuate addiction to coal as a primary energy source.

We see this addiction as a hopeless situation that perpetuates environmentally devastating means of economic development. All these documentaries draw on the voices of the same activists, highlight some of the same battles with MTR companies, and, except for the B.J. Gudmundsson films, foreground the same MTR spokesperson. Yet this repetition fails until, as in the Gudmundsson films, coal as an energy source is removed from the mix. *The Last Mountain* does offer wind power as an alternative to coal, while offering an evenhanded argument for moving coal mining back underground. In Gudmundsson's films, however, coal mining and coal-generated energy are replaced with clean alternative energy sources, progressive fair-use politics are withdrawn, and a hopeless dependence on coal-burning power plants is replaced with promising alternatives to fossil fuels for our future electricity.

Hope in the Face of Hopelessness in the Context of Mountaintop Removal Films

In most of the anti–mountaintop removal films we screened, protesters are faced with astronomical personal losses: poisoned wells, a shattered ecosystem, and a loss of faith in the compromised political system, partly because, as stated in each film foregrounding mountaintop removal, coal produced 50 percent of all the electricity in the United States until the rise of shale gas dropped it to 36 percent. But we also hear them sing, as in *Mountain Top Removal*, "There was always hope, because that's all I have," even in the face of what looks like irrevocable disaster in the film's context.

And, as in other documentaries examining mountaintop removal mining, we see this hope illustrated in the film's ending. After a minister prays, "Turn back this evil time and be healers of this land," the film highlights the August 2006 decision by the West Virginia Department of Environmental Protection that revokes a permit to expand a coal-processing plant near a school, and representatives of Pennies for Promise, a protest organization raising funds to build a new school and move children away from the plant, arrive in Washington DC. Even though title cards indicate that the Department of Environmental Protection's ruling was overturned, a Massey Energy Company settlement of twenty million dollars ends the film, as if the minister's prayers had been answered. This same hope resonates in more-recent documentaries addressing mountaintop removal mining, *Coal Country*, which ends with a blatantly hopeful message in the face of continuing MTR, and *On Coal River*, which focuses more specifically on the fight to move Marsh Fork Elementary School. As one activist explains in *Coal Country*, "Even in the face of a David and Goliath struggle, I will stand up here and speak. This is an insurmountable mountain, but you never give up."

Collective hope in the face of disaster drives the rhetoric of most anti–mountaintop removal films, but that hope rests on the mythology of America and the American dream. In an exploration of Americans' and Europeans' conflicting responses to the recent global crises of 2008–9, for example, Dominique Moisi, a leading geo-strategic thinker and founder of the French Institute of International Affairs asserts, "Today there is more collective hope and more individual fear in America.

But the reverse is true in Europe. Here one encounters less collective hope and less individual fear." Moisi believes there is one reason for the contrast: "The U.S. has Obama, and Europe has the welfare state." Although Barack Obama has certainly reignited the spark of optimism and rewritten the politics of hope through his own *The Audacity of Hope* and his national speeches from 2004 forward, a rhetoric of hope has grounded American ideology since its inception. That rhetoric of hope drives arguments for change in arenas from the civil rights movement to climate change initiatives. According to Deborah F. Atwater, a rhetoric of hope "use[s] . . . symbols to get Americans to care about this country, to want to believe in this country, to regain hope and faith in this country, and to believe that we are more alike than we are different with a common destiny and a core set of values" (123). This move toward hope rests on defining shared values and common goals, a communal faith building.

Such a vision of hope functions as a tool to bring Americans together and encourage them to care about one another because of shared values. This belief also serves as the chief rhetorical tool of the anti–mountaintop removal mining movement, as reflected in most of the documentaries we screened, but that hope seems groundless in most of these films, since protesters are faced with such insurmountable obstacles from not only MTR mining corporations but also politicians at all levels: local politicians and governors in Appalachia, representatives in the U.S. House and Senate, and the president of the United States. Even Senator Jay Rockefeller of West Virginia, who fought against strip-mining in the early 1970s, changed his stance when he lost the gubernatorial race in 1972 against Republican Arch Moore. In a speech he gave at Morris Harvey College the same year, Rockefeller provided a powerful argument against surface mining, asserting,

Government has turned its back on the many West Virginians who have borne out of their own property and out of their own pocketbooks the destructive impact of stripping. We hear that our Governor once claimed to have wept as he flew over the strip mine devastation of this state. Now it's the people who weep. They weep because of the devastation of our mountains, because of the disaster of giant high walls, acid-laden benches, and bare, precipitous out slopes, which support no vegetation at all but erode thousands of tons of mud and rocks into streams and rivers below. Strip-mining must be abolished because of those who have given most to the cause—West Virginians who have suffered actual destruction to their homes; those who have put up with flooding, mud slides, cracked foundations, destruction of neighborhoods, decreases in property values, the loss of fishing and hunting, and the beauty of the hills. (Burns 200)

When he lost the governor's race, however, Rockefeller recalibrated his position, thinking it had caused his defeat, and began publicly supporting strip-mining in West Virginia. In fact, according to Burns, "Rockefeller was the most vehement among West Virginia Senators and Congressman Rahall in extolling the virtues of MTR" (89). With politicians like this representing West Virginians, there seems to be no possibility of an end to MTR; yet most documentaries opposing MTR maintain their rhetoric of hope despite these defeats and ground that hope in a hopeless alternative, underground mining.

Documenting Anti-Mountaintop Removal Protests, Progress, and a Fragile Hope

Razing Appalachia (2002), for example, documents the battle with Arch Coal over an expansion of the Dal-Tex Strip MTR site in West Virginia but advocates the economic benefits that underground mining might provide. The film effectively argues against mountaintop removal mining but fails to support alternatives to fossil fuels as a more sustainable means of development for the region. After a Gary Singer quotation, the film argues against MTR by highlighting West Virginia as "the old home place" before images of blasting on screen show the destruction of the West Virginia landscape. Images of coal extraction are reinforced with the music in the background, "Take My Dreams Away," a song that illustrates the loss felt by residents in Blair, West Virginia. Four women conversing outside a restaurant argue that the EPA doesn't protect them, but Rich Abraham, an independent coal contractor, wants the last crawdad to belly up in Blair, if it means more coal.

With this context clarified, the film explains, in May 1998 in Pigeon Roost Hollow near Blair, West Virginia, Arch Coal Inc. applied for a new mountaintop removal contract for the largest site ever mined. Joe Lovett, an environmental attorney, led the fight against Arch Coal. The Weekleys are the only family left in the hollow, and the couple laments the endless blasting that destroyed Mrs. Weekley's previous home. David G. Todd from Arch Coal, on the other hand, argues that he and his company are "stewards of the land" and seek "productive post-mine land use." Todd claims that large-scale operations will shut down if the permit is not is-sued, and 350 workers will lose their jobs, "tragic effects," Todd explains.

Regulatory agencies and protest groups in the Ohio Valley argue against claims from coal companies, highlighting environmental, economic, and social destruction caused by MTR. Yet their arguments rest on populist visions of development, arguing not for an end of coal mining but for a redistribution of wealth and a return to underground mining, seen as a viable solution to MTR and a viable means of restoring thousands of min-ing jobs. For example, Patricia Bragg, from the West Virginia Organizing Project, asks, "Where's the tax money going, and why are counties not benefiting?" Her message counters beliefs that "they'll be in poverty if MTR is halted" but also reinforces populist views of development. MTR not only destroys the land without contributing to the area income; it also obliterates family homes and ancestral cemeteries. Other forms of mining would preserve the land and distribute wealth more equally, the film implies. Freda Williams of the West Virginia Organizing Project sums up the problem: "Coal companies were always greedy," she as-serts, and now they're also "destructive," while more images of blasting support these claims.

The film supports coal mining employment, however, as long as it moves back underground. For example, one elderly retired coal miner explains that he once earned $1.15 per day but still believes, "I lived a good life." And his daughter holds contrasting memories of fears that he wouldn't survive and happiness when he brought home nickel cakes for the children. To highlight the need for a return to UMWA-led underground mining, the film focuses on the history of the UMWA and its emphasis on tradition versus change through Trish Bragg's memories. The film sug-gests that some UMWA workers believe coal miners are hurt by protests against MTR, arguing that people benefit from coal mining, no matter what. Without coal jobs they take whatever they can get—minimum wage jobs at Wal-Mart or McDonald's. Their kids are going to college and moving on anyway, they say. But others explain that they've been put into a position of no choice. They have to do this kind of work.

Distribution of profits from MTR mining is also discussed in the film, again reinforcing its populist position. Few benefit from MTR in Logan County, the film asserts. Citizens talk about how the coal companies have destroyed their town. A view of a valley fill works as evidence. The companies have filled in the hollow with debris, so the men ask about the kind of development possible in their county. MTR doesn't employ the numbers it used to, the film argues, with a drop from 120,000 mining jobs in West Virginia in 1950 to 16,000 in 2000, according to this film, numbers that vary in other films but remain similarly devastating.

The film then documents protests over Arch Coal's new permits for the Dal-Tex MTR mine, showing how Judge Charles Haden intervened, with help from CBS's *60 Minutes*, and stopped new permits until Arch Coal shut down the mine and laid off nearly four hundred UMWA workers. Judge Haden's ruling was overturned in 2001, and the Supreme Court declined to hear the case's appeal. In spite of setbacks, however, the film ends with hope. Trish Bragg tells us that the strength of the region lies in its simple life; "Home and community should be protected," she explains, and a child looks at a frog and a crawdad from the creek bed that opens the film and then lets them go. Although Joe Lovett does note the need for energy diversity in the film, the film also ends with a populist message that perpetuates exploitation of resources for wealth, as long as that wealth is distributed more widely and moves mining underground.

Catherine Pancake's *Black Diamonds: Mountaintop Removal and the Fight for Coalfield Justice* (2006) advocates the work of the Coal Mountain River Watch, a group fighting MTR in southern West Virginia and surrounding states, yet it too perpetuates populist positions of development. Opening on fog-covered hills called "heaven" by a narrator, the film reveals rhododendron, waterfalls, and wildflowers, but, as the narrator exclaims, when the coal companies surface mine, it's like "watch [ing] somebody drop a bomb on it." Protests from May 2004 highlight the battle to stop this destruction, but William R. Raney, the president of the

West Virginia Coal Association, explains that since more than half of the electricity in the United States comes from coal-powered plants, we should "capitalize on all the economic activity that surrounds the extraction of coal." According to Raney, West Virginia is second to Wyoming in coal production in the United States.

Activists such as the late Julia (Judy) Bonds are highlighted in the film, illustrating the fight against the repercussions of this unbridled coal extraction, but they battle not for the end of coal mining but for a return to earlier underground methods that, at least in memory, pro- vide more employment, distribute capital more equitably, and preserve the mountains and their resources. Bonds explains that West Virginia is the poorest state in the union in spite of the coal companies' prom- ises. The mountains, Bonds asserts, "should be mined responsibly for the people of West Virginia and for our children." Raney nonetheless proclaims, "Nobody in this world is extracting coal like we are in West Virginia" and praises the technology that allows the massive surface mining he advocates. Protesters, on the other hand, assert that "terror- ism is legal in West Virginia," based on the environmental destruction in the coal companies' wake. A narrator emphasizes the breadth of that destruction, explaining that 244 plant and animal species are affected by MTR. Once the mountains are destroyed, most plants no longer can root. But the argument critiques only differing mining techniques, not coal-generated energy in general, so it fails to maintain its nod toward sustainable development.

Instead, the film demonizes one form of mining, MTR, while embrac- ing the products of coal: electricity and a culture based in coal mining. Clearly, MTR is the most devastating form of coal mining now in existence, and *Black Diamonds* effectively documents the technique's hazardous environmental consequences.

Footage from mountaintop removal blasting reinforces the film's rhetoric and illustrates the power of film, since home movies of blast- ing's effect on homes in the area led Arch Coal to settle a lawsuit with area residents, with help from their attorney, Pat McGurly. Footage of dust from blasts in 1999 highlights the power of these coal companies, however. The film explains, "People had no choice; if people wanted to get anything out of their homes, they had to go to the coal companies.

The coal companies already had the money allocated—not fair market value price—and banned them from living in the area the rest of their lives. They signed certificates with the company. People had no choice."

The film explains that the Blair Mountain court case, *Bragg v. Robertson*, rested on a history of conflicts between the coal industry and West Virginia citizens. The film shows some of that history, from the underground coal mining conditions of the late nineteenth and early twentieth centuries to John Lewis's and Mother Jones's fight for miners, and explains that the Surface Mining Control and Reclamation Act, signed by President Carter in 1977, also applied to MTR. MTR could occur only if the company rebuilt the mountain within fifty feet of its original height or provided a plan for reclaiming the area for business.

Even the reclaimed sites are inferior, the film asserts. William Massey explains, while flying over reclaimed MTR sites, that the mountain is left decapitated, leveled for more acreage, so after mining ends, the flat top is hydro-seeded with inferior or hybrid weeds on which no animal will graze. Mulch comes back only in grass. Hardwood trees native to the region won't grow there. In the film Raney argues the coal company response: "If we had planted more trees, we'd have been okay." It was easier to replant grass. Yet the film turns to Jamie Hiler, a coal industry analyst, who explains that underground mines can be cheaper than MTR, offering underground mining as a viable alternative to the surface destruction caused by MTR. There is more and better technology for all kinds of mining, some of which is imported from Wyoming, he explains. Underground mining, the film suggests, would alleviate problems caused by MTR. Underground mining would solve this problem and provide a viable economic solution to Massey and to West Virginia, the film implies, a "solution" that predicts a hopeless future that maintains our addiction to coal and the environmentally devastating environmental effects of fossil fuel–generated electricity.

Black Diamonds maintains its argument against MTR and for underground mining as a viable solution rather than arguing that coal mining should be eliminated altogether because the film's subjects still wish to profit from coal. They just hope to spread the wealth more equitably and move mining back underground to, as they see it, better preserve the mountains and the culture they sustain. Activists from Julia (Judy) Bonds to Maria Gunnoe drive suvs and watch televisions on big-screen tvs. And they support their argument against mtr with statistics that highlight the loss of mining jobs and the destruction of their culture caused by mtr.

In the face of multiple failures, too, the film attempts to maintain hope, but that hope seems baseless by the film's end. In spite of strong arguments for halting mtr, Judge Haden's ruling was overturned by an appeals court in 2001 on a technicality, for example. According to the film, even flooding in 1997, 2001, and 2002 caused by mountaintop removal's repercussions—valley fills, slurry ponds, and drainage systems—has not convinced coal companies and politicians to halt mtr. And when a three-year-old was killed by a boulder falling from the A and G Coal Company because of blasting, the film explains, the company was fined only $1,500. As a result Bonds has built a multistate organization with direct actions against the mining companies, beginning with a protest in May 2005 over slurry impoundments in Sundial, West Virginia; the film shows police arresting Bonds and others in Sundial and near other mtr sites. Yet by 2005, 1,200 miles of streams were covered by valley fills. The film predicts that in ten years at such a rate, 2,200 square miles of Appalachia will be permanently blasted apart, an area the size of Delaware.

Despite such evidence against any possibility of success, however, the film ends with hope, contrasting the devastation of a mountaintop removal site with the pristine biodiverse mountains beyond. A sunset ends the film, but the fight against mtr continues, and this film seeks to join the fight, succeeding through its visual imagery, but also diluting its message through its disjointed storyline, irrelevant details, and ineffective argument. *Black Diamonds* fails to argue a message of sustainable development not only because the battle with mtr corporations seems hopeless, but also because the film perpetuates coal mining (as long as it is underground), fossil fuel consumption, and mythic values that endorse progress at any cost, as long as that progress serves the many instead of the few.

David Novack's *Burning the Future: Coal in America* (2008) comes closer to offering alternatives to coal and coal mining but fails as a call to action because it attempts to take an evenhanded approach to the issues surrounding mtr, juxtaposing opposing arguments from anti-mtr protestors and representatives from coal mining companies without definitively siding with either one. Instead of opening on the devastation of MTR, the film warns against overuse of electricity during a heat wave. "Conserve power," advises an announcer before the percentage of electricity in America produced by coal (51 percent) is explained. The film, however, attempts to take an evenhanded approach to the issue of MTR, showing coal miners who see mining as the last frontier. The mechanism of support is on display in these images—shovels, belts, cleaners, and other machinery, all dirty and underground—but the miner explains, "Look at coal. God doesn't do futile work."

The film contrasts these images with views of the majestic mountains above the mine, helicopter shots of hills and valleys of southern West Virginia that move closer to reveal images of the railroad that runs near activist Maria Gunnoe's house in Bobwhite. According to Gunnoe her family survived on roots, mushrooms, venison, and wild boar from the mountains, and she wishes to pass on this culture of survival. When she heard the chainsaws associated with clear-cutting, however, she knew things would change, and mountaintop removal would fill and plug her valley, completely altering the landscape.

Gunnoe's narration contrasts with that of Bill Raney from the West Virginia Coal Association, who explains that MTR is not only cheaper but also dictated by geography. Gunnoe shows results of valley fill, but a corporate spokesperson sees the landscape differently: "The process is ready to be restored." The coal company will rebuild the mountain and plant seed, so that the trees will return years later. For Gunnoe, however, MTR and the erosion it causes leads to flooding, lost property, and destroyed bridges. Five of her acres have washed away. There is no place for the rain to go. Bill Raney, on the other hand, believes flooding is natural and explains it was an act of God.

As a way to address these opposing points, the film highlights the work of biologist Ben Stout, who, as in other films, explains that Appalachia is the second most diverse land in the world and contrasts lush forests with the dynamiting of a mountain for MTR. The film shows two huge explosions, a spectacular display of destruction witnessed by riders in four-wheelers. At the top of an operation, we see the results. A mountain decreases from 2,555 feet to 1,755 feet. A million acres of hardwood forest are set for MTR and valley fill, Jim Hecker, a lawyer for Public Justice, warns, calling MTR the single most environmentally destructive activity in America.

The film also contrasts views of our dependence on coal. Although Sierra Club representatives argue for energy diversity, and a school tour of a coal electric plant shows the extent of our dependence on coal, tour guides explain that coal is cheapest because it is most abundant. West Virginia governor Joe Manchin sees the coal industry as heroic and thinks that the companies are doing something valuable for the state and the country.

According to the film the popularity of clean coal technology drives much of the market for MTR, but both Peter Lehner and Ben Stout see the idea of "clean coal" as flawed due to both carbon dioxide emissions and black water left from coal cleaning. The Clean Air Act and the Clean Water Act are in conflict here. Flooded impoundments support their claims. There are at least 130 active slurry impoundments in the region and 110 billion gallons of toxic water in West Virginia, with equal amounts in Kentucky, Tennessee, Virginia, Pennsylvania, Ohio, Indiana, and Illinois. These are the legacy costs of burning coal as a fuel. The Ohio Valley Environmental Organization fights back with help from activists led by Judy Bonds. Maria Gunnoe, however, is at the center of the film and personalizes its message. She waxes nostalgic about what the mountains once looked like before MTR. As one activist explains, stories are their most powerful tool, a counter to the governor and his support for corporate exploitation of the miners and their land. The fact that jobs have decreased is repeated in this film, too, this time with numbers showing jobs dropping from 125,000 to 15,000 in the mines when MTR and other strip-mining techniques became the dominant method of coal extraction.

The battle over water in some communities, however, is won, according to the film. In Williamson, for example, citizen activists have convinced the state government to provide rural areas with city water, since their wells have been completely contaminated and people poisoned by the mine runoff. Ben Stout reinforces what is lost when MTR destroys the pristine hardwood forests and warns against more permits. Gunnoe and her colleagues continue their fight against the permits for over three thousand acres of MTR and travel by car and train to attend a United Nations Commission for Sustainable Development meeting in New York City, hoping to convince the world that MTR should be stopped. When UN officials continue to talk about "clean coal," however, Gunnoe exclaims, "America doesn't care." The activists are told that the destruction of their land and people is "acceptable collateral damage." Wilbur Ross, CEO of International Coal Group Inc., refuses to meet them in New York, but the film begins to make the connection between the city and Appalachia here. Without coal city dwellers wouldn't have sufficient electricity. Train cars and subway cars connect this message, one accelerated in Times Square. Standing at night in the middle of Times Square, a carnival of lights, Gunnoe screams, "Turn out the lights!"

Both Gunnoe and Stout explain, "We have to do something else." A final protest with a West Virginia State Police intervention and a final shot of an MTR site in contrast to the remaining mountains reinforce one side of the film's message. Yet a 2007 national energy bill calls for drastic increases in coal production. A Steve Earle song opposing strip-mining ends the film, but MTR continues, and so does hope, even in the face of the unbeatable odds presented in the film. *Burning the Future* fails because of this ill-fated rhetoric of hope but also because of its attempt to document both sides of the MTR argument. The film seems to argue against MTR, especially in its concluding scenes, but its evenhanded approach muddies its message, especially since the film also advocates continuing and even increasing coal production to stimulate the Appalachian economy, as long as the mining moves underground.

Segments of the third installment of *The Appalachians* (2005), a Nashville Public Television series directed by Phylis Geller, also highlight MTR, especially in conjunction with strip-mining in the region begun in the 1970s, but it too attempts an evenhanded approach, so its arguments break down as Bill Raney again valorizes MTR mining techniques and their benefits for the region. *Mountain Top Removal* too attempts a balanced approach, not only by highlighting Raney's arguments but also by including pro-MTR viewpoints from miners and local business owners. Like *Razing Appalachia* the film argues for a return to underground mining as a way to increase job opportunities in the area. Despite its strong arguments against MTR as destructive to the land and water sources in the region, this film also validates populist views, asserting the need to distribute the spoils of resource exploitation more widely. New schools should be built away from mines, for example, argue representatives of Pennies for Promise. The film asserts that coal mining should continue, as long as it moves underground. And this film also attempts to maintain hope in the face of defeat, highlighting a minister's prayer at a cemetery in the middle of an MTR site and Pennies for Promise's arrival in Washington DC. A shot of an MTR explosion ends the film, but with a parting note that Massey Mining paid twenty million dollars in fines in a water pollution lawsuit with the U.S. Environmental Protection Agency. This fine seems to provide hope for a future without MTR, but because the film also promotes underground mining, it too perpetuates a coal culture that exploits both a land and its people.

   Coal Country (2009), directed by Phylis Geller, attempts the same evenhanded approach taken in other MTR documentaries and in her own *Appalachians*. Even with its strong connection to the Sierra Club, the film follows the same patterns found in *Mountain Top Removal* by including multiple conflicting perspectives on MTR without clearly supporting any one over the others. The film foregrounds mine workers, past and present, musicians like Kathy Mattea, and scholars like Phillippe Jamet, who seem to argue against MTR, but it also provides a sympathetic portrait of an environmental reclamation engineer for the coal companies. The same voices from previous films are also here: Joe Lovett and Julia (Judy) Bonds, for example. It also foregrounds Michael Shnayerson, author of *Coal River*, in conjunction with conflicting voices from union workers and coal company personnel, voices that might be included to show the complexity of the MTR argument but dilute the possible rhetoric of a film so evenhanded that its message is lost.

   Julia (Judy) Bonds provides an emotional anti-MTR perspective, but the film also highlights the views of workers at the MTR sites, workers reclaiming leveled mountains, and others both advocating for MTR and for keeping mining, as a chief source of income and jobs, in Appalachia. Ultimately *Coal Country*, too, ends with hope, suggesting that alternative energy sources might be viable options in the future, but the film also advocates for underground coal mining and looks back to a coal economy that employed more than one hundred thousand workers with living wages that could eventually contribute to the development of the Appalachian region. Instead of looking toward a future without coal and all the negative environmental consequences associated with it, *Coal*

Country looks to the past for answers that might have devastating results to the land and its people.

Sustainable Anti-Mountaintop Removal Films

B. J. Gudmundsson's *Rise Up! West Virginia* and *Mountain Mourning* and, to a lesser extent, Bill Haney's *The Last Mountain* present new, radical arguments. The films demand alternative energy sources to meet sustainable development goals and effectively maintain their rhetoric against MTR. Even though these films and their subjects strive for and build their arguments on the need for wider distribution of fair-use commodities, they also argue against coal mining in general and maintain their position against MTR and corporate coal mining throughout the films. The fact that 50 percent of America's power is coal generated does not sway them from their demand for new forms of less destructive energy production and consumption.

Rise Up! West Virginia presents George Daughtery, a West Virginia attorney, arguing that "coal mining hasn't saved the state yet" by juxtaposing images of the pristine mountains that may soon vanish with the nightmare resulting from MTR. Judy Bonds's narration accompanies pristine images of West Virginia mountains that provide, as Bonds explains, the "sense of place [that] pulls at you" and "makes Appalachians who they are." With authentic Appalachian music performed by West Virginia musicians, the film highlights this need for a sense of place, even providing a "Bambi shot" of a doe in a hardwood forest. The pure scene is contrasted with shots of mammoth blasting destroying a mountain in Boone County, so that, as the film states, the mountain's "guts are blown out" in a "man-made destruction." The film also presents Appalachians as victims like the mountains: both are exploited by corporate mining companies with progressive views of resource exploitation. The film argues that West Virginia has been turned into a Third World colony and will be abandoned after all the coal has been brutally extracted.

After this opening, which establishes the film's conflict, a focus on "sustainable energy and jobs" is reinforced with a musical celebration of the land that remains at the Mountain Keepers Music Festival with Larry Gibson, a landowner surrounded by MTR because he refused to sell his land or mineral rights. The festival is meant to provide a voice for the anti-MTR movement and to support alternative and sustainable energy sources that will provide jobs for the region. These anti-MTR protesters align with the pristine nature that could become only a memory, like the fish in "hollers," thousands of acres of virgin forest, and sandstone rocks now lost because of MTR.

Although this film also documents jobs lost because of the move to MTR, arguments against coal mining chiefly rely on its environmental consequences: timber lost to clear-cutting, sludge dams breaking and destroying towns and water sources, valley fills polluting wells and clogging rivers and streams, blasting not only decapitating mountains but covering whole towns with toxic coal dust, even after a processing plant has been covered with a dome.

The coal mining companies, especially Massey, are established as the culprits for this destruction of the land and the people of West Virginia. A child in the film explains, "These coal mines are making us kids sick," while describing Massey's attempts to expand a coal preparation plant near a school. The government, too, is held responsible for ongoing destruction, since it has overturned stays on permits and allowed MTR and its consequences to continue.

The film's ending maintains both the bifurcation between the big guys—corporate mining interests—and the little guys—citizens of West Virginia. But it also continues its argument for sustainable development. Back at the music festival protestors argue, "Turn off electric gadgets and demand renewable energy." And they offer suggestions for winning the war against MTR. According to the film Appalachians should elect responsible people to public office and think of their neighbors. They should make phone calls and write letters. In a nod to nostalgia, the film ends with another Bambi shot in a pristine forest and an exclamation: "She's worth more than all the power in the world," so "Rise Up! West Virginia," the film asserts, providing a sense of hope that moves beyond the seemingly hopeless context established in other anti-MTR documentaries. With viable solutions to not only MTR but also coal mining and our reliance on coal for our electricity, hope is preserved.

Mountain Mourning stands out because it explicitly states its Christian position but also because it too argues for sustainable development without attempting an evenhanded approach to MTR. The film was presented by Christians for the Mountains and bases its opposition to mountaintop removal mining on biblical assertions like "the Earth is the Lord's." As in other MTR documentaries, *Mountain Mourning* highlights the richness of mountain resources and the cultures they have sustained for centuries, but here facts are delivered with sacred music in the background. "Blessed Jesus" accompanies information about the hardwood forests in Appalachia, along with pristine scenes of deer, ginseng, and black cohosh. A billboard declaring, "This is Coal Country" breaks the meditative tone of the film, and the narration reinforces the conflict. The billions of tons of coal used to produce over 50 percent of our electricity results in sulfur dioxide pollutants that are the main cause of acid rain. To more easily reach this coal commodity, MTR has replaced much of underground mining, the narrator reveals, explaining the destruction left behind when six hundred feet of a mountaintop is removed to reach the exposed coal seams, so that dragline cranes can scoop out all the mineral like seeds out of a split melon.

Damages to the landscape range from loss of forests through clear-cutting, erosion, runoff, and black water spills; streams buried by valley fills; construction of slurry sludge ponds to store black water left from coal processing; and slurry spills resulting from weakened dams. The film shows floods caused by slurry spills and erosion to illustrate the dangerous repercussions of MTR. According to Gudmundsson, half the mountains in southern West Virginia will be gone in the next twenty years if permits are submitted and approved at the current rate.

Other costs are economic but negatively affect humans and the natural world as well. Generated in part by MTR erosion, devastating floods destroyed five thousand homes and businesses in 2001 and four thousand in 2002. MTR's repercussions are pushing people out of the "hollers" and into Federal Emergency Management Agency trailers. Whole communities must be relocated away from MTR sites because of blasting, contaminated drinking water, and dust. An enormous number of jobs have been lost in the state in the last three decades, decreasing the number of miners from 120,000 to fewer than 15,000. Counties in West Virginia are now like Third World countries, the film declares, noting that McDowell County,

West Virginia, is now the eighth poorest in the United States. Over three thousand children there live in poverty, asserts the narrator.

In spite of these dire conditions, however, the film begins and ends with hope as it supports sustainable development and maintains its anti-MTR stance. Musicians support a "Vigil for the Mountains" that opens and closes the film, an attempt to raise awareness of mountaintop removal mining and its consequences. Instead of experts offering underground mining as a viable solution to MTR, this film shows us a banner behind musicians at the vigil arguing for alternative energy sources. The film also ends with its beginning biblical message: "The Earth is the Lord's, and the fullness thereof," a vision that points to the power of a rhetoric of hope, this time based in a more powerful argument for sustainable development that maintains its opposition to corporate coal mining and its exploitation of the natural world. With perhaps a more diluted message because it relies on the outsider perspective of its narrator, Robert Kennedy Jr., and highlights opposing views of coal company executives such as Don Blankenship, *The Last Mountain* continues this vigil for alternative energy with focus on wind power as a way to save what has been called the last mountain on Coal River.

A New Rhetoric of Hope

Although most of the anti–mountaintop removal mining films we viewed perpetuate coal mining and its repercussions, as long as it moves back underground, they seek to extend the dissemination of the rewards of development to "the many" instead of "the few," taking a populist approach to progress. Even the Gudmundsson films foreground the need to share wealth with the economically deprived Appalachians protesting MTR and its repercussions. Gudmundsson, as an ethnographer, provides multiple portraits of West Virginians fighting corporate coal mining companies on a local level while illustrating the Appalachian culture that will be lost if the mountains are destroyed.

Her films, like other documentaries opposing MTR, also rest on a rhetoric of hope, but because Gudmundsson offers alternative non–fossil fuel energy sources as a solution to coal mining of all kinds and its effects, hope has a stronger foundation in her films. In most of these

Mountain Mourning: Flooding caused by mountaintop removal

films, government officials, politicians, and even leaders in the UMWA promote MTR as an economic savior for the region in spite of the evidence against such claims highlighted therein. These films document a continuing history of exploitation not only of the mountains but also of their people, exploitation valorized by those in power to serve their definitions of progress. Senator Jay Rockefeller's decision to turn his back on the land and the people of West Virginia to gain the support of those in power and win elected office highlights the breadth of this history, a history that continues in the face of powerful evidence: spectacular shots of exploding mountaintops and flooded communities, personal narrative, scientific evidence of toxic waste destroying streams and other water sources, and thousands of examples of code violations by energy corporations.

Still, hope continues, and there are signs that it may have grounding: Judy Bonds, who passed away in January 2011, lived to see a new school at the Marsh Fork Elementary location in Sundial, West Virginia. Students will "start attending class there in the fall of 2012," according to Dennis Hevesi of the *New York Times* (24). And as of January 2011, the EPA revoked the permit for Arch Coal Inc.'s Spruce Mine MTR project. According to *Wall Street Journal* reporters Stephen Power and Kris Maher, this "is only the second time in the 39-year history of the federal Clean Water Act that the agency has canceled a water permit for a project of any kind after it was issued" (A3). Although federal judge Reggie Walton ruled that the National Mining Association can challenge the EPA's interpretation of the Clean Water Act, the EPA delayed more than seventy-nine MTR permits in 2010 and 2011 because they violate the Clean Water Act. Both the EPA and the Army Corps of Engineers have sixty days to review the permits (Schoof).

This abrupt change of policy from the nearly universal approval of permits in May 2009, as documented in the *Charleston (WV) Gazette*, and the recent overarching hold on permits provides powerful grounding for hope, especially with the added support of the most recent anti-MTR documentary, supported by Robert Kennedy Jr., *The Last Mountain* (2011) and a March on Blair Mountain led by a diverse group seeking to end MTR, build sustainable jobs, and implement stronger labor laws (Ward). The march commemorates the ninetieth anniversary of the 1921 Battle of Blair Mountain, in which ten thousand miners marched as rednecks in red bandanas to protest coal mining conditions. With multiple levels of evidence supporting the dangers of MTR, these films' messages may provide the call to action that Benson and Snee describe in *The Rhetoric of the New Political Documentary*. Audiences may not merely mimic the action on the screen. They may interpret the actions documented and invent and engage in acts of their own.

CHAPTER EIGHT

THE SEARCH FOR THE "GOLDEN SHRIMP"

The Myth of Interdependence in Oil Drilling Films

According to John Ezell's *Innovations in Energy: The Story of Kerr-McGee*, after the first successful oil well was drilled out of sight of land in the Gulf of Mexico in 1947 by the Kerr-McGee Company, the January 1948 issue of *Oil* declared, "The Kerr-McGee well definitely extends the kingdom of oil into a new province that is of incalculable extent and may help assuage the all-devouring demand for gasoline and fuel oils" (quoted in Ezell 169). A reporter from the *Kermac News* illustrated this valorization of the success of the oil well: "Everybody shook hands with everybody twice. . . . Congratulations came pouring in . . . [as] other radios had picked up our surprising hit and the telephone began to squeal from Houston to New Orleans. . . . The newspapers gave it banner notices" (quoted in Ezell 164–65).

Completion of British Petroleum's Deepwater Horizon oil rig in 2009 resulted in similar kudos. As the deepest oil and gas well ever drilled offshore, the Deepwater Horizon was lauded by Robert L. Long, Transocean Ltd.'s chief executive officer. In his congratulatory message Long declared, "This impressive well depth record reflects the intensive planning and focus on effective operations by BP and the drilling crews

Louisiana Story: The Cajun boy celebrates on the oil well "Christmas tree"

of the Deepwater Horizon" ("Deepwater Horizon"). On Vermont Public Radio, Debbie Elliot asserted the same positive response to oil drilling in the Gulf. According to Elliot, fishermen and oil companies had built an interdependent relationship: "The local fishermen feared their way of life was in jeopardy when the first oilmen arrived in Cajun south Louisiana. But over the last half century, the two industries learned to live together. Oil and gas brought jobs and opportunity for many families."

It is this interdependent relationship between the fishing and the oil industries that has taken center stage in media discussions after the Gulf of Mexico Deepwater oil rig explosion and spill in April 2010, in spite of the 1989 *Exxon Valdez* disaster, which seemed to demonstrate that oil and wild nature don't mix. From a contemporary perspective the conflict between these two industries seems new, a product of the rig explosion and its aftermath. In fact, the conflict began with the first oil well in and around the Gulf in the second decade of the twentieth century, culminating with the Kerr-McGee's successful well in 1947. Any conflict between the two industries, however, has been whitewashed by media representations of their relationship, building toward Elliot's conclusion that they have learned to live together because oil brought money and jobs to the region.

Filmic representations following Kerr-Mcgee's success draw on this drive to minimize the conflict between the fishing and the oil industries and valorize oil drilling and the opportunities it brings. Both Robert Flaherty's *Louisiana Story* (1948) and Anthony Mann's *Thunder Bay* (1953), for example, commend the oil industry for bringing wealth to an otherwise impoverished region, with differing levels of interdependence between local residents and oil company outsiders on display. Whereas *Louisiana Story* makes the case that an oil company can build its rig, drill for oil, build a pipeline, and disappear, leaving the bayou untouched and the Cajuns around the well a little richer, *Thunder Bay* asserts that oil drillers and shrimpers can work together. In fact, in *Thunder Bay* oil drilling provides more than jobs and money. According to the film, it offers access to "the golden shrimp" that fishermen have been seeking for generations, stimulating a more productive shrimp season. As a testament to a continuation of this vision of interdependence, *Dead Ahead: The Exxon Valdez Disaster* (1992), *Black Wave: The Legacy of the Exxon Valdez* (2009), and *Crude* (2009) draw on this same mythology, asserting that the oil and the fishing industries can work interdependently once appropriate safety precautions are in place.

Approaches to Progress and Ecology in *Louisiana Story* and *Thunder Bay*

Louisiana Story and *Thunder Bay* therefore illustrate differing visions of oil drilling, visions that draw on conflicting views of both progress and ecology. Whereas *Louisiana Story* advocates for a progressivist vision of progress in which corporate "big guys" rather than local "innocent" Cajuns successfully reap the benefits of modernization and an economic, or "fair-use," approach to ecology, *Thunder Bay* demonstrates a populist view of progress and an organismic, or "wise-use," approach to ecology. Yet both films' representations rest on fabricated American myths, which fall flat under scrutiny.

Louisiana Story's progressivist perspective connects Cajuns to the natural world around them in the film. In reality it exploits them and their land, an exploitation that demonstrates the negative consequences of economic and fair-use approaches to ecology. Economic consequences affect both locals and their environment in a series of negative externalities, once again made blatant after the Deepwater Horizon disaster sixty-two years later.

Thunder Bay's populist presentation of progress and organismic, or wise-use, approaches to ecology seem like more-viable choices for both local shrimpers and their environment. But those visions also collapse in the face of the negative externalities ever present during offshore oil drilling. Although the film suggests shrimpers and oil drillers can build and maintain interdependent relationships that serve them both economically while preserving the sea and its marine life, implying the possibility of sustainable development in the Gulf, those claims are all based in fiction (myth) rather than fact (reality).

Progressivist versus Populist Visions of Progress

In *Gunfighter Nation* and *Regeneration through Violence*, Richard Slotkin argues that the frontier myth rested on both progressive and populist schools of American ideology (*Gunfighter Nation* 22). According to Slotkin "the 'progressive' style . . . reads the history of savage warfare and westward expansion as a Social Darwinian parable, explaining the emergence of a new managerial ruling class and justifying its right to subordinate lesser classes to its purposes" (22). In contrast the populist style rests on premises that "combined the agrarian imagery of Jeffersonianism and the belief in economic individualism and mobility characteristic of pre–Civil War 'free labor' ideology. Progress in the populist style is measured by the degree to which the present state of society facilitates a broad diffusion of property, of the opportunity to 'rise in the world,' and of political power" (22).

According to Slotkin, however, both progressive and populist styles draw on a common myth/ideological language in which there is substantial agreement on such central concerns as the exceptional character of American life and history, the necessity and desirability of economic development, "the vitality of 'democratic' politics, and the relevance of something called 'The Frontier' as a way of explaining and rationalizing what is most distinctive and valuable in 'the American way'" (*Gunfighter Nation* 23–24). Ultimately both progressive and populist views of progress rest on an empire-building model that exploits resources and desecrates the environment. Whether the empire sustains either the few or the many, the environment suffers, since both "draw on a common myth" of a pristine frontier (23).

An Overview of Organismic (Wise-Use) and Economic (Fair-Use) Approaches to Ecology

These films not only move toward a more populist vision of progress; they also seem to embrace an organismic approach to ecology that encourages sustainability. According to environmental historian Carolyn Merchant, organismic ecology is based on Frederic Clements's view of a plant community as a living organism that evolves through succession, a process in which invading pioneer species develop into climax plant communities. A plant community is also vulnerable to disruption or death by technologies such as those that caused the dust bowl and "strives for a nature of cooperation among individuals in animal and human communities" (Merchant 184), a view that ecologist Aldo Leopold applied to human communities in his manifesto, "The Land Ethic," which encouraged an ecologically centered view of the land as a biotic pyramid in which humans were a part.

Whereas the organismic approach to ecology encourages preservationist policies toward the environment, the economic approach, in which ecosystems are seen as sums of their parts, not living organisms, encourages fair-use politics that call for the exploitation of resources for human gain. Such an approach valorizes humans as managers who are "above nature and able to control it" (Merchant 186) and use environmental resources for human benefit. Economic ecologist Kenneth Watt asserts, for example, that human beings are economic animals, and "economic ecology's goal is to maximize the productivity of each type of ecosystem and each level of that ecosystem for human benefit" (quoted in Merchant 188). Although ecologist Eugene Odum has connected the tenets of organismic ecology with those of the economic to demonstrate ways in which humans can repair the natural world, the ultimate goal of economic ecology—maximizing benefits of nature for humans—serves more as a means of disruption than a tool for healing.

Louisiana Story and Separation between Humans and the Natural World

The support for oil drilling and its benefits illustrated in *Louisiana Story* should come as no surprise because the Standard Oil Company financed the film. In his biography of Robert Flaherty, *The Innocent Eye*, Arthur Calder-Marshall asserts that Standard Oil began negotiating with Flaherty as early as 1944 for "a film dramatizing to the public the risk and difficulties of getting oil from beneath the earth" (211). Roy Stryker, Standard Oil's public relations officer in New Jersey, suggested that "Flaherty would produce an idea, not yet perceived, which would discover in the romance of oil-drilling a theme so compelling that it would play the commercial theatres" (211). In *The World of Robert Flaherty*, biographer Richard Griffith associates Standard Oil's choice of Flaherty to direct its public relations film with the success of *Nanook of the North*, which had also been sponsored by a commercial company and "hailed as a classic with no complaint from anyone that its finances might be tainted" (148).

In her biography of her husband, Frances Hubbard Flaherty takes this relationship between Flaherty and Standard Oil further, claiming that Standard Oil commissioned Flaherty despite a cynical response from a film industry that saw Flaherty as a freelance filmmaker without the professional resources to support a film project of this size. According to Frances Flaherty, instead of the superficial films Hollywood produced, Standard Oil wanted "a classic, a permanent and artistic record of the contribution which the oil industry has made to civilization" presented "with the dignity and epic sweep it deserved," a film that would "assure this story a lasting place on the highest plane of literature of the screen" (quoted in Flaherty 34). All these biographical sources suggest that Flaherty had created an art piece that, as did *Nanook of the North*, transcends its corporate funding.

Contemporaneous reviews of the film support the claim that the film's source of financing does not detract from its success as a work of art. Bosley Crowther of the *New York Times* asserts that the film "is not a submissive nod" to technology; yet "it is recognition that the machine can be a useful friend of man, no more rapacious, in some way, than primitive man or nature themselves." Crowther declares the scenes highlighting the oil drilling operation "the most powerful and truly eloquent phases" of *Louisiana Story*. Despite the sympathetic portrayal of the oil drillers, however, Crowther doubts that money supplied by Standard Oil encouraged Flaherty's perspective. Instead, Crowther asserts, "the ring of sincerity is clear in Flaherty's film."

Variety calls the film "a documentary-type story told almost purely in camera terms" ("*Louisiana Story* Review"). The *Variety* review mentions that Standard Oil of New Jersey funded the production only in passing, asserting instead that *Louisiana Story* "has a slender, appealing story, moments of agonizing suspense, vivid atmosphere and superlative photography." Instead of valorizing either the Cajuns or the oil drillers, the review suggests that "there are no real heroes or villains" in the film. According to *Variety* "the simple Cajun family is friendly, and the oil-drilling crew is pleasant and likable." The stylistic choices deserve the most kudos, the review asserts, with "long sequences being told by the camera, with eloquent sound effects and Virgil Thomson's expressive music in the background" rather than through concentrated dialogue-driven scenes.

None of these contemporaneous reviews suggests that financing by Standard Oil in any way skewed the rhetoric of *Louisiana Story*, even though the offshore drilling on display here is shown from the perspective of a Cajun boy. Instead, the reviews and biographical overviews of the film agree with and substantiate the message on display in the film: offshore oil drilling, even in a fragile bayou, will have no effect on the pristine wild nature around a well or on the innocent Cajuns who are enriched by mineral rights contracts and lease payments received from the drilling company, a company that enters the bayou and then all but disappears by the end of the film.

Despite clear evidence that oil drilling cannot leave the water and land around it untouched, the film and its reviewers assert the opposite, demonstrating through the experience of oil drillers and a Cajun boy that humans and the natural world can maintain separate existences and thrive. Instead of emphasizing the interdependent relationship between humans and the natural world, *Louisiana Story* suggests that to maintain the innocence of nature in the bayou, and of its more natural

Cajun inhabitants, a humanity more aligned with culture and technology must leave wild nature behind, entering it only briefly and with caution to avoid an indelible affect. Two myths are perpetuated by the film, then: the myth that oil drilling can leave a natural setting untouched, and the myth that humans are somehow separate from nature rather than interconnected with it.

Louisiana Story perpetuates these two myths through both its aesthetic and its narrative. Close-ups of a pristine bayou open *Louisiana Story*. Flowers, an alligator, and a heron on an evergreen tree emphasize the film's naturalistic setting. A lone boy poles through weeping cypress trees in a small boat. We see the bayou from his point of view, including water below him. A narrator describes the scene, even mentioning werewolves to set the mythic tone of this innocent scene. The boy wears salt on his waist and something inside his shirt to protect him from all that bubbles, we are told, and smiles at a raccoon in a tree, connecting him to both natural and supernatural elements. A snake, gators, and grasses blowing in the wind continue the scene.

When the boy shoots at an animal, and the pristine scene is disrupted, the conflicting element in the film is introduced: modernism in the shape of oil drilling in the bayou. Other explosions take the gunshot's place, then, as a wheeled machine drives into the bayou. The machine looks like a tractor, a cultivator cutting a path through the grass. The boy floats away, demonstrating the separation between culture and nature that the film perpetuates.

The boy and his Cajun family represent an innocence untouched by civilization. When the boy heads home to his family, a family structure more in touch with the natural world is introduced. The family's cabin sits beside the bayou and can be accessed only by boat. Inside the cabin the boy's father talks about "gators" in a Cajun accent to a clean-cut younger man, reinforcing his connection to nature. The boy's mother does offer coffee, a connection with culture, but the boy's entrance by boat at his parent's dock again highlights how isolated this family is from society. The blasting that continues, however, contrasts and conflicts with this innocent, more "natural" scene, highlighting the intervention on display. Modern culture has entered the pristine wilderness of the bayou and infiltrated the innocent Cajun family that is still tied to the natural world. To seal this connection the oil drillers offer lease agreements to the boy's father: "Can that thing really tell where oil is?" the older man asks and signs his name to a contract.

Evidence in the film, however, suggests that nature and culture can and must remain separated. The oilmen, representing culture, leave the rustic cabin in their speedboat. Later the boy and his raccoon, representing nature, watch the oilmen from their rowboat as the drillers prepare to build their rig and platform. The boy fishes while Cajuns hunt along a pristine shore, further connecting them to the natural world. We get a view of homes on the shore from a houseboat and a shore view of the motorboat and its wake. The boy and the raccoon continue watching, and the wake of the motorboat throws him out of his boat, so he is literally connected with the natural world. But the boy seems fascinated with the elements of culture brought by the oilmen and watches a man survey the area and a tall rig rolling up the bayou to the spot the surveyor has indicated. The boy and his raccoon watch this modern scene from the safety of nature—the waters and fecund grasses of the bayou. They remain innocent, smiling as they observe without relinquishing their connection with the natural world.

The rig contrasts with the natural scene around it, maintaining its separation from the natural world. The technology of the rig and the oil drilling it represents become a beautiful and powerful opposition to the peaceful bayou. Steam surrounds the rig, and we hear the pumping sounds of the drill. Although the boy talks to a couple of oilmen and asks what they are doing, he does not board the rig when invited. Instead, he paddles away, reinforcing his separation, and watches from his boat as the long drill comes out of the well, so worn down that the drillers must replace it. A sunset over the bayou further separates the mechanization of oil drilling from the natural scene, which the boy and his boat both envelop and represent.

The separation between culture and nature continues even after the boy boards the rig for a closer look. The film shows the whole process of preparing the drill before the boy goes on board to see for himself. The rig is loud as chains swing around pipes to tighten and loosen connections. We cannot hear the boy and the oilman's conversation, but we see them smile, suggesting a connection between them and, consequently, a connection between culture and nature beyond the economic vision of ecology supported by the film's narrative.

After this long segment demonstrating the process of oil drilling, however, the scene shifts back to the boy and his raccoon in the bayou and, in a long sequence, highlights a battle between elements of nature. The boy leaves his raccoon and examines eggs left by an alligator. When the gator comes back on shore, the boy and we see the gator eggs hatch. The boy holds a baby gator until the mother gator roars, and the boy runs away. The raccoon is now loose and swims up on a log, but the gator is close behind. The boy searches for his pet and passes representatives of wild nature: a spider in a web, a rabbit, a skunk, singing birds, and a deer. When he sees the broken line on the boat and realizes the raccoon has escaped, he fears the gator has killed the raccoon. In a parallel to the boy's fears, the gator devours a water bird, so the boy sets a gator trap to avenge his friend's death. His attempts fail, however, but his father has been searching for him and helps him out of the water, telling him, "We'll get him." Together they kill the alligator, it seems. Although we do not see the actual slaughter, we assume it occurs because father and son visit the oil rig and bring the gator's skin to show the drillers on board, holding it up for them to admire from their rowboat.

This resolution of the battle between humans and the natural world is paralleled on the rig with a battle between humans and elements of culture when one of the oilmen, Tom, tests oil levels. The father kids him about never finding oil, while the boy fishes from the platform, and his father sets traps for game. We hear a rushing sound and see water spurting over machinery—a blowout that illustrates a battle between human and nonhuman culture in the context of *Louisiana Story*. The boy runs, and the father watches water spurt up the rig. It is gas and salt water, according to a newspaper headline, so the well must be capped using a blowout preventer. This initial drilling has failed, just as the boy's attempts to kill the alligator were thwarted.

Yet just as the alligator is ultimately killed when the boy's father intervenes, the oil drilling improves when, according to the film's narrative, the boy helps, seemingly connecting the natural and the supernatural with the culture of modernism represented by the oil rig and its men. The boy, still enraptured by the derrick, climbs it as if it were a Christmas tree and tries dropping salt into the well for good luck, spitting on the salt for good measure. The oilmen laugh when he tells them what he has done, but later when the boy is at home peeling potatoes, he tells his family, "I know she won't go away." Then they hear the drill. According to an onscreen newspaper headline, "angling the hold to bypass the pressure area" has saved the well and brought the oil drillers success.

Any connection between culture and nature ends once the oilmen test the oil and find it good. The lease money from the father's contract buys groceries and a new pot for Mom and a new rifle for the boy, but the family members continue to speak Cajun without translation. Despite the relative prosperity that the lease money brings to the family, the last two scenes from the film perpetuate the separation between nature and culture and suggest that human intervention—even oil drilling—can leave the natural world pure and untouched. In the first of these scenes, the boy sees his raccoon in the tree, complete with the rope collar around its neck, so boy and raccoon are reunited, and consequently the boy is reconnected with the natural world. In the second and last of these two scenes, the derrick leaves slowly, and oil is pumped through a pipeline under the bayou and hidden from the natural world. The boy and his pet watch the process and wave good-bye to the rig, its oilmen, and the culture they represent. Only a lone Christmas tree–like pole remains, and it is now more tree than derrick, a tangible claim in the film that human exploitation of nature's resources can leave its pure innocence untouched.

Thunder Bay and the Myth of Interdependence

Unlike *Louisiana Story*, *Thunder Bay* approaches offshore oil drilling from a strictly fictional point of view, without claiming a more fact-based documentary approach to the subject, but it also illustrates a skewed view of oil drilling perhaps reinforced by one of the film's star's (James Stewart) connections to the oil industry. In her updated biography of Anthony Mann, for example, Jeanine Basinger recounts James Stewart's connection to the film and its subject, explaining that *Thunder Bay* was one of three projects that Stewart found and asked Mann to direct, in this case because Stewart had joined a partnership with a Texas oilman (132). With a weak script, Anthony Mann's "mastery of physical space" (Basinger

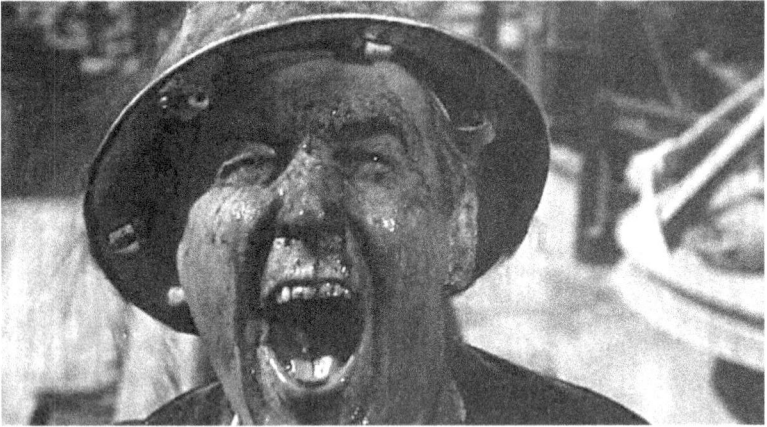

Thunder Bay: Steve Martin (James Stewart) celebrating after the well begins to produce oil

132) stands out in *Thunder Bay*. According to Basinger "although it is somewhat unsettling today to watch a movie that sets a conflict between oil-drilling and nature—and oil-drilling is the hero—the machinery and the rig are photographed as things of beauty and majesty" (132). From Basinger's perspective "hard industrial grays and reds replace the greens and blues of nature and become the 'colors' of the modern era" (132). A.W. of the *New York Times* agrees, asserting that visually "the complex off-shore drilling apparatus is the most distinctive aspect of *Thunder Bay*." Shot in Technicolor and shown on an innovative "wide, curved screen [with] stereophonic [stereo] (or directional) sound" (A.W.) in the Loew's State Theatre, *Thunder Bay* features a vast setting that takes center stage, overshadowing its weak narrative.

Basinger calls the film and its ending "a modern environmentalist's worst nightmare" based on her reading of the film as a conflict between oil drilling and nature in which oil drilling wins, perhaps missing the film's implausible environmental message: shrimpers and oil men can live together interdependently because the elusive golden shrimp are not only undamaged by oil drilling but attracted to the rig. Other reviewers address this move toward interdependence. Reviewer Dennis Schwartz claims that the film's resolution "has shrimpers and oil men willing to live with each other in harmony, saying there's room for both." Reviewer Dan Jardine asserts that Anthony Mann establishes a conflict of worldviews between what he calls Hispanic shrimp fishermen and speculative oilmen but "backs away from the dialectic he has established from the get-go and gives us a soppy and completely implausible restorative ending."

Although we agree that the film's ending is implausible, we argue that the seeds of a resolution to the conflict between shrimpers and oilmen are planted early in the film when the romantic plot between Johnny Gambi (Dan Duryea) and Francesca Rigaud (Marcia Henderson) is broached. *Thunder Bay* moves beyond *Louisiana Story*, then, not only claiming that oil drilling can leave the natural world untouched but also asserting that oil drilling and shrimping can coexist interdependently.

Set in 1946 Louisiana, *Thunder Bay* connects oil drilling and shrimping from its opening shot of Johnny Gambi and Steve Martin (James Stewart) walking down a long, deserted road. They carry a heavy chest and discuss a moneymaking idea that will require a two-million-dollar investment, but then a Port Filliay Fish Company truck picks them up and takes them into town for a 2:00 p.m. appointment, aligning their oil drilling plan with the community's fishing industry. The connection between fishing and oil drilling broached by the film is emphasized here, especially since, once they reach town, Gambi rents a shrimp boat for fifty dollars a day, so the two can, they hope, form a partnership with a big oilman, Kermit MacDonald (Jay C. Flippen).

At first, however, the relationship between oil drilling and fishing is seen as conflicting rather than interdependent. To offset any hostility their enterprise might ignite, Gambi and Martin encourage area fishermen to think that they are opening a fish cannery. But when their potential investors arrive by seaplane and, despite company troubles, agree to fund Steve Martin's project, an offshore drilling platform and rig, the film's major conflict is introduced. Even though business investor MacDonald gives Martin money in advance to pay off debts and promises to deposit five hundred thousand dollars the next day, the area shrimpers are skeptical of this possible disruption to their means of survival and way of life.

The daughters of the shrimp boat owner Dominique (Antonio Moreno) serve as love interests for Gambi and Martin and another source of conflict between local fishermen and the oil drillers: the elder sister, Stella (Joanne Dru), eventually partners with Martin, and the younger sister, Francesca (Marcia Henderson), pairs up with Gambi. Primarily, however, the townspeople oppose Martin and Gambi, believing that oil and shrimp can't mix. The main conflict of *Thunder Bay*, then, is between those who make a living from the sea—shrimpers and other fishermen—and those who would like to make a living from what lies beneath its waters—oilmen. Although history suggests this conflict is irresolvable, the film negotiates a resolution between these two worldviews and sources of income that is based in organismic approaches to ecology.

Ultimately *Thunder Bay* reinforces Steve Martin's position on offshore oil drilling. Martin effectively argues for the offshore drilling by stressing interdependence, an organismic approach to ecology, claiming that oil and shrimp can not only mix but also bring prosperity to all: "There's oil down there," Martin proclaims, and "this is going to be good for the town, good for the people."

The conflict is not so easily resolved, however, and must first rise to a climax. Because of his opposition to oil drilling, for example, Dominique will no longer rent his shrimp boat to Martin and Gambi, but his friend Teche (Gilbert Roland) will, perhaps only as another income source. The other shrimpers remain concerned: "Don't they know they're killing the shrimp?" Dominique asks. Stella, Dominique's older daughter, agrees, exclaiming, "The town's not enough. They have to kill the whole bay."

During the initial seismic blasting that will locate the best areas for underwater drilling, Martin disagrees and reinforces his claims that oilmen and shrimpers can build a prosperous community together: "Those shrimp can withstand ten times the blast," he asserts. After the blasting, however, the townspeople plan to stop Martin and Gambi because they believe their dynamite may have destroyed the shrimp beds. When Stella warns Martin that the townspeople may confront him, however, he continues to stress the potential for an interdependent relationship between shrimpers and oilmen. He tells her that dynamite won't "do any harm," insisting, "If it hurt the shrimp, I'd stop it." When the townspeople nearly attack him, Martin continues to espouse his claims for an interdependent relationship between them: "Nothing we do spoils the fish or the town. . . . Oil is going to do good things for the place."

Dominique remains unconvinced, however, and induces Mr. Parker (uncredited) from the Department of Wildlife and Fisheries to intervene with a cease-and-desist order for Martin and Gambi. When Dominique and Parker arrive with the order, Martin has already stopped the blasting, since they have chosen a drilling site. Now Martin's financial support, Macdonald, "Mac," gives him twenty-six days to find oil below the rig and, perhaps, even less time to convince the locals that oil and shrimp can build prosperity.

During the initial drilling process, shrimpers and oilmen remain in opposition. Martin is so dedicated to this mission that he stays on the rig during a possible hurricane. But when Stella comes to make sure her younger sister, Francesca, does not marry Gambi, Martin explains the challenge of oil drilling and establishes a foundation for his own beliefs in mutual progress: "Now oil was found. . . . It was found from things dying millions of years ago" and can build a future from the past, bringing all time together. This is an evolutionary argument that highlights a desire for a progress built on a rich past and, of course, on oil.

The climax of the film occurs, however, when Francesca's fiancé, Phillipe (Robert Monet), who violently opposes oil drilling, tries to blow up the rig, causing Martin to think that Stella is part of the plan. Martin stops the blasting, but Phillipe falls, and Martin can't save him. Drilling continues despite this disaster, with a montage sequence illustrating progress. With eight days to go, however, Mac must pull out of the operation. The company would not finance the drilling, Mac explains, so Mac has, and he is out of money. Now the corporate board will no longer support the project, and it seems as if the shrimpers have won.

The consequence of the looming deadline provides an exciting spectacle to heighten tension and, in a parallel to the shrimping families ashore, to demonstrate the strong community built on the oil rig. Drilling is going so fast to meet the deadline that a warning bell goes off. It is a saltwater blow, and Gambi is not on the rig to stop it, since he has not yet returned from his secret shore visit with Francesca. All men run to their stations and use the blowout prevention system to stop the blow. When the automatic system fails, they must rely on the manual operation, turning the wheels together. Mac and Martin work alongside the men, and the system works.

The oil rig community seems to be working to ensure a successful drilling process. With Gambi still away, Martin offers the men a two-hundred-dollar bonus if they hit oil, explaining that they will need to work for free for the last week of the operation, since their funding has fallen through. Martin exclaims, "There's enough oil there to lubricate the universe."

When Gambi returns, however, he and Martin fight because Gambi had abandoned his post. Gambi is ready to leave the rig with the rest of the crew, but when he hears about the new financial situation, he claims, "We oughta have some of the glory for bringing in the first offshore rig," and convinces the crew to continue work. He tells Martin he was gone because he has married Francesca, building the first tangible link between oilmen and shrimpers. The second link between fisheries and oil occurs when pumping equipment is clogged by enormous "golden shrimp"; solving one problem leads to the bonanza of bounty in rare seafood. The area now produces wealth from both shrimp and oil.

Before Martin can reveal the good news, however, Dominique nearly eradicates the possibility of this effective connection. Instead, he wants to fight Martin and Gambi, rescue Francesca, and destroy the rig. Dominique proclaims, "They'll kill our fish. They will take everything from us." The conflict between oil drilling and shrimping is still in place but, in the film's context, only because the "truth" has not yet been revealed to Dominique and his friends.

Once one of the shrimpers, Teche, learns that golden shrimp, which have eluded them for decades, are attracted to the rig, interdependence becomes possible. Martin shows Teche the golden shrimp off camera, so when Dominique and the townspeople arrive to take Francesca away, a symbiotic relationship between oilmen and shrimpers is established instead of the continuing conflict that Dominique predicts. On camera Martin tells Teche that the golden shrimp foul up their intake valves at night and asks Teche what he might do for him. Teche declares, "What a dumb oilman," but the ice has been broken, and the battle between the shrimpers and oilmen is a short one.

Martin connects that relationship between the two worldviews to Francesca's marriage to Gambi, telling the townspeople, "She's here to stay, and so are we," when they ask for Francesca. "We won't hurt ya.

We never will. You look for one thing in the gulf. We look for something else. That's the only business. . . . Without oil this country would die." The rig begins to shake as if it will blow. "It's going to be the richest oil field in the world." And a gusher rushes up the rig: "Cap that thing fast!"

Now both oilmen and shrimpers can reap the benefits of oil drilling in the fantasy narrative on display in *Thunder Bay*. The oilmen rejoice, covered in oil, and Teche shows fellow shrimpers how to catch the golden shrimp. There are thousands of these wondrous shrimp, and a biotic community is established between oilmen and fishermen. This symbiotic relationship extends to marriage: Gambi marries Francesca, and Martin follows Stella to New Orleans in a truck borrowed from Teche. In a fantastic resolution to a realistic conflict between shrimpers and oilmen, *Thunder Bay* asserts interdependence, an organismic approach to ecology suggesting that humans and the natural world can maintain a thriving relationship that benefits all.

Dead Ahead: The Exxon Valdez Disaster, Black Wave: The Legacy of the Exxon Valdez, and *Crude: The Real Price of Oil*: When Externalities Become Transparent

While *Louisiana Story* and *Thunder Bay* suggest that oil production will either leave the landscape untouched or benefit its ecosystem, films responding to major oil spills, including the March 24, 1989, *Exxon Valdez* ecocatastrophe in Alaska's Prince Edward Sound, highlight the negative effects that oil disasters may have on the environment and the cultures and economies it supports. Instead of condemning the oil industry in general, however, these films attack individuals and promote safe production practices. In a move similar to that of *Louisiana Story*, *Dead Ahead: The Exxon Valdez Disaster* (1992), *Black Wave: The Legacy of the Exxon Valdez* (2009), and *Crude: The Real Price of Oil* (2009) assert that because oil and the natural environment don't mix, they must remain separate.

Unlike *Thunder Bay*, which asserts that humans and the natural world can share an interdependent relationship, *Dead Ahead, Black Wave,* and, to a certain extent, *Crude* suggest that human and environmental disasters occur when safety precautions fail, because of either human error or blatant neglect. If, as in *Louisiana Story*, oil companies enter the natural world briefly and with caution to avoid an indelible effect, then, the films suggest, they can avoid such disasters. Ultimately these films perpetuate the same two myths upheld by *Louisiana Story*: if implemented correctly and safely, oil drilling can leave a natural setting untouched, so that humans and their technology can remain separate from nature rather than interconnected with it.

Dead Ahead: The Exxon Valdez Disaster, for example, focuses primarily on the reasons behind both the spill and its slow cleanup, rather than on the inherently dangerous consequences of oil production and shipment. To reinforce this assertion that safety regulations, not the oil industry per se, caused this horrendous disaster and its catastrophic consequences, the film provides a reenactment of the 1989 *Exxon Valdez* tanker catas-trophe, from the moments before the tanker ran aground in Alaska's Prince William Sound, rupturing its storage tanks and spilling millions of gallons of oil, through its devastating aftermath. According to *Los Angeles Times* staff writer Susan King, "the behind-the-scenes catastrophes *after* the mammoth oil spill . . . shocked the British creative team of HBO's docudrama *Dead Ahead*." The film's researcher-writer Michael Baker and executive producer Leslie Woodhead called the disaster "a black comedy" (King) because of the neglect and greed of oil and pipeline companies and the disastrous choices made by the Coast Guard, the EPA, and the first Bush administration.

As King declares, the film "depicts the bureaucracy, fighting, and finger-pointing among officials at Exxon, the Alyeska Pipeline Com-pany . . . , the Coast Guard, the U.S. Environmental Protection Agency and the Bush Administration, while the spill was left basically unattended for days." Anger with these multiple groups' mistakes prompted Baker and Woodhead to move forward with the film. As Woodhead explains, "It is so infuriating, the revelation that the oil laid there for three days in beautiful weather. It was just a tangle of priorities and people trying to tidy up their own images which left the oil lying there in the water" (King). Baker agrees, asserting, "People started kind of blaming each other. . . . It became a question of controlling the media, not cleaning up the oil, but controlling the spill as an event" (King).

From its opening scenes showing Captain Joseph Hazelwood's (Jack-son Davies) absence from the bridge because of alcohol abuse to its dramatization of conflicts between the EPA and its local representative, Dan Lawn (John Heard), and between Exxon and its spokesperson, Frank Iarossi (Christopher Lloyd), the film effectively addresses the postspill disaster, arguing through both its narrative and its cinematic portrayals of once-pristine waters and landscapes for double hulls in oil tankers and better implementation of protocols if and when another spill occurs. It does not, however, argue against the production and transporting of oil because, as Woodhead states, "America cannot afford to be without [an oil] supply, but we better try to do a lot better in controlling how we get it out of there" (King).

The powerful cinematic representations of the landscape became possible because "establishing shots and aerial footage were shot of the Port of Valdez," even though *Dead Ahead* was filmed primarily in Vancouver, British Columbia. According to director Paul Seed, "it would have been difficult to shoot inside Alaska because of the unpredictable weather" (King). The wild shorelines of Vancouver overlap effectively with the establishing shots of Valdez and contrast well with the postdisaster shots of a spill (recreated with a gelatin-based food thickener) to accentuate the dangerous consequences of the spill: loss of the pristine beauty of wild nature.

These contrasting shots parallel the positions voiced by Lawn and Iarossi, who both in some ways oppose the organizations they see as responsible for the spill. Iarossi's character becomes more authentic because Iarossi willingly answered interview questions, revealing, as he had during the actual spill's aftermath, Exxon's reactions to the spill. His focus on safety, however, reinforces the film's emphasis on accident prevention rather than the eradication of oil production and shipment. Then president of the Exxon Shipping Company, Iarossi represented the company during public forums in Valdez and informed investigators that Captain Joseph Hazelwood was legally drunk during the tanker disaster.

More importantly, Iarossi revealed that Exxon knew about Hazelwood's drinking problem but allowed him to continue as captain of the *Valdez*. Iarossi resigned from Exxon in 1990 and became president of the American Bureau of Shipping, "a nonprofit corporation that classifies ships for insurers, inspects blueprints during construction and surveys vessels to make sure they are seaworthy" ("Where Are They Now?"). According to a 1999 *Anchorage Daily News* article, Iarossi told the *Business*

Times of Singapore, "What we need to do is to try to develop much more of a safety culture, the mentality which is very much safety oriented on the part of shipping companies and ship operating officers." The film draws on this same representation of Iarossi as a figure disillusioned by Exxon's failure to address safety issues to reinforce its argument for double-hulled tankers but not against oil.

Representations of Dan Lawn parallel that of Iarossi and, again, validate the film's call for safer transporting of oil. As chief of the Valdez office of the Alaska Department of Environmental Conservation, Lawn confronts an unresponsive state government, a complaisant EPA, and an unprepared Alyeska Pipeline Service Company, asserting the need for both better preventative systems and emergency plans to tackle oil spills and their consequences. The film's portrayal of Lawn draws authentically on his attempts to improve both prevention and response strategies. In a 1989 *Seattle Times* article, for example, Lawn asserts, "We are all to blame. . . . We demand petroleum products, but we're unwilling to be taxed. We thought someone was taking care of it. We put in pro-industry officials, and our ability to control things went away." Although the film effectively argues for better safety standards to prevent future oil spill disasters, *Dead Ahead* reinforces the arguments broached in *Louisiana Story*: if we successfully maintain the bifurcation between nature and culture—between a pristine Alaska and its oil—both can be preserved.

Black Wave: The Legacy of the Exxon Valdez, on the other hand, examines the ongoing negative consequences of the *Exxon Valdez* disaster from a contemporary perspective. It too, however, blames ineffective choices made by the EPA and the corrupt practices of Exxon for the spill's continuing negative effects. Like *Dead Ahead* the film reasserts the reasons for the economic and environmental devastation still rampant in the Valdez area—an oil spill that could have been prevented if appropriate safety measures had been in place. *Black Wave* takes this position further, effectively condemning Exxon not only for its failures during and immediately after the disaster but for its reluctance to clean up Prince Edward Sound and provide relief funds to fishermen and spill workers still affected by the catastrophic repercussions of this unchecked spill.

In a move similar to that made in both *Louisiana Story* and *Dead Ahead, Black Wave* contrasts pristine images of Alaskan waters and shorelines near Cordova with testimonies of fishermen and oil spill workers still affected by the disaster. The film highlights scenes of a fisherman's daughter fishing alongside her father for the first time since the spill, for example, as a powerful portrait of a family's connection with Prince Edward Sound and its bounty. But the joy the daughter demonstrates in her ode to "the earth, the water, and the fish" is broken once the film reveals that this is the first time the daughter has fished with her father in twenty years because fishing was not financially feasible until then. Her father, Peter O'Toole, had saved enough money to buy a fishing boat and permit in February 1989. The spill in March of the same year fore-stalled all fishing and devastated his fishing business for twenty years, all because, as Riki Ott, a marine biologist, reveals, both the salmon and the herring runs collapsed. Of the twenty-four species devastated by the spill, the film explains, fifteen have not recovered.

The lasting effects of the spill permeate the communities around Prince Edward Sound, the film explains, with permanent economic crises contributing to increased levels of alcoholism and suicide. The spill's negative effects extend beyond the sound's economy, too, and include health problems faced by spill workers who inhaled oil and dispersants, toxic chemicals used to clean up the spill. Of the 6,724 workers who filed upper-respiratory illness claims and the two dozen lawsuits, only seven were settled. Recollections of Prince Edward Sound immediately after the spill reinforce the cause of both economic and health crises. Docu-mentary footage shows mountains glowing with a glossy pink, the tanker beside them now blood red because inky stained waters have evaporated, forming a haze in the sky, the toxic hydrocarbon vapors inhaled by oil spill workers and residents of villages around the sound.

Ultimately, however, the film centers on Exxon and its greedy and corrupt practices as the cause of these continuing crises. A mandatory class action suit begun in 1994 with thirty-two thousand plaintiffs, for example, seems to bring victory to the plaintiffs, validating Exxon's claim that it "will consider whatever it takes to make [them] whole." Ultimately, however, a U.S. Supreme Court decision reduces an initial $5 billion settlement to $500 million, despite the fact that only 3 percent of the spill was cleaned up. Oil residue remains in the water and along the shore-line, buried in soil only inches from the surface. Polycyclic hydrocarbon aromatics are a thousand times more toxic than expected, according to the film, affecting both workers and wildlife in and around the sound. Illnesses attack the respiratory and nervous systems of former workers. The ongoing negative effects of the spill, however, are blamed on Exxon's negligence and greed rather than the oil industry as a whole.

Here, as in other documentaries, the $100 million a year lost in the Prince Edward Sound economy and the fifteen lost species of marine and shore life are blamed on one particular oil company's practices. The film ends, then, by condemning Exxon Mobile for its greed. The company's profits are at least $160 billion per year, the film explains, yet the company fought a lawsuit asking for less than 3 percent of its annual income and refused to be interviewed. *Black Wave* effectively documents the reasons for and long-term consequences of the *Exxon Valdez* disaster, but it fails to revile oil as an industry. As in earlier documentaries, the film suggests that if better safety and restoration practices were in place, oil spills could be avoided, as would their dire consequences.

Crude follows a pattern similar to that of *Black Wave*, highlighting the need to maintain the separation between nature and culture, while suggesting that oil production, if implemented effectively, can maintain a pristine wilderness. The film documents the battle between Ecuadorian indigenous tribes and Chevron over the oil company's rampant toxic-waste dumping and consequent destruction of both the Indians' rainforest home and their sources of water. With help from Trudie Styler, Sting's wife, filmmaker Joe Berlinger provides a balanced portrait of both the dangerous outcomes of toxic-waste dumping and the lawsuit between the tribes and Chevron continuing from 1993. According to *Rolling Stone's* Peter Travers review of *Crude*, however, "the most telling arguments come from watching tribes living in a toxic wasteland with children ravaged by skin diseases and cancer." According to Travers "the shattering sight of sludge creating a poison rainbow on a river argues eloquently about why oil and water don't mix." In the film, however, the focus is not on the inherent incompatibility of oil and water but on Chevron's negligent practices, just as *Dead Ahead* and *Black Wave* highlight the need for a safer approach to oil shipping but not the elimination of our reliance on oil or the oil industry. Recent Ecuadorian court decisions claiming that Chevron owes five billion dollars for damages were stopped by appeals in the U.S. courts.

Can Oil and Water Mix?

Oil tanker spills like those documented by *Dead Ahead* and *Black Wave* seemed to be "a much larger threat" (Bourne 42) than an offshore oil drilling catastrophe like the BP Deepwater Horizon Disaster, according to Joel K. Bourne's report in the October 2010 *National Geographic*. From the first offshore oil well forward, efforts to tap what Bourne calls "the largest U.S. oil discoveries in decades" went further offshore and deeper into the Gulf of Mexico. BP's Macondo Deepwater Horizon well was fifty miles offshore and a mile below sea level. Despite the obvious risks involved in such offshore drilling, Bourne asserts that "the industry had acted as if such a catastrophe would never occur. So had its regulators. Nothing like it had happened in the Gulf of Mexico since 1979, when a Mexican well called Ixtoc I blew out in the shallow waters of the Bay of Campeche" (42). As Bourne explains, "drilling technology had become so good since then, and the demand for oil so irresistible, that oil companies had sailed off the continental shelf into ever deeper waters" (42).

Both *Louisiana Story* and *Thunder Bay* draw on this same belief regarding offshore oil drilling. Unlike comparatively more fragile oil tankers, offshore oil wells are regulated by the Minerals Management Service (MMS), which claimed, according to Bourne, "that the chances of a blowout were less than one percent, and that even if one did happen, it wouldn't release much oil" (42). Despite biogeochemist Mandy Joye's call "to green power" (quoted in Bourne 53), however, Bourne focuses primarily on BP's decisions when it became clear that its well was not stable. According to Robert Bea, a University of California, Berkeley expert in technological disasters and offshore engineering, for example, "one problem . . . was a loss of core competence. After [a] merger BP forced thousands of older, experienced oil field workers into retirement. That decision, which made the company more dependent on contractors for engineering expertise, was a key ingredient in BP's 'recipe for disaster'" (quoted in Bourne 47).

As of March 2011, the effects of the BP oil disaster continue. A *Guardian* article from Suzanne Goldenberg suggests that the spill may have caused the death of ninety bottle-nosed dolphins, for example. Yet according to the final report of the National Commission on the BP Deepwater Horizon Oil Spill and Offshore Drilling, "drilling in deep water does not have to be abandoned. It can be done safely." The last chapter of the report outlines how best to implement the safety precautions that will avoid such disasters and facilitate more offshore oil drilling.

The media responses to the BP Deepwater Horizon disaster, then, draw on the more separatist philosophy represented by *Louisiana Story*. Although few would suggest that oil, fishing, and the water that sustains it are inherently interdependent, most media representations do assert the need for controlling oil production to maintain pristine nature rather than eliminating it altogether. As Elliot asserts, the oil and the fishing industries may have learned to live together because oil brought money and jobs to the region. What remains unanswered, however, is whether those jobs are worth the risk to fragile ecosystems in the Gulf, as documented in *Dead Ahead, Black Wave,* and *Crude* and illustrated by *Louisiana Story* and *Thunder Bay*, films responding to the development of the first offshore oil rigs in the Gulf of Mexico. Oil and water can mix, they argue, at least if appropriate safety precautions are in place.

CONCLUSION

Can the Film Industry and the Environmental Movement Mix?

Even though the oil drilling films we examined attempt to show us that oil and water can mix, at least if appropriate safety precautions are in place, the filmic representations of everyday eco-disasters explored throughout this book all highlight the negative consequences (externalities) of fulfilling our basic needs. They also demonstrate that more often than not, these eco-disasters also jeopardize those needs. *Total Recall*, for example, illustrates the repercussions of oxygen deprivation, but it also emphasizes the cause of unequal distribution of air: turning resources into commodities. *Quantum of Solace*, despite its James Bond action-adventure genre, demonstrates similar consequences, this time in relation to water as a necessary resource. *Our Daily Bread, The Cove, Norma Rae, Blue Vinyl: The World's First Toxic Comedy, The Last Mountain* (and the other eleven mountaintop removal mining documentaries), and *Black Wave: The Legacy of the Exxon Valdez* primarily emphasize the eco-disasters associated with fulfilling our basic needs, yet they also effectively illustrate how these everyday eco-disasters threaten the needs of both humans and the natural world.

All these films, to a greater or lesser extent, provide an environmental reading based on everyday eco-disasters associated with our everyday lives. Some focus on how satisfying our needs sometimes causes an everyday

Mountain Mourning: Homes overturned by mountaintop removal–related flooding

eco-disaster. Others highlight how our drive to commodify those needs endangers both the resources and ourselves. And still others show how our consumption practices risk the resources that sustain us. Yet because these works are all products of the film industry, whether made independently or as a Hollywood blockbuster, they all also contribute to the environmental degradation that translates into an everyday eco-disaster when it affects our ability to meet our basic needs.

Total Recall, for example, was one of the last major blockbusters to make large-scale use of miniature effects rather than CGI, a carbon-heavy approach that draws on multiple resources, leaving behind waste that is typically disposed of in landfills rather than recycled. According to Eric Lichtenfeld, five different companies were brought in to handle the film's effects. The only CGI sequence was a forty-two-second scene produced by MetroLight Studios that showed the x-rayed skeletons of commuters and their concealed weapons (258). In contrast only a year later, blockbusters such as James Cameron's *Terminator 2: Judgment Day* (1991) moved almost entirely to CGI. In spite of its message about the negative ramifications of turning oxygen into a commodity available to the privileged rather than the "commons," *Total Recall* integrated production practices with a heavy carbon footprint.

More-recent films rely more fully on CGI and digital production, but even when the films blatantly address the detrimental effects on our basic needs or the dire consequences of meeting them, they still struggle with maintaining the realism expected by both Hollywood and its audiences while encouraging environmentally friendly production practices. With a budget of $200 million and a gross profit of $586 million, *Quantum of Solace*, a blockbuster with a blatantly environmental message against commodifying water, serves as an apt example of the dilemma filmmakers face: How can a film company provide an effective and lucrative film product and limit negative environmental externalities?

In many ways this Bond film failed to achieve the "green" message of the story in its production practices. According to Randee Daniel of *Hollywood Reporter*, for example, *Quantum of Solace* was shot in six countries, and this on-location filming is, according to RPS Group, "among the most expensive and carbon-intense stages of film production. Large crews and quantities of equipment must be flown abroad, and diesel generators are used to power the lighting and heating of temporary sets." In Bregenz, Austria, during the scenes of the performance of *Tosca* and its aftermath, 1,500 extras were used, and for a later scene, the Palio di Siena at the Piazza del Campo in Siena was recreated in Italy; for a scene where Bond emerges from the Fonte Gaia, 1,000 extras were hired, according to the film's production diary on the M16 website. Bill Dawes of *FX Guide* also reveals that a full-scale replica of the hotel building's exterior was used for the exploding segment in which Bond and Camille escape in South America.

Yet efforts were made to "green" this film production. Although six Aston Martins were destroyed during the making of *Quantum of Solace*, the film also featured environmentally friendly Ford Motor Company cars: A Ford Ka electric vehicle (EV), which seems to be electrically powered, and a fleet of Ford Edge Fuel-Cell EVs. The film also relied heavily on CGI, with over nine hundred visual effects shots stirring up adventure, according to a *VFX World* interview recorded by Bill Desowitz. Like other

James Bond films, *Quantum of Solace* was produced at Pinewood Studios, whose carbon footprint was recently evaluated by RPS Group to support its plan to build a "1400 unit residential development—that also doubles as a giant 15-location film set for Pinewood Studios." The assessment report suggests that between 60 percent and 90 percent reductions of greenhouse gas emissions may be possible if the development is approved, and using "streetscapes for filming will achieve a 44% annual reduction over business-as-usual location shooting abroad."

These changes to the studio seemed to bode well for future James Bond productions until the carbon footprint–heavy *Skyfall* (2012), but other action-adventure films have more successfully implemented "green" production practices. With a budget of $90 million, *Sherlock Holmes: A Game of Shadows* (2011), for example, "exemplifies eco-friendly filmmaking," according to Gerri Miller of the *Mother Nature Network* and still has already grossed $543 million. Because the film was part of Warner Brothers' Green Initiative, the studio brought in Greenshoot as a consultant to "assist the production in lowering the carbon footprint [of the film] and to help implement more sustainable production practices in conjunction with and to complement the Green initiatives already set out by Warner Bros" ("Sustainability"). According to coproducer Lauren Meek, "Construction set waste and food waste were key issues for us" (quoted in Miller). As Meek explains, "We diverted 756 tons of film waste from landfills with a recovery rate of 98.6 percent which was a zero landfill achievement. We saved 2500 tons of CO^2 from being emitted by using Greenshoot and adopting green practices throughout the production, and saved money through Greenshoot's services into the productions" (quoted in Miller). Some of this was achieved by making the film digitally, but "visual effects enabled the production to cut down on travel and shoot everything in England, except for a few establishing shots" (Miller).

Warner Bros. Pictures, the studio that brought us both *Sherlock Holmes: Game of Shadows* and *Harry Potter and the Deathly Hallows: Part II* (2011), has made an effort to maintain carbon neutrality and nurture conservation initiatives on its movie productions. According to its website, "all Warner Bros. Pictures Productions use a carbon calculator to measure their footprint and inform future green production initiatives." It notes the success of the 2005 film *Syriana* and 2010's New Line Cinema film

Valentine's Day as films that have "implemented numerous sustainable practices, including a first-of-its kind hybrid base camp utilizing solar power and bio-diesel-fueled generators; reusable water bottles, to eliminate the use of single-use plastic water bottles; clean-air vehicles, for both talent and equipment transportation; recycling and composting efforts; and biodegradable food ware." According to the site, eight of the studio's last twenty-five films were carbon neutral, including *Due Date* (2010), *Flipped* (2010), *Green Lantern* (2011), *Inception* (2010), *The Town* (2010), and *Sherlock Holmes: A Game of Shadows*. Warner Bros.' animated films also lessen their carbon footprint (as well as their production costs) by implementing digital cinematography and distribution.

Other studios have made the move to digital cinematography for their live-action films, such as Paramount Pictures' *Hugo* (2011), or live-action/animated films, such as Twentieth-Century Fox's *Avatar* (2009). Since 2007 sales of film cameras have rapidly declined, and all new cinema cameras introduced since 2007 are digital, a change that contributed to Eastman Kodak's bankruptcy in January 2012. The success of this move to digital is demonstrated by the preponderance of digital films winning the Academy Award for Cinematography. *Slumdog Millionaire* (2009) and *Avatar*'s digital production is regarded by most as a large step toward "greening" Hollywood, a move that has not negatively affected either film's profits.

The success of digital blockbusters creates an even more inviting atmosphere for digital filmmaking and video digital projection. The ultimate goal is that all theatrical projectors will be digital video. This goal of transforming all theaters to digital projection will mean the end of using film in the production process. Computer-generated video production and exhibition, like that used for *Hugo* and *Avatar*, ends the chemical links of producing film prints, eliminates the need to create and deliver thousands of prints for exhibition, and obviates the need to destroy the prints after their theatrical runs. This transformation also means millions of dollars will be saved on every major release, while also substantially reducing the carbon footprint that creating, delivering, and exhibiting films has caused since their invention in the late nineteenth century. In *Greening the Media*, Richard Maxwell and Toby Miller provide a detailed description of the environmental destruction associated with celluloid film (71–75).

As we write, the rapid technological changeover from film to digital projection is reaching high speed. As Nick Leiber of *Bloomberg Business-week* explains, "To induce exhibitors to purchase the equipment, celluloid prints of new movies from majors will no longer be available in the U.S. by the end of 2013, according to John Fithian, president of the National Association of Theater Owners" (53). According to Leiber, "about 26,000 of the 40,0000 screens in the U.S. have already converted" to digital (54). The conversion to digital eliminates production of celluloid, chemical processing, and the physical delivery of thousands of film prints per major feature release. This "greening" of film production distribution and exhibition had been jump-started by the success of digital films and 3-D blockbusters such as *Harry Potter and the Deathly Hallows: Part II* (1.3 billion in worldwide ticket sales) and *Avatar* (2.75 billion in worldwide ticket sales). Since 3-D is now a major theatrical draw for audiences, theaters have been forced to adapt quickly by phasing in digital projection at a far faster rate than previously anticipated. IMAX theaters, for example, have completely transitioned to digital projection. A majority of theaters worldwide will soon be projecting feature films digitally, now that box office potential for 3-D has become a financial reality.

This success now forces far greater beneficial environmental results throughout the whole process of filmmaking and film viewing. The digital age may reduce the carbon footprint of film companies in major ways that are still being calculated. As Maxwell and Miller suggest, "the question is whether the digital transition will make motion pictures less ecologically destructive" despite their high energy use and toxic-waste production, especially if home viewing screens are included (75). With studio practices becoming more environmentally sound and environmental messages becoming more audience friendly, however, digital films like *Sherlock Holmes: A Game of Shadows* can reach worldwide audiences, serving audiences with a potentially lighter carbon footprint. In fact, as Gendy Alimurang states in an April 12, 2012, *Los Angeles Weekly* piece, studios "no longer want to physically print and ship movies" because it costs only $150 for a digital copy, rather than the $1,500.00 per print times four thousand theaters for 35mm film. Although, as Alimurang suggests, the shift to digital will have negative consequences for independent theaters, projectionist jobs, and classic film distribution, it may also help "green" the movie business.

But these changes also beg a final question: How green is the theater experience? The changeover to total digital production in both the film-making process and the delivery and projection of film may create a new manufacturing paradigm that is greener than the nineteenth-century model being phased out. But the final third leg of the nineteenth-century model still exists: the theater, which is dependent on enormous energy expenditures to entertain and inform mass audiences in locations that usually average 300–1,200 seats per screen, not to mention the enormous amount of energy used to get people from home to theater and back. Light-ing, heating, and cooling these multiplexes (numbering approximately 35,000 screens in the United States in 2012) is seen as an economically feasible expenditure. Spending billions of dollars alone to transition theaters worldwide to digital projection means the industry calculates that the mass consumption of films will continue well into the future.

Digital filmmaking does make it possible to produce the low-budget independent films we explore in this book. The digital cinematography used in the powerful anti–mountaintop removal mining films of B. J. Gudmundsson and the humorous call to address climate change found in Jon Cooksey's *How to Boil a Frog* lower their budgets, making them more financially feasible to produce and distribute. Even larger-budget documentaries such as *The Last Mountain* and *Blue Vinyl* lower production costs using digital filmmaking processes. Technologies such as digital cameras and computer-generated editing for both image and sound have made the whole process of filmmaking truly democratic.

Yet making those films accessible to a wider audience creates other economic and financial problems. *New York Times* reporter Nancy Ramsey highlights the hidden costs of documentaries in her exploration of Jona-than Caouette's distribution experience with *Tarnation* (2003). Although the film cost as little as $218 to make, once it gained distribution, costs exceeded $500,000, with rights to the music included in the film ac-counting for $230,000 of the total. The difficulty of attaining distribution also limits low-budget documentaries' accessibility. Peter Judson's *Nobody Wants Your Film* (2005) provides a sometimes comic perspective on the problems that director Alexandre Rockwell and writer Brandon Cole face when attempting to market their film, *Thirteen Moons*. *Nobody Wants Your Film* collects and augments footage shot on the set of *Thirteen Moons*, as well as a series of interviews with cast and crew members and e-mails between Rockwell and possible distributors to provide a semifictionalized story of the difficulties of gaining distribution, illustrating the problem that many of the filmmakers explored here face when their films are available only through a small distributor's website.

Of the twelve mountaintop removal mining films we watched, for example, only two gained a wide release: *Coal Country*, as a regional festival favorite, was broadcast on PBS in the fall of 2009, perhaps because it was directed by Mari-Lynn Evans and Phylis Geller, the filmmakers who brought *The Appalachians* to PBS in 2005. With Robert F. Kennedy Jr. at its center, Bill Haney's *The Last Mountain* acquired a limited theatrical release after premiering at the Sundance and Seattle Film Festivals. Another documentary examining mountaintop removal mining, *On Coal River* (2010), is becoming a festival favorite like *Coal Country* and *The Last Mountain*, but it has chosen a different distribution route: iTunes. The film is available as a DVD for schools, libraries, and universities, but individual films are available only through the iTunes library. Even though only two of these films have found limited distribution success, however, all twelve draw on the experiences of nearly the same anti-MTR activists, including Maria Gunnoe, Joe Lovett, and especially (before her death) Julia (Judy) Bonds. They also all highlight MTR incidents primarily in and near Boone County, West Virginia, even though other parts of Appalachia are suffering the results of MTR, including Kentucky, Virginia, Tennessee, and other counties in West Virginia.

Which brings us back to the original question: can the film industry and environmental movements mix? With cautious optimism, we can give only a qualified "yes" to the new attempts because of the enormous energy expenditures used to create film and the yet-uncalculated waste levels associated with its distribution and exhibition. Hollywood film studios are making the move to "green," partly because of economic issues, partly because of California's environmental laws, which regulate greenhouse gas emissions more stringently than the federal government, and partly because Hollywood film stars from George Clooney to Leonardo DiCaprio demand it. As the Warner Brothers website declares, "It takes creativity to entertain the world while conserving resources on our planet." Although some succeed more than others, the films we explore in *Film and Everyday Eco-disasters* attempt to do both.

FILMOGRAPHY

Abuela Grillo. Dir. Denis Chapon. Perf. Luzmila Carpio. Bolivia, 2009. YouTube.

Anchors Aweigh. Dir. George Sidney. Perf. Frank Sinatra, Kathryn Grayson, Gene Kelly. MGM, 1945. DVD.

Animals. Dir. Jason Young. National Film Board of Canada, 2003. DVD.

The Appalachians. Dir. Phylis Geller. Evening Star Productions, 2005. DVD.

Arthur. Dir. Jason Winer. Perf. Russell Brand, Helen Mirren, Jennifer Garner. Warner Brothers, 2011. DVD.

Atomic Café. Dir. Jayne Loader, Kevin Rafferty, and Pierce Rafferty. The Archives Project, 1982. DVD.

Avatar. Dir. James Cameron. Perf. Sam Worthington, Zoe Saldana. Twentieth Century Fox, 2009.

Bacon: The Film. Dir. Hugo Latulippe. National Film Board of Canada, 2002. DVD.

The Ballad of Cable Hogue. Dir. Sam Peckinpah. Perf. Jason Robards, Stella Stevens, David Warner. Warner Brothers, 1970. DVD.

Battle: Los Angeles. Dir. Jonathan Liebesman. Perf. Aaron Eckhart, Michelle Rodriguez. Columbia, 2011. Film.

Baytar Environmental Clothing Industry. Dir. Allie Taylor. 2010. YouTube.

Beef, Inc. Dir. Carmen Garcia. National Film Board of Canada, 1999. DVD.

Black Diamonds: Mountaintop Removal & the Fight for Coalfield Justice. Dir. Catherine Pancake. Bullfrog Films, 2006. DVD.

Black Wave: The Legacy of the Exxon Valdez. Dir. Robert Cornellier. Macumba DOC, 2009. DVD.

Blood of the Beasts. Dir. Georges Franju. The Criterion Collection, 1949 (2004). DVD.

Blue Gold: World Water Wars. Dir. Sam Bozzo. Purple Turtle Films, 2008. DVD.

Blue Vinyl: The World's First Toxic Comedy. Dir. Daniel B. Gold and Judith Helfand. Perf. William Baggett. Docurama Films, 2002. DVD.

Burning the Future: Coal in America. Dir. David Novack. Firefly Pix, 2008. DVD.

Chang: A Drama of the Wilderness. Dir. Merian C. Cooper and Ernest B. Schoedsack. Paramount, 1927. DVD.

China Blue. Dir. Micha X. Peled. Teddy Bear Films, 2005. DVD.

Chinatown. Dir. Roman Polanski. Perf. Jack Nicholson, Faye Dunaway, John Huston. Paramount Pictures, 1974. DVD.

A Civil Action. Dir. Steven Zaillian. Perf. John Travolta, Robert Duvall, Kathleen Quinlan. Touchstone Pictures, 1998. DVD.

Coal Country. Dir. Phylis Geller. Alliance for Appalachia, 2009. DVD.

The Corporation. Dir. Mark Achbar, Jennifer Abbott. Big Picture Media Corporation, 2003. DVD.

Cotton Road. Dir. Laura Kissel and Li Zhen. 2013. DVD.

The Cove. Dir. Louie Psihoyos. Perf. Richard O'Barry. Lionsgate, 2009. DVD.

Crude. Dir. Joe Berlinger. Entendre, 2009. DVD.

Dark Days. Dir. Marc Singer. Palm Pictures, 2000. DVD.

Darwin's Nightmare. Dir. Hubert Sauper. International Film Circuit, 2004. DVD.

The Day after Tomorrow. Dir. Roland Emmerich. Perf. Dennis Quaid, Jake Gyllenhaal, Emmy Rossum. Twentieth Century Fox, 2004. DVD.

Dead Ahead: The Exxon Valdez Disaster. Dir. Paul Seed. HBO, 1992. VHS.

The Devil Wears Prada. Dir. David Frankel. Perf. Anne Hathaway, Meryl Streep. Fox 2000 Films, 2006. DVD.

Due Date. Dir. Todd Phillips. Perf. Robert Downey Jr., Zach Galifianakis, Michelle Monaghan. Warner Brothers, 2010. DVD.

Earth. Dir. Alastair Fothergill and Mark Linfield. Disneynature, 2007. DVD.

Easter Parade. Dir. Charles Walters. Perf. Judy Garland, Fred Astaire. MGM, 1948. DVD.

The End of the Line. Dir. Rupert Murray. Arcane Pictures, 2009. DVD.

Erin Brockovich. Dir. Steven Soderbergh. Perf. Julia Roberts, Albert Finney. Universal, 2000. DVD.

Even the Rain (También la lluvia). Dir. Icíar Bollaín. Perf. Gael García Bernal, Luis Tosar, Karra Elejalde. AXN, 2010. DVD.

Farmingville. Dir. Carlos Sandoval. Camino Bluff Productions, 2004. DVD.

Flipped. Dir. Rob Reiner. Perf. Madeline Carroll, Callan McAuliffe, Rebecca De Mornay. Castle Rock, 2010. DVD.

Flow: For Love of Water. Dir. Irena Salina. Group Entertainment, 2008. DVD.

Food, Inc. Dir. Robert Kenner. Magnolia Pictures, 2008. DVD.

Friends with Benefits. Dir. Will Gluck. Perf. Justin Timberlake, Mila Kunis. Sony Pictures, 2011. DVD.

Gasland. Dir. Josh Fox. HBO Documentary Films, 2010. DVD.

Gomorra. Dir. Matteo Garrone. Perf. Salvatore Abruzzese, Simone Sacchettino, Gianfelice Imparato. Fandango, 2008. DVD.

The Grapes of Wrath. Dir. John Ford. Perf. Henry Fonda, Jane Darwell, John Carradine. Twentieth Century Fox Films, 1940. DVD.

Grass. Dir. Merian C. Cooper and Ernest B. Schoedsack. Paramount, 1925. DVD.

Green Lantern. Dir. Martin Campbell. Perf. Ryan Reynolds, Blake Lively, Peter Sarsgaard. Warner Brothers, 2011. DVD.

Happy Feet Two. Dir. George Miller. Perf. Elijah Wood, Robin Williams, Pink. Warner Brothers, 2011. DVD.

Harry Potter and the Deathly Hallows: Part II. Dir. David Yates. Perf. Daniel Radcliffe, Emma Watson. Warner Bros. Pictures, 2011. DVD.

The Help. Dir. Tate Taylor. Perf. Emma Stone, Viola Davis. DreamWorks SKG, 2011. DVD.

The History of Ready Meals. BBC Four, 2009. DVD.

A Home of Our Own. Dir. Tony Bill. Perf. Kathy Bates, Edward Furlong. MGM, 1993. DVD.

Housekeeping. Dir. Bill Forsyth. Perf. Christine Lahti, Sara Walker. Columbia Pictures, 1987. DVD.

How Green Was My Valley. Dir. John Ford. Perf. Walter Pidgeon, Maureen O'Hara, Anna Lee. Twentieth Century Fox, 1941. DVD.

How to Boil a Frog. Dir. Jon Cooksey. Perf. Jon Cooksey. Fools Bay Entertainment, 2009. DVD.

Hugo. Dir. Martin Scorsese. Perf. Ben Kingsley, Asa Butterfield. Paramount Pictures, 2011. DVD.

Imitation of Life. Dir. John M. Stahl. Perf. Claudette Colbert, Warren William, Rochelle Hudson. Universal, 1934. DVD.

Imitation of Life. Dir. Douglas Sirk. Perf. Lana Turner, John Gavin, Sandra Dee, Susan Kohner. Universal, 1959. DVD.

Inception. Dir. Christopher Nolan. Perf. Leonardo DiCaprio, Joseph Gordon-Levitt, Ellen Page. Warner Brothers, 2010. DVD.

An Inconvenient Truth. Dir. Davis Guggenheim. Perf. Al Gore. Paramount Classics, 2006. DVD.

It Happened on Fifth Avenue. Dir. Roy Del Ruth. Perf. Don DeFore, Ann Harding, Charles Ruggles. Roy Del Ruth Productions, 1947. DVD.

Keeper of the Mountains. Dir. B. J. Gudmundsson. Patchwork Films, 2006. DVD.

King Corn. Dir. Aaron Woolf. Mosaic Films, 2007. DVD.

The Last Mountain. Dir. Bill Haney. Perf. Susan Bird, Don Blankenship, Ron Burris, Robert Kennedy Jr. Massachusetts Documentary Productions, 2011. DVD.

The Last Train Home. Dir. Lixin Fan. Perf. Changhua Zhan, Yang Zhang, Sugin Chen. Canada Council for the Arts, 2009. DVD.

Libby, Montana. Dir. Durry Gunn Carr. High Plains Films, 2004. DVD.

Life and Debt. Dir. Stephanie Black. Perf. Belinda Becker, Buju Banton, Horst Kohler. Tuff Gong Pictures, 2001. DVD.

Live-In Maid. Dir. Jorge Gaggero. Perf. Norma Aleandro, Norma Argentina. Aquafilms, 2004. DVD.

The Living Daylights. Dir. John Glen. Perf. Timothy Dalton, Maryam d'Abo. United Artists, 1987. DVD.

Look What They've Done. Dir. B. J. Gudmundsson. Patchwork Films, 2006. DVD.

Louisiana Story. Dir. Robert Flaherty. Robert Flaherty Productions, 1948. DVD.

The Maid. Dir. Sebastian Silva. Perf. Catalina Saavedra, Claudia Celedon, Mariana Loyola. Forastero Films, 2009. DVD.

Make Way for Tomorrow. Dir. Leo McCarey. Perf. Victory Moore, Beulah Bondi. Paramount Pictures, 1937. DVD.

Man of Aran. Dir. Robert J. Flaherty. Gainsborough Pictures, 1934. DVD.

Man with a Movie Camera. Dir. Dziga Vertov. VUFKU, 1929. DVD.

Maquilapolis: City of Factories. Dir. Vicky Funari, Sergio de la Torre. California Newsreel, 2006. DVD.

Mardi Gras: Made in China. Dir. David Redmon. Carnivalesque Films, 2005. DVD.

Meat. Dir. Frederick Wiseman. PBS, 1976. DVD.

Milk of Sorrow. Dir. Claudia Llosa. Perf. Magaly Solier, Susi Sanchez. Olive Films, 2009. DVD.

Moana. Dir. Robert J. Flaherty. Famous Players-Lasky Productions, 1926. DVD.

The Molly Maguires. Dir. Martin Ritt. Perf. Sean Connery, Richard Harris, Samantha Egger. Paramount, 1970. DVD.

Money Pit. Dir. Richard Benjamin. Perf. Tom Hanks, Shelley Long. Amblin Entertainment, 1986. DVD.

Mountain Mourning. Dir. B. J. Gudmundsson. Patchwork Films, 2006. DVD.

Mountain Top Removal. Dir. Michael Cusack O'Connell. The Group Entertainment, 2007. DVD.

Mr. Blandings Builds His Dream House. Dir. H. C. Potter. Perf. Cary Grant, Myrna Loy. RKO Radio Pictures,1948. DVD.

Nanook of the North. Dir. Robert J. Flaherty. Les Freres Revillon, 1922. DVD.

No Blade of Grass. Dir. Cornel Wilde. Perf. Nigel Davenport, Jean Wallace, John Hamill. Theodora Productions, 1970. VHS.

Nobody Wants Your Film. Dir. Peter Judson. Perf. Alexandre Rockwell, Brandon Cole. NWYF, 2005. DVD.

Norma Rae. Dir. Martin Ritt. Perf. Sally Field, Beau Bridges, Ron Leibman. Twentieth Century Fox, 1979. DVD.

Northfork. Dir. Michael Polish. Perf. Duel Farnes, James Woods, Nick Nolte, Daryl Hannah. Paramount, 2003. DVD.

The Oblongs. Creators: Angus Oblong and Jace Richdale. Perf. Pamela Adlon, Will Ferrell, Jean Smart. Akom Production Company, 2001–2. DVD.

Ocean. Dir. Jacques Perrin and Jacques Cluzaud. Disneynature, 2009. DVD.

On Coal River. Dir. Francine Cavenaugh. 7 Spencer Productions. 2010. iTunes.

On the Town. Dir., Stanley Donen. Perf. Gene Kelly, Frank Sinatra, Betty Garrett. MGM, 1949. DVD.

Our Daily Bread. Dir. King Vidor. Perf. Karen Morley, Tom Keene, Barbara Pepper. United Artists, 1934. DVD.

Our Daily Bread. Dir. Nikolaus Geyrhalter. Nikolaus Geyrhalter Filmproduktion, 2005. DVD.

Our Man Flint. Dir. Daniel Mann. Perf. James Coburn, Lee J. Cobb, Gila Golan. Twentieth Century Fox, 1966. DVD.

The Pajama Game. Dir. George Abbott. Perf. Doris Day, John Raitt, Carol Haney. Warner Brothers, 1957. DVD.

The Plow That Broke the Plains. Dir. Pare Lorenz. Resettlement Administration, 1936. DVD.

Quantum of Solace. Dir. Marc Forster. Perf. Daniel Craig, Olga Kurylenko. MGM, 2008. DVD.

A Raisin in the Sun. Dir. Daniel Petrie. Perf. Sidney Poitier, Claudia, McNeil, Ruby Dee. Columbia, 1961. DVD.

A Raisin in the Sun. Dir. Bill Duke. Perf. Starletta DuPois, Lou Ferguson. Monterey Home Video,1989. VHS.

A Raisin in the Sun. Dir. Kenny Leon. Perf. Sean Combs, Sanaa Lathan. Sony Pictures Television, 2008. DVD.

Rango. Dir. Gore Verbinski. Perf. Johnny Depp, Isla Fisher. Paramount Pictures, 2011. Film.

Razing Appalachia. Dir. Sasha Waters. 2002. DVD.

Ready to Wear. Dir. Robert Altman. Perf. Sophia Loren, Julia Roberts, Marcello Mastroianni. Miramax Films, 1994. DVD.

The Real Dirt on Farmer John. Dir. Taggart Siegel. KAVU Releasing, 2005. DVD.

Red Desert. Dir. Michelangelo Antonioni. Perf. Monica Vitti, Richard Harris, Carlo Chionetti. Film Duemila, 1964. DVD.

Red River. Dir. Howard Hawks. Perf. John Wayne. United Artists, 1948. DVD.

Repas de Bebe. Dir. Louis Lumière. Lumière, 1895. DVD.

Rise Up! West Virginia. Dir. B. J. Gudmundsson. Patchwork Films, 2007. DVD.

The Road to Wellville. Dir. Alan Parker. Perf. Anthony Hopkins, Bridget Fonda, Matthew Broderick. Columbia Pictures, 1994. DVD.

The Road Warrior. Dir. George Miller. Perf. Mel Gibson, Bruce Spence, Michael Preston. Kennedy Miller Productions, 1981. DVD.

Safe. Dir. Todd Haynes. Perf. Julianne Moore, Xander Berkeley, Dean Norris. American Playhouse Theatrical Films, 1995. VHS.

Sex and the City. Dir. Michael Patrick King. Perf. Sarah Jessica Parker, Kim Cattrall. New Line Cinema, 2008. DVD.

Sex and the City 2. Dir. Michael Patrick King. Perf. Sarah Jessica Parker, Kim Cattrall. New Line Cinema, 2010. DVD.

Sherlock Holmes: A Game of Shadows. Dir. Guy Ritchie. Perf. Robert Downey Jr., Jude Law. Warner Bros. Pictures, 2011. DVD.

Silent Running. Dir. Douglas Trumbull. Perf. Bruce Dern, Cliff Potts, Ron Rifkin. Universal Pictures, 1972. DVD.

Sin Nombre. Dir. Cary Joji Fukunaga. Perf. Marco Antonio Aguirre, Paulina Gaitan. Scion Films, 2009. DVD.

Skyfall. Dir. Sam Mendes. Perf. Daniel Craig, Judi Dench, Javier Bardem. MGM, 2012. Film.

Slumdog Millionaire. Dir. Danny Boyle, Loveleen Tandan. Perf. Dev Patel, Saurabh Shukla, Anil Kapoor. Celador Films, 2008. DVD.

Soylent Green. Dir. Richard Fleicher. Perf. Charlton Heston, Edward G. Robinson, Leigh Taylor-Young. MGM, 1973. DVD.

Supersize Me. Dir. Morgan Spurlock. Kathbur Pictures, 2004. DVD.

Sweetgrass. Dir. Ilisa Barbash. Harvard Sensory Ethnography Lab, 2009. DVD.

Syriana. Dir. Stephen Gaghan. Perf. George Clooney, Matt Damon, Amanda Peet. Warner Brothers, 2005. DVD.

Tapped. Dir. Stephanie Soechtig, Jason Lindsey. Atlas Films, 2009. DVD.

Tarnation. Dir. Jonathan Caouette. Wellspring Media, 2003. DVD.

Thread: A Documentary. Dir. Michele Vey. Tree Media, 2013. DVD.

Thunder Bay. Dir. Anthony Mann. Universal, 1953. DVD.

The Town. Dir. Ben Affleck. Perf. Ben Affleck, Rebecca Hall, Jon Hamm. Warner Brothers, 2010. DVD.

Total Recall. Dir. Paul Verhoeven. Perf. Arnold Schwarzenegger, Sharon Stone, Michael Ironside. Carlco International N.V., 1990. DVD.

Treme. Dir. Eric Overmyer. Perf. Khanki Alexander, Rob Brown. HBO, 2010. DVD.

Trouble the Water. Dir. Carl Deal. Elsewhere Films, 2008. DVD.

T-Shirt Travels. Dir. Shantha Bloeman. Perf. Ishmael Patel. PBS Independent Lens, 2001. DVD.

A View to a Kill. Dir. John Glen. Perf. Roger Moore, Christopher Walken, Tanya Roberts. MGM, 1985. DVD.

A Visit to Peek Frean and Co.'s Biscuit Works. Cricks and Martin Films, 1906. DVD.

WALL-E. Dir. Andrew Stanton. Perf. Ben Burtt, Elissa Knight, Jeff Garlin. Disney, 2008. DVD.

War Horse. Dir. Steven Spielberg. Perf. Jeremy Irvine, Emily Watson. Dreamworks SKG. DVD.

Water Wars. Dir. Jim Burroughs. Cinema Libre Studio, 2009. DVD.

We Feed the World. Dir. Erwin Wagenhofer. Allegro Film, 2005. DVD.

When the Clouds Roll By. Dir. Victor Fleming. Perf. Douglas Fairbanks, Kathleen Clifford. Douglas Fairbanks Pictures, 1919. DVD.

When the Levees Broke: A Requiem in Four Acts. Dir. Spike Lee. 40 Acres and a Mule Filmworks and HBO, 2006. DVD.

Which Way Home. Dir. Rebecca Cammisa. HBO Documentaries, 2009. DVD

The World according to Monsanto. Dir. Marie-Monique Robin. Image et Compagnie, 2008. DVD.

The World Is Not Enough. Dir. Michael Apted. Perf. Pierce Brosnan, Sophie Marceau, Robert Carlyle. MGM, 1999. DVD.

WORKS CITED

A.W. "*Thunder Bay* Shown at State on New Wide, Curved Screen." *New York Times* 21 May 1953. Web.

Ackerman, Frank and Massey, Rachel. "The Economics of Phasing Out PVC." *Healthy Building.net.* Dec. 2003.Web. 1 Jan. 2012.

Alimurang, Gendy. "Movie Studios Are Forcing Hollywood to Abandon 35 Millimeter Film." *Los Angeles Weekly* 12 Apr. 2012. Web. 21 Dec. 2012.

Al-Sharrah, G. K., et al. "Planning an Integrated Petrochemical Industry with an Environmental Objective." *Industrial Engineering Chemical Research* 40.9 (2001). Web. 20 Oct. 2011.

Allen, David T. "Chapter 14. *Industrial Ecology.*" www.epa.gov. 2002. Web. 10 Oct. 2011.

Anderson, Alison. *Media, Culture, and the Environment.* New Brunswick NJ: Rutgers University Press, 1997. Print.

Anderson, John. "Food, Inc." *Variety* 11 Sept. 2008. Web. 3 June 2009.

Anderson, Terry Lee and Snyder, Pamela. *Water Markets: Priming the Invisible Pumps.* Washington DC: Cato Institute, 1997. Print.

Atkinson, Michael. "Painted Wasteland: Antonioni's *Red Desert* at BAM." *Village Voice* 31 Aug. 2011. Web. 27 Dec. 2011.

Atwater, Deborah F. "Senator Barack Obama: The Rhetoric of Hope and the American Dream." *Journal of Black Studies* 38.2 (November 2007): 121–29. Print.

Bailey, Ronald. "The Law of Increasing Returns." *New York Salon* 13 Feb. 2007. Web. 2 Oct. 2011.

Barlow, Maude and Clarke, Tony. *Blue Gold: The Fight to Stop the Corporate Theft of the World's Water.* New York: New York Press, 2002. Print.

Basinger, Jeanine. *Anthony Mann*. Middleton CT: Wesleyan University Press, 2007. Print.

"*Battle: Los Angeles* Production Notes." *Cinemareview.com*. 2011. Web. 2 June 2011.

Bennet, Michael Dana, and David W. Teague, eds. *The Nature of Cities: Ecocriticism and Urban Environments*. Tucson: University of Arizona Press, 1999. Print.

Benson, Thomas W., and Brian J. Snee. *The Rhetoric of the New Political Documentary*. Carbondale: Southern Illinois Press, 2008. Print.

"*Blue Vinyl* Review." *Philadelphia City Paper* 2 May 2002. Web. 14 Oct. 2011.

"Bolivia: Celebrating Community Management of Water in Cochabamba." *E-Source.com*. 9 May 2011. Web. 12 June 2011.

Bolston, Homes, III. "Environmental Ethics." *The Blackwell Companion to Philosophy*. 2nd ed. Oxford: Blackwell, 2003. 517–29. Print.

Bourne, Joel K., Jr. "The Deep Dilemma." *National Geographic* October 2010: 40–53. Print.

Bouse, Derek. *Wildlife Films*. Philadelphia: University of Pennsylvania Press, 2000. Print.

Brody, Richard. "Getting Wasted." *New Yorker* 14 June 2010. Web. 27 Dec. 2011.

Bullard, Robert D. "Waste and Racism: A Stacked Deck?" *Forum for Applied Research and Public Policy*. Spring 1993. 29–35. Print.

Burns, Shirley Stewart. *Bringing Down the Mountains: The Impact of Mountaintop Removal Surface Coal Mining on Southern West Virginia Communities, 1970–2004*. Morgantown: West Virginia University Press, 2007. Print.

Calder-Marshall, Arthur. *The Innocent Eye: The Life of Robert J. Flaherty*. London: W. H. Allen, 1963. Print.

Callicott, J. Baird. "Animal Liberation and Environmental Ethics: Back Together Again." *The Animal Rights/Environmental Ethics Debate: The Environmental Perspective*. Ed. Eugene C. Hargrove. Albany: SUNY Press, 1992. 249–61. Print.

Canby, Vincent. "Norma Rae: Mill-Town Story; Unionism in the South." *New York Times* 2 Mar. 1979. Web. 3 Aug. 2011.

Carmichael, Deborah A., ed. *The Landscape of the Hollywood Western: Ecocriticism in an American Film Genre*. Salt Lake City: University of Utah Press, 2006. Print.

Center for Health, Environment, and Justice. *Louisiana*. Summer 2010. Web. 16 Oct. 2011.

Chang, Justin. "*The Cove.*" *Variety* 30 Jan. 2009. Web. 3 June 2011.

Christley, Jaime N. "*Red Desert* Review." *Slant Magazine* 29 Aug. 2011. Web. 27 Dec. 2011.

Cifuentes, Enrique, and Howard Frumkin. "Environmental Injustice: Case Studies from the South." *Environmental Research Letters* 2 (2007): 1–9. Print.

Clarke, Robert. *Ellen Swallow: The Woman Who Founded Ecology*. Chicago: Follett, 1973. Print.

Claudio, Luz. "Waste Couture: Environmental Impact of the Clothing Industry." *Environmental Health Perspectives* 1 Sept. 2007. Web. 3 July 2011.

"Climate Change and Air Quality." *Our Nation's Air: Status and Trends through 2010*. Research Triangle Park NC: Environmental Protection Association, Feb. 2012. 22–24. Print.

Clover, Joshua. "Cinema for a New Grand Game." *Film Quarterly* 62.4 (Summer 2009): 6–9. Print.

Corliss, Richard. "*Ready to Wear* Review." Time.com. 20 Dec. 1994. Web. 31 May 2011.

Crowther, Bosley. "*Louisiana Story*: A Flaherty Film about a Boy in the Bayou Country, at the Sutton." *New York Times* 29 Sept. 1948. Web. 1 Jan. 2012.

Cubitt, Sean. *Eco-Media*. Amsterdam: Rodopi Press, 2005. Print.

Danko, Sheila. "Indoor Ecology: Designing Health and Wellness into the Workplace. *Human Ecology* 19.1 (Fall 1990): 2–7. Print.

Dargis, Manohla. "*Happy Feet 2*: A Search for Self-Discovery, Two Left Feet and All." *New York Times* 17 Nov. 2011. Web. 23 Nov. 2011.

———. "*Our Daily Bread* Review." *New York Times* 24 Nov. 2006. Web. 1 June 2011.

"*Darwin's Nightmare* Production Notes." *International Film Circuit and Celluloid Dreams* 2004. Web. 3 June 2011.

Davies, Sam. "Film Review: *Gasland.*" *Sight and Sound* Feb. 2011. Web. 31 May 2011.

Dawes, Bill. "Back into Bondage." *FX Guide* 16 Nov. 2008. Web. 7 Jan. 2012.

Dawn, Randee. "Quantum Is Marc Forster's 007 Art Film." *Hollywood Reporter* 11 Nov. 2008. Web. 3 Jan. 2012.

"Deepwater Horizon." *Transocean Ltd.* Aug. 2010. Web. 2010.

Denby, David. "Candid Cameras: Three New Documentaries." New Yorker 6 Mar. 2006. Web. 20 Mar. 2010.

————. "*The Help* Review." *New Yorker* 8 Aug. 2011. Web. 3 Sept. 2011.

Desowitz, Bill. "MK12 Has a Blast with Quantum Main Titles." *Animation World Network* 16 Jan. 2009. Web. 3 Sept. 2011.

Donohew, Zachary. "Property Rights and Western United States Water Markets."
Australian Journal of Agricultural and Resource Economics 53 (2009): 85–103. Print.

Durodie, Bill. "*Blue Vinyl* Review." *Culture Wars* Jan. 2003. Web. 8 Oct. 2011.

Ebert, Roger. "*The End of the Line* Review." *RogerEbert.com.* 15 July 2009. Web. 5 June 2010.

————. "Food, Inc." *Chicago Sun Times* 17 June 2009. Web. 30 June 2009.

————. "*Quantum of Solace*: A Q Only in Quantum." *RogerEbert.com.* 12 Nov. 2008. Web. 12 June 2011.

————. "*Rango* Review." *RogerEbert.com.* 2 Mar. 2011. Web. 19 Sept. 2013.

————. "*Ready to Wear* Review." *RogerEbert.com.* 25 Dec. 1994. Web. 31 May 2011.

————. "*Safe* Review." *RogerEbert.com.* 28 July 1995. Web. 6 June 2011.

Elliott, Debbie. "A Love-Hate History: Oil and Fishing in the Gulf." NPR. Web. 22 July 2010.

Ellis, Curt. "Meeting King Corn: Earl Butz Was a Product of His Time." *Culinate* 19 Feb. 2008. Web. 3 June 2009.

Ellis, Jack C., and Betsy A. McLane. *A New History of Documentary Film.* New York: Continuum, 2005. Print.

"Environmental Justice Definition." *Environmental Protection Agency.* 26 Oct. 2011. Web. 26 Oct. 2011.

Evelyn, John. *Fumifugium, or the Inconvenience of the Aer and the Smoake of London Dissipated. Together with Some Remedies Humbly Proposed.* London: By His Majesties Command, 1661. Web. 21 Dec. 2011.

Ezell, John Samuel. *Innovations in Energy: The Story of Kerr-McGee.* Norman: University of Oklahoma Press, 1979. Print.

Felperin, Leslie. "Our Daily Bread." *Variety* 23 Dec. 2005. Web. 5 June 2009.

Fishman, Charles. *The Big Thirst: The Secret Life and Turbulent Future of Water*. New York: Free Press, 2011. Print.

Flaherty, Frances Hubbard. *The Odyssey of a Film-Maker: Robert Flaherty's Story*. New York: Arno Press, 1972. Print.

"Food for Thought: *We Feed the World*. *Lumière Reader* 16 Feb. 2007. Web. 5 June 2009.

Gelbspan, Ross. *Boiling Point: How Politicians, Big Oil and Coal, Journalists, and Activists Have Fueled a Climate Crisis—and What We Can Do to Avert Disaster*. New York: Basic Books, 2005.

Giroux, Henry. "*Norma Rae*: Character, Culture, and Class." *Jump Cut* 22 May 1980. Web. 2 Aug. 2011.

Gleiberman, Owen. "Food, Inc." *Entertainment Weekly* 10 June 2009. Web. 30 June 2009.

Godard, Jean-Luc. "The Night, the Eclipse, the Dawn: Godard Interviews Antonioni." *Michelangelo Antonioni's Red Desert Insert*. Criterion. 2010. Print.

Goldenberg, Suzanne. "BP Oil Spill May Be Responsible for Dolphin Deaths." *Guardian*. 4 Mar. 2011. Web. 18 Mar. 2011.

Goldsmith, David, and Robert Ries. "Biocentric Development Ethics." *Smart and Sustainable Built Environments* 18 June 2009. Web. 22 Oct. 2011, 8 Dec. 2011.

Goodwin, Neva, et al. "Externality." *The Encyclopedia of Earth*. 20 Nov. 2008. Web. 20 July 2010.

Greenberg, Paul. *Four Fish: The Future of the Last Wild Food*. New York: Penguin, 2011. Print.

Griffith, Richard. *The World of Robert Flaherty*. New York: Little Brown, 1953. Print.

Guthmann, Edward. "Even in Suburbia, No One is 'Safe.'" *San Francisco Chronicle* 28 July 1995. Web. 31 Dec. 2011.

Hageman, Andrew. "Ecocinema and Ideology: Do Ecocritics Dream of Clockwork Green?" *Ecocinema Theory and Practice*. Ed. Stephen Rust et al. New York: Routledge, 2013. 63–86. Print.

Harvey, Dennis. "China Blue." *Variety* 13 Oct. 2005. Web. 2 Aug. 2011.

———. "King Corn." *Variety* 22 Oct. 2007. Web. 3 June 2009.

Heider, Karl G. *Ethnographic Film*. Austin: University of Texas Press, 1976. Print.

Hevesi, Dennis. "Judy Bonds, 58, an Enemy of Mountaintop Coal Mining." *New York Times* 15 Jan. 2011: 24. Print.

Hochman, Jhan. *Green Cultural Studies: Nature in Film, Novel, and Theory.* Caldwell: University of Idaho Press, 1998. Print.

Hochscherf, Tobias. "Quantum of Solace." *Film and History* 39.2 (Fall 2009): 77–79. Print.

Hornaday, Ann. "Giving Yellow Journalism a Good Name." *Washington Post* 19 Oct. 2007. Web. 5 June 2009.

Howe, Desson. "*Safe* Review." *Washington Post* 4 Aug. 1995. Web. 31 Dec. 2011.

Ingram, David. *Green Screen: Environmentalism and Hollywood Cinema.* Exeter: University of Exeter Press, 2000. Print.

Jacobson, Mark Zachary. *Atmospheric Pollution: History, Science and Regulation.* Cambridge: Cambridge University Press, 2002. Print.

Jardine, Dan. "*Thunder Bay.*" *Apollo Guide Review* 1998–2008. Web. 1 Jan. 2012.

"Judge Approved $43 Million Settlement for People of Libby, Montana." *Mesothleioma News* 20 Sept. 2011. Web. 22 Oct. 2011.

Kates, Robert W., et al. "What Is Sustainable Development? Goals, Indicators, Values and Practice." *Environment: Science and Policy for Sustainable Development* 47.3: 8–21. Print.

Kempley, Rita. "Safe Review." *Washington Post* 4 Aug. 1995. Web. 31 Dec. 2011.

Kennedy, Lisa. "*The Help* Review." *Denver Post* 9 Aug. 2011. Web. 30 Sept. 2011.

King, Susan. "Crude Filmmaking: Producer of HBO's Exxon Valdez Docudrama Calls It a Black Comedy as Well as a Tragedy." *Los Angeles Times.* Web. 6 Dec. 1992.

Koehler, Robert. "Gasland." *Variety* 25 Jan. 2010. Web. 30 May 2011.

Lane, Anthony. "Soul Survivor: *Quantum of Solace.*" *New Yorker* 17 Nov. 2008. Web. 12 June 2011.

Lawn, Dan. "The Lost Frontier: A Whiff of Petroleum, and Burial by Paperwork." *Seattle Times* 24 Sept. 1989. Web. 3 June 2011.

Lease, Gary. "Introduction: Nature under Fire." *Reinventing Nature: Responses to Postmodern Deconstruction.* Washington DC: Island Press, 1995. 3–16. Print.

Lee, Nathan. "Consumption and Extinction." *New York Times* 19 June 2009. Web. 2 June 2010.

Leiber, Nick. "For Small Theaters, the Digital Future Is Dark." *Bloomberg Businessweek*. Feb. 20–26, 2012: 53–54. Print.

Leopold, Aldo. *A Sand County Almanac: And Sketches Hear and There.* London: Oxford University Press, 1949. Print.

Leydon, Joe. "We Feed the World." *Variety* 7 Nov. 2005. Web. 21 May 2009.

"Libby Site Background." *epa.gov.* 2009. Web. 22 Oct. 2011.

Lichtenfeld, Eric. *Action Speaks Louder: Violence, Spectacle, and the American Action Movie.* Middletown CT: Wesleyan University Press, 2007. Print.

"*Louisiana Story* Review." *Variety* 31 Dec. 1947. Web. 10 Aug. 2010.

MacDonald, Scott. *The Garden in the Machine: A Field Guide to Independent Films about Place.* Berkeley: University of California Press, 2001. Print.

Maxwell, Richard, and Toby Miller. *Greening the Media.* New York: Oxford University Press, 2012. Print.

Maxwell, Trevor. "Poland Spring Wins Fryeburg Battle." *Portland Press Herald.* 12 Mar. 2010. Web. 31 May 2011.

Merchant, Carolyn. *American Environmental History: An Introduction.* New York: Columbia University Press, 2007. Print.

Meyers, Robert J. "Viability of Common Law Actions for Pollution Caused Injuries and Proof of Facts." *New York Law Journal* 18 (Spring 1973). Web. 31 Dec. 2011.

Midgley, Mary. "The Mixed Community." *The Animal Rights/Environmental Ethics Debate: The Environmental Perspective.* Ed. Eugene C. Hargrove. Albany: State University of New York Press, 1992. 211–25. Print.

Miller, Gerri. "How *Sherlock Holmes: A Game of Shadows* Kept It Green on Set." *Mother Nature Network* 14 Dec. 2011. Web. 8 Jan. 2012.

Mitman, Gregg. *Reel Nature: America's Romance with Nature on Film.* Seattle: University of Washington Press, 1999. Print.

Moberg, David. "Whose Subsidy Is It, Anyway?" *In These Times* 4 June 2007. Web. 30 May 2009.

Moisi, Dominique. "More European Hope, Less American Fear." *Japanese Times Online.* 29 June 2009. Web. 12 July 2010.

"More Heartbreak for Asbestos Superfund Town Libby, Montana: Wood Chips, Tree Bark Contaminated." *New York Daily News.com.* 5 July 2011. Web. 22 Oct. 2011.

Morgenstern, Joe. "*The Help:* '60s Racism in Black and White." *Wall Street Journal* 12 Aug. 2011. Web. 30 Sept. 2011.

Morris, Gary. "Antonioni's *Red Desert.*" *Bright Lights Film Journal* 26 (Nov. 1999). Web. 27 Dec. 2011.

Murray, Noel. "*The Cove.*" *A. V. Club* 30 July 2009. Web. 20 Mar. 2010.

———. "*Darwin's Nightmare.*" *A. V. Club* 9 Nov. 2005. Web 20 Mar. 2010.

Nathan, Robert, and Jo-Ann Mort. "Remembering *Norma Rae.*" *Nation* 12 Mar. 2007: 1–4. Print.

Newton, Julianne Lutz, et al. "Land Ecology and Democracy: A Twenty-First Century View." *Politics and Life Sciences* 25.1–2 (Mar.–Sept. 2006): 42–56. Print.

Nichols, Bill. *Introduction to Documentary.* Bloomington: University of Indiana Press, 2001. Print.

"*Norma Rae* Review." *Variety.com.* 31 Dec. 1978. Web. 30 June 2011.

Null, Christopher. "*Blue Vinyl* Review." *Filmcritic.com.* 16 May 2002. Web. 8 Oct. 2011.

O'Hehir, Andrew. "Behind the Food Industry's Iron Curtain." *Salon.com.* 12 June 2009. Web. 20 June 2009.

———. "Bond and Cousteau Track the Dolphin Killers." *Salon.com.* 30 July 2009. Web. 30 Mar. 2010.

———. "Beyond the Multiplex." *Salon.com.* 11 Oct. 2007. Web. 20 Mar 2010.

———. "Rango and the Rise of Kidult-Oriented Animation." *Salon.com.* 2 Mar. 2011. Web. 1 June 2011.

"Open Statement to the Fans of *The Help.*" *Association of Black Women Historians* 28 Oct. 2011. Web. 28 Oct. 2011.

Pearce, Diana, and Jennifer Brooks. "The Self-Sufficiency Standard for Illinois." *WomenEmployed.org.* Dec. 2001. Web. 19 Dec. 2011.

Perelman, Dalia. "We Feed the World." *Bullfrog Films* 2009. Web. 2009.

Phelps, Norm. *The Longest Struggle: Animal Advocacy from Pythagoras to PETA.* New York: Lantern, 2007. Print.

Phipps, Keith. "Quantum of Solace." *The Onion A.V. Club* 13 Nov. 2008. Web. 12 June 2011.

Pinheiro, Ethel, and Cristiane Rose Duarte. "*Panem et circenses* at *Largo da Carioca,* Brazil: The Urban Diversity Focused on People-Environment Interactions." *Anthropology Matters Journal* 6.1 (2004). 19 Nov. 2006. Web. 20 Feb. 2008.

Power, Stephen, and Kris Maher. "EPA Blasted as It Revokes Mine's Permit." *Wall Street Journal* 14 Jan. 2011. Print.

Quart, Leonard. "The Intricacy and Beauty of *Red Desert*." *Dissent* 7 Oct. 2011. Web. 27 Dec. 2011.

Raglon, Rebecca, and Marion Scholtmeijer. "'Animals Are Not Believers in Ecology': Mapping Critical Differences between Environmental and Animal Advocacy Literatures." *Isle: Interdisciplinary Studies in Literature and Environment* 14.2 (2007): 121–40. Print.

Ramsey, Nancy. "The Hidden Cost of Documentaries." *New York Times* 16 Oct. 2005. Web. 7 Jan. 2012.

Richards, Ellen Swallow. *The Art of Right Living*. Boston: Whitcomb and Barrows, 1911. Print.

———. *Conservation by Sanitation*. Boston: F. H. Gilson, 1911. Print.

———. *The Cost of Cleanness*. New York: John Wiley and Sons, 1908. Print.

———. *Sanitation in Daily Life*. Boston: Whitcomb and Barrows, 1907. Print.

Richards, Ellen Swallow, and Alpheus G. Woodman. *Air, Water, and Food*. New York: Scientific Press, 1909. Print.

Rooney, David. "*Darwin's Nightmare*." *Variety* 21 Sept. 2004. Web. 20 Mar. 2010.

Ross, Benjamin, and Steven Amter. *The Polluters: The Making of Our Chemically Altered Environment*. New York: Oxford University Press, 2010. Print.

"RPS Evaluates Carbon Footprint of Iconic Film Studios." *RPS Group*. 28 Feb. 2011. Web. 6 Jan. 2012.

Rust, Stephen, Salma Monani, and Sean Cubitt, eds. *Ecocinema Theory and Practice*. New York: Routledge, 2013. Print.

Sachs, Ben. "*The Help* Review." *Chicago Reader* 11 Aug. 2011. Web. 28 Sept. 2011.

"Save Japan Dolphins." *An Earth Island Institute Project*. Web. 3 June 2011.

Scanlan, Sean. "Introduction: Nostalgia." *Iowa Journal of Cultural Studies*. 5.1 (2005). 20 Nov. 2006. Web. 21 Mar. 2008.

Schenker, Andrew. "*The End of the Line*." *Slant Magazine* 14 June 2009. Web. 2 June 2010.

Schmidt, Robert H. "Why Do We Debate Animal Rights?" *Wildlife Society Bulletin* 18.4 (1990): 459–61. Print.

Schoof, Renee. "EPA Holds Up 79 Permits for Appalachian Surface Mines." *McClatchy Newspapers* 3 Nov. 2009. Web. 11 Sept. 2009.

Schwarzbaum, Lisa. "*Happy Feet 2.*" *Entertainment Weekly* 22 Nov. 2011. Web. 30 Nov. 2011.

Schwartz, Dennis. "*Thunder Bay.*" *Ozus' World Movie Reviews.* Web. 14 Jan. 2006.

Scott, A. O. "007 Is Back, and He's Brooding." *New York Times* 13 Nov. 2008. Web. 12 June 2011.

———. "A Dust-to-Dust Attachment Till Salary Did Them Part." *New York Times* 18 July 2007. Web. 30 Sept. 2011.

———. "There's a New Sheriff in Town, and He's a Rootin', Tootin' Reptile." *New York Times* 3 Mar. 2011. Web. 31 May 2011.

Sharrett, Christopher. "*Red Desert* Review." *Cineaste* 36.1 (2010). Web. 27 Dec. 2011.

Shiva, Vandana. *Water Wars: Privatization, Pollution, and Profit.* Cambridge MA: South End Press, 2002. Print.

Shnayerson, Michael. *Coal River.* New York: Farrar, Straus, and Giroux, 2008. Print.

Singer, Peter. *Animal Liberation.* New York: Avon Books, 1975. Print.

Slotkin, Richard. *Gunfighter Nation: The Myth of the Frontier in Twentieth-Century America.* New York: Harper Perennial, 1992. Print.

———. *Regeneration through Violence: The Mythology of the American Frontier: 1600–1800.* Norman: University of Oklahoma Press, 2000. Print.

Smith, Kyle. "Bean There, Bun That." *New York Post* 11 June 2009. Web. 30 June 2009.

Snitow, Alan and Kaufman, Deborah. *Thirst: Fighting the Corporate Theft of Water.* San Francisco: John Wiley and Sons, 2007. Print.

Snyder, Rachel Louise. *Fugitive Denim.* New York: W. W. Norton, 2008. Print.

Stewart, Kathleen. "Nostalgia: A Polemic." *Cultural Anthropology* 3.3 (Aug. 1988): 227–41. Print.

Stopper, Tim. "*Blue Vinyl* Review." *World Film About.com.* 2002. Web. 14 Oct. 2011.

Sullivan, Patricia A. "Vermiculite, Respiratory Disease, and Asbestos Exposure in Libby, "Montana: Update of a Cohort Mortality Study." *Environmental Health Perspectives* 115.4 (Apr. 2007): 579–85. Print.

"Summary of the Clean Water Act." *epa.gov.* 2 Mar. 2011. Web. 2 June 2011.

"Superfund Strategy Recommendation—Region 06." *U.S. Environmental Protection Agency* 12 May 2011. Web. 10 Oct. 2011.

"Sustainability." *Warner Bros. Entertainment: Corporate Responsibility.* 13 Feb. 2012. Web. 13 Feb. 2012.

Travers, Peter. "*Crude.*" *Rolling Stone* 10 Sept. 2009. Web. 1 Oct. 2011.

Ward, Ken, Jr. "Obama's EPA clears 42 of 48 New Mountaintop Removal Mining Permits." *Charleston (wv) Gazette* 24 Nov. 2009. Web. 17 May 2009.

Weinman, Jaime. "A Good Enviro-toon." *Something Old, Nothing New: Thoughts on Popular Culture and Unpopular Culture.* 6 Sept. 2004. Web. 10 Oct. 2005.

"What's the Plan?: U.S. Farm Subsidies, 1995 through 2003." *Environmental Working Group.* 2007. Web. 3 June 2009.

Wilensky, Joe. "Protection and Comfort?" *Human Ecology* Dec. 2001: 5. Print.

Willoquet-Maricondi, Paula, ed. *Framing the World: Explorations in Ecocriticism and Film.* Charlottesville: University of Virginia Press, 2010. Print.

Winter, Metta. "Engineering Textiles to Protect Workers from Toxic Chemicals." *Human Ecology* May 2004: 18–21. Print.

Yacowar, Maurice. "The Bug in the Rug: Notes on the Disaster Genre. *Film Genre Reader III.* Ed. Barry Keith Grant. Austin: University of Texas Press, 2003. 277–95. Print.

Zacharek, Stephanie. "Quantum of Solace." *Salon.com.* 14 Nov. 2008. Web. 12 June 2011.

INDEX

175, 182; and organismic approaches, 163; and water, 43

eco-warrior, vi, xxi, 24, 25, 44, 45

Elliott, Debbie, 160, 161, 182

Ellis, Curt, 69, 75; and *King Corn*, 79–81

Ellis, Jack C., 72, 73. *See also* McLane, Betsy A.

The End of the Line, vii, xxii, 73, 92, 93; and biotic community, 97–99, 104, 111, 112; and environmental ethics, 94–97

environmental justice, xxii; and clothing, 48–50, 55–57, 59; and housing, 115–16, 118, 121–23, 125, 127–28, 131, 135

Environmental Protection Agency (EPA): and air, 8; and clothing, 56, 64; and housing, 122, 130–34; and MTR, 158; and oil, 176, 177, 178; and water; 26, 28–29, 39, 43–44

environmental racism, 115, 121–22, 127, 132, 135

enviro-toon, xix

Erin Brockovich, 38, 93

Evelyn, John, 7

Even the Rain (También la lluvia), 31

externalities, v, xiii, xvi–xix, xxi, xxii, xxiii; and air, 15; and clothing, 48; and film, 183, 185; and oil, 162, 175; and water, 44

Ezell, John Samuel, 159

fair use economics, xiii, xiv, xvi, xvii; and ecology, 22; and fishing, 98; and MTR, 140, 153; and oil, 161–63

Farmingville, 73

fast fashion, 55, 63, 65

Felperin, Leslie, 87

Fishman, Charles, 32

Flaherty, Frances Hubbard, 164

Flipped, 187

Flow: For Love of Water, xxi, 31, 44

Food, Inc., xii, xviii, xxi, 69–72, 76; and pastoral fantasy, 76–79, 80, 81, 86, 87, 91

Friends with Benefits, 117

Frumkin, Howard, 57, 135, 136. *See also* Cifuentes, Enrique

Gasland, vii, xvi, 39; and groundwater, 39–41, 44

Gelbspan, Ross, 20

genetically modified organism (GMO): and clothing, 62; and food, 83

Giroux, Henry, 50–51

Gleiberman, Owen, 77

global warming, xi, 5, 6; and atmospheric pollution, 17–23

Godard, Jean-Luc, 10–11

Goldenberg, Suzanne, 181

Goldsmith, David, 129–30. *See also* Ries, Robert

Gomorra, xxii, 137

Goodwin, Nevam, xvi

The Grapes of Wrath, 27

Grass, 73

Greenberg, Paul, 92

Green Lantern, 187

Griffith, Richard, 164

groundwater, 28, 30, 38; and *Gasland*, 39–41; and *Tapped*, 41–43, 44

the Gulf (of Mexico), xvi, 159, 160, 162, 175, 181, 182

Guthmann, Edward, 16, 16

Hageman, Andrew, 31

Happy Feet Two, vii, xvii, xix, *xviii*, 4

Harry Potter and the Deathly Hallows: Part II, 186, 188

Harvey, Dennis: and *China Blue*, 53; and *King Corn*, 79

Heider, Karl G., xv; and food films, 72–73, 91; and MTR, 139

The Help, 120–21, 122

Hevesi, Dennis, 158

The History of Ready Meals, 73

Hochman, Jhan, xx

A Home of Our Own, 118

Hornaday, Ann, 79

Housekeeping, 117

Howe, Desson, 15

How Green Was My Valley, 5

How to Boil a Frog, vii, xii, xx, 4, 10, 189; and climate change, 17–21, *18*, 22–23

Hugo, 187

human ecology movement, xiv; and clothing, 43, 47, 49; and Ellen Richards,
9–10; and global warming, 12, 15–17,
21–23

Imitation of Life (1934), 120
Imitation of Life (1959), 120
Inception, 187
An Inconvenient Truth, 4–5, 17, 19, 71, 82
Ingram, David, xx
It Happened on Fifth Avenue, 117

Jacobson, Mark Zachary, 7, 8
Jardine, Dan, 171

Kates, Robert W., xvii
Keeper of the Mountains, 139
Kempley, Rita, 15
Kennedy, Lisa, 120
King, Susan, 176
King Corn, xxi; and nostalgia, 69, 70, 71,
74–76; and process documentary, 79–
81, 86, 87, 91
kino-pravda, 73
Koehler, Robert, 39

land ethic, xxii; and air, 121; and Aldo Leo-
pold, 105, 163; and fishing, 94, 96
Lane, Anthony, 35, 205
The Last Mountain, xxii, xxiii; and alterna-
tives to mtr, 138–40, 153, 156, 158; and
film industry, 183, 189, 190
The Last Train Home, xxi, 48, 49, 54–55, 65
Lease, Gary, 117
Lee, Nathan, 97
Leiber, Nick, 188
Leopold, Aldo, xxii, 21–22, 94, 96, 101,
105–6, 163
Leydon, Joe, 82
Libby, Montana, vii, ix, xxii; and Blue Vinyl,
130–31, 131; and superfund, 132–35
Lichtenfeld, Eric, 184
Life and Debt, xxi, 58
Live-In Maid, 120–22
The Living Daylights, 34
Look What They've Done, 139

Louisiana Story, vii, xxii; and progress,
160, 161–62; and separation from
nature, 164–69, 171, 175–76, 178,
181–82
Lumière brothers, 4, 72

MacDonald, Scott, xx
Maher, Kris, 158. See also Power, Stephen
The Maid, 119
Make Way for Tomorrow, 117
Man of Aran, 72, 73
Man with a Movie Camera, 73
Maquilapolis, vii, xxi; and free zones, 48,
57, 58–59, 59, 64, 65
Mardi Gras: Made in China, vii, xxi, 47, 48,
57–58, 65
Massey, Rachel, 128, 129, 199. See also
Ackerman, Frank
Maxwell, Richard, 87, 188. See also Toby
Miller
McLane, Betsy A., 72, 73. See also Ellis,
Jack C.
Meat, 72, 74
Merchant, Carolyn, 95–96, 163
Meyers, Robert J., 7
Midgley, Mary, 100–101, 106
Milk of Sorrow, 118
Miller, Gerri, 118
Miller, Toby, 87, 188. See also Maxwell,
Richard
Mitman, Gregg, xx
Moana, 72
Moberg, David, 81
Moisi, Dominique, 141, 142
The Molly Maguires, 5
Monani, Salma, xiii. See also Cubitt, Sean;
Rust, Stephen
Money Pit, 118
Morgenstern, Joe, 20
Morris, Gary, 11
Mort, Jo-Ann, 52, 53. See also Nathan,
Robert
Mountain Mourning, vii, xxiii, 138, 153, 184;
and Christianity, 154–56, 157
Mountain Top Removal, xxii, 139, 141,
151–52